Sunset

BEST HOME PLANS

One-Story Living

Classic columned porch, high ceilings, and indoor-outdoor living spaces highlight this handsome single-story home. See plan E-1710 on page 110.

Sunset Publishing Corporation ■ **Menlo Park, California**

SUNSET BOOKS

VP, General Manager:
Richard A. Smeby
VP, Editorial Director:
Bob Doyle
Production Director:
Lory Day
Art Director:
Vasken Guiragossian
Contributing Editor:
Don Vandervort

A Dream Come True

In response to the success of Sunset's first edition of *One-Story Living,* we present this new, updated edition, a collection of proven plans for more than 200 of the latest, most popular one-story home designs available. All of these plans have been created for families just like yours by architects and professional designers. In addition to viewing a myriad of designs, you'll learn how to plan and manage your home-building project—and how to ensure its success.

Peruse the following pages and study the floor plans to find a home that's just right for you. When you're ready to order blueprints, you can simply call or mail in your order, and you'll receive the plans within days.

Enjoy the adventure!

Fourth printing March 2001
Copyright © 1996, 1992 Sunset Publishing
Corporation, Menlo Park, CA 94025.
Second edition. All rights reserved, including
the right of reproduction in whole or in part
in any form. ISBN 0-376-01146-7. Library of
Congress Catalog Card Number 95-072512.
Printed in the United States.

Visit our website at
www.sunsetbooks.com

Contents

Charming rustic home has two porches: a country-style front porch and a screened-in side porch between the house and the garage. The compact floor plan includes a large kitchen, a living room with a fireplace, a master suite, and two more bedrooms. See plan C-8650 on page 217.

Single-Story Living

Are you thinking or dreaming about building a custom home? One of your first decisions will be whether to build a one-story or a multi-level house, a choice based on the building site you have in mind and your family's needs and preferences.

What are the benefits of a single-story house? Young families often prefer a home where bedrooms and bathrooms are in convenient proximity, where the master bedroom is within easy earshot of the nursery, and where the dangers posed by staircases are avoided. For older people or those with limited mobility, the ease of getting around a one-story home is primary.

Moreover, a low-profile, one-story house won't overwhelm a neighborhood with its bulk, as a two-story house can. Single-story homes are also easier to build, simpler to maintain, and have more flexible interiors—living spaces without floors overhead allow for dramatic vaulted ceilings, clerestory windows, and generous use of skylights.

The two keys to success in building a home are capable project management and good design. The next few pages will walk you through some of the most important aspects of project management: you'll find an overview of the building process, directions for selecting the right plan and getting the most from it, and methods for successfully working with a builder and other professionals.

The balance of the book presents professionally designed stock plans for homes in a wide range of styles and configurations. Once you find a plan that will work for you—perhaps with a few modifications made later to personalize it for your family—you can order construction blueprints for a fraction of the cost of a custom design, a savings of many thousands of dollars (see pages 12–15 for information on how to order).

Wide, covered porch evokes an earlier era, but this home has all the modern amenities, including a large island kitchen, a bayed breakfast area, and a master suite with two walk-in closets and a raised spa tub. See plan J-86140 on page 172.

Despite its dramatic frontage, this luxurious home is on a single level. Inside the tall double doors, a central foyer provides direct access to the formal dining room, generous gourmet kitchen and breakfast room, living room, master suite, and den/bedroom. See plan HDS-99-177 on page 210.

Distinctive windows and a gable design give this home an elegant yet friendly exterior. Inside, the foyer leads to an open-plan family room/kitchen area. Both the dining room and master bedroom have tray ceilings; the master bath and breakfast room are vaulted. See plan FB-5009-CHAD on page 136.

Gracefully arching windows accent this expansive family home. The symmetrical plan offers a central foyer and living room, flanked on the right by public spaces—family room, dining room, and kitchen—and on the left by the master suite, two more bedrooms, and a study. See plan DD-2802 on page 163.

The Art of Building

As you embark on your home-building project, think of it as a trip—clearly not a vacation but rather an interesting, adventurous, at times difficult expedition. Meticulous planning will make your journey not only far more enjoyable but also much more successful. By careful planning, you can avoid—or at least minimize—some of the pitfalls along the way.

Start with realistic expectations of the road ahead. To do this, you'll want to gain an understanding of the basic house-building process, settle on a design that will work for you and your family, and make sure your project is actually doable. By taking those initial steps, you can gain a clear idea of how much time, money, and energy you'll need to invest to make your dream come true.

The Building Process

Your role in planning and managing a house-building project can be divided into two parts: prebuilding preparation and construction management.

■ **Prebuilding preparation.** This is where you should focus most of your attention. In the hands of a qualified contractor whose expertise you can rely on, the actual building process should go fairly smoothly. But during most of the prebuilding stage, you're generally on your own. Your job will be to launch the project and develop a talented team that can help you bring your new home to fruition.

When you work with stock plans, the prebuilding process usually goes as follows:

First, you research the general area where you want to live, selecting one or more possible home sites (unless you already own a suitable lot). Then you choose a basic house design, with the idea that it may require some modification. Finally, you analyze the site, the design, and your budget to determine if the project is actually attainable.

If you decide that it is, you purchase the land and order blueprints. If you want to modify them, you consult an architect, designer, or contractor. Once the plans are finalized, you request bids from contractors and arrange any necessary construction financing.

After selecting a builder and signing a contract, you (or your contractor) then file the plans with the building department. When the plans are approved, often several weeks—or even months—later, you're ready to begin construction.

■ **Construction management.** Unless you intend to act as your own contractor, your role during the building process is mostly one of quality control and time management. Even so, it's important to know the sequence of events and something about construction methods so you can discuss progress with your builder and prepare for any important decisions you may need to make along the way.

Decision-making is critical. Once construction begins, the builder must usually plunge ahead, keeping his carpenters and subcontractors progressing steadily. If you haven't made a key decision—which model bathtub or sink to install, for example—it can bring construction to a frustrating and expensive halt.

Usually, you'll make such decisions before the onset of building, but, inevitably, some issue or another will arise during construction. Being knowledgeable about the building process will help you anticipate and circumvent potential logjams.

Selecting a House Plan

Searching for the right plan can be a fun, interactive family experience—one of the most exciting parts of a house-building project. Gather the family around as you peruse the home plans in this book. Study the size, location, and configuration of each room; traffic patterns both inside the house and to the outdoors; exterior style; and how you'll use the available space. Discuss the pros and cons of the various plans.

Browse through pictures of homes in magazines to stimulate ideas. Clip the photos you like so you can think about your favorite options. When you visit the homes of friends, note special features that appeal to you. Also, look carefully at the homes in your neighborhood, noting their style and how they fit the site.

Mark those plans that most closely suit your ideals. Then, to narrow down your choices, critique each plan, using the following information as a guide.

■ **Overall size and budget.** How large a house do you want? Will the house you're considering fit your family's requirements? Look at the overall square footage and room sizes. If you have a hard time visualizing room sizes, measure some of the rooms in your present home and compare.

It's often better for the house to be a little too big than a little too small, but remember that every extra square foot will cost more money to build and maintain.

■ **Number and type of rooms.** Beyond thinking about the number of bedrooms and baths you want, consider your family's life-style and how you use space. Do you want both a family room and a living room? Do you need a formal dining space? Will you require some extra rooms, or "swing spaces," that can serve multiple purposes, such as a home office–guest room combination?

■ **Room placement and traffic patterns.** What are your preferences for locations of formal living areas, master bedroom, and children's rooms? Do you prefer a kitchen that's open to family areas or one that's private and out of the way? How much do you use exterior spaces and how should they relate to the interior?

Once you make those determinations, look carefully at the floor plan of the house you're considering to see if it meets your needs and if the traffic flow will be convenient for your family.

■ **Architectural style.** Have you always wanted to live in a Victorian farmhouse? Now is your chance to create a house that matches your idea of "home" (taking into account, of course, styles in your neighborhood). But don't let your preference for one particular architectural style dictate your home's floor plan. If the floor plan doesn't work for your family, keep looking.

■ **Site considerations.** Most people choose a site before selecting a plan—or at least they've zeroed in on the basic type of land where they'll situate their house. It sounds elementary, but choose a house that will fit the site.

When figuring the "footprint" of a house, you must know about any restrictions that will affect your home's height or proximity to the property lines. Call the local building department (look under city or county listings in the phone book) and get a very clear description of any restrictions, such as setbacks, height limits, and lot coverage, that will affect what you can build on the site (see "Working with City Hall," at right).

When you visit potential sites, note trees, rock outcroppings, slopes, views, winds, sun, neighboring homes, and other factors. All will impact on how your house works on a particular site.

Once you've narrowed down the choice of sites, consult an architect or building designer (see page 8) to help you evaluate how some potential houses will work on the sites you have in mind.

Is Your Project Doable?

Before you purchase land, make sure your project is doable. Although it's too early at this stage to pinpoint costs, making a few phone calls will help you determine whether your project is realistic. You'll be able to learn if you can afford to build the house, how long it will take, and what obstacles may stand in your way.

To get a ballpark estimate of cost, multiply a house's total square footage (of livable space) by the local average cost per square foot for new construction. (To obtain local averages, call a contractor, an architect, a realtor, or the local chapter of the National Association of Home Builders.) Some contractors may even be willing to give you a preliminary bid. Once you know approximate costs, speak to your lender to explore financing.

It's a good idea to discuss your project with several contractors (see page 8). They may be aware of problems in your area that could limit your options—bedrock that makes digging basements difficult, for example. These conversations are actually the first step in developing a list of contractors from which you'll choose the one who will build your home.

Working with City Hall

For any building project, even a minor one, it's essential to be familiar with building codes and other restrictions that can affect your project.

■ **Building codes,** generally implemented by the city or county building department, set the standards for safe, lasting construction. Codes specify minimum construction techniques and materials for foundations, framing, electrical wiring, plumbing, insulation, and all other aspects of a building. Although codes are adopted and enforced locally, most regional codes conform to the standards set by the national Uniform Building Code, Standard Building Code, or Basic Building Code. In some cases, local codes set more restrictive standards than national ones.

■ **Building permits** are required for home-building projects nearly everywhere. If you work with a contractor, the builder's firm should handle all necessary permits.

More than one permit may be needed; for example, one will cover the foundation, another the electrical wiring, and still another the heating equipment installation. Each will probably involve a fee and require inspections by building officials before work can proceed. (Inspections benefit *you*, as they ensure that the job is being done satisfactorily.) Permit fees are generally a percentage (1 to 1.5 percent) of the project's estimated value, often calculated on square footage.

It's important to file for the necessary permits. Failure to do so can result in fines or legal action against you. You can even be forced to undo the work performed. At the very least, your negligence may come back to haunt you later when you're ready to sell your house.

■ **Zoning ordinances,** particular to your community, restrict setbacks (how near to property lines you may build), your house's allowable height, lot coverage factors (how much of your property you can cover with structures), and other factors that impact design and building. If your plans don't conform to zoning ordinances, you can try to obtain a variance, an exception to the rules. But this legal work can be expensive and time-consuming. Even if you prove that your project won't negatively affect your neighbors, the building department can still refuse to grant the variance.

■ **Deeds and covenants** attach to the lot. Deeds set out property lines and easements; covenants may establish architectural standards in a neighborhood. Since both can seriously impact your project, make sure you have complete information on any deeds or covenants before you turn over a spadeful of soil.

Recruiting Your Home Team

A home-building project will interject you and your family into the building business, an area that may be unfamiliar territory. Among the people you'll be working with are architects, designers, landscapers, contractors, and subcontractors.

Design Help

A qualified architect or designer can help you modify and personalize your home plan, taking into account your family's needs and budget and the house's style. In fact, you may want to consider consulting such a person while you're selecting a plan to help you articulate your needs.

Design professionals are capable of handling any or all aspects of the design process. For example, they can review your house plans, suggest options, and then provide rough sketches of the options on tracing paper. Many architects will even secure needed permits and negotiate with contractors or subcontractors, as well as oversee the quality of the work.

Of course, you don't necessarily need an architect or designer to implement minor changes in a plan; although most contractors aren't trained in design, some can help you with modifications.

An open-ended, hourly-fee arrangement that you work out with your architect or designer allows for flexibility, but it often turns out to be more costly than working on a flat-fee basis. On a flat fee, you agree to pay a specific amount of money for a certain amount of work.

To find architects and designers, contact such trade associations as the American Institute of Architects (AIA), American Institute of Building Designers (AIBD), American Society of Landscape Architects (ASLA), and American Society of Interior Designers (ASID). Although many professionals choose not to belong to trade associations, those who do have met the standards of their respective associations. For phone numbers of local branches, check the Yellow Pages.

■ **Architects** are licensed by the state and have degrees. They're trained in all facets of building design and construction. Although some can handle interior design and structural engineering, others hire specialists for those tasks.

■ **Building designers** are generally unlicensed but may be accredited by the American Institute of Building Designers. Their backgrounds are varied: some may be unlicensed architects in apprenticeship; others are interior designers or contractors with design skills.

■ **Draftspersons** offer an economical route to making simple changes on your drawings. Like building designers, these people may be unlicensed architect apprentices, engineers, or members of related trades. Most are accomplished at drawing up plans.

■ **Interior designers,** as their job title suggests, design interiors. They work with you to choose room finishes, furnishings, appliances, and decorative elements. Part of their expertise is in arranging furnishings to create a workable space plan. Some interior designers are employed by architectural firms; others work independently. Financial arrangements vary, depending on the designer's preference.

Related professionals are kitchen and bathroom designers, who concentrate on fixtures, cabinetry, appliances, materials, and space planning for the kitchen and bath.

■ **Landscape architects, designers, and contractors** design outdoor areas. Landscape architects are state-licensed to practice landscape design. A landscape designer usually has a landscape architect's education and training but does not have a state license. Licensed landscape contractors specialize in garden construction, though some also have design skills and experience.

■ **Soils specialists and structural engineers** may be needed for projects where unstable soils or uncommon wind loads or seismic forces must be taken into account. Any structural changes to a house require the expertise of a structural engineer to verify that the house won't fall down.

Services of these specialists can be expensive, but they're imperative in certain conditions to ensure a safe, sturdy structure. Your building department will probably let you know if their services are required.

General Contractors

To build your house, hire a licensed general contractor. Most states require a contractor to be licensed and insured for worker's compensation in order to contract a building project and hire other subcontractors. State licensing ensures that contractors have met minimum training standards and have a specified level of experience. Licensing does not guarantee, however, that they're good at what they do.

When contractors hire subcontractors, they're responsible for overseeing the quality of work and materials of the subcontractors and for paying them.

■ **Finding a contractor.** How do you find a good contractor? Start by getting referrals from people you know who have built or remodeled their home. Nothing beats a personal recommendation. The best contractors are usually busily moving from one satisfied client to another prospect, advertised only by word of mouth.

You can also ask local real estate brokers and lenders or even your building inspector for names of qualified builders. Experienced lumber dealers are another good source of names.

In the Yellow Pages, look under "Contractors–Building, General"; or call the local chapter of the National Association of Home Builders.

■ **Choosing a contractor.** Once you have a list of names of prospective builders, call several of them. On the telephone, ask first whether they handle your type of job and can work within your schedule. If they can, arrange a meeting with each one and ask them to be prepared with references of former clients and photos of previous jobs. Better still, meet them at one of their current work sites so you can get a glimpse of the quality of their work and how organized and thorough they are.

Take your plan to the meeting and discuss it enough to request a rough estimate (some builders will comply, while others will be reluctant to offer a ballpark estimate, preferring to give you a hard bid based on complete drawings). Don't hesitate to probe for advice or suggestions that might make building your house less expensive.

Be especially aware of each contractor's personality and how well you communicate. Good chemistry between you and your builder is a key ingredient for success.

Narrow down the candidates to three or four. Ask each for a firm bid, based on the exact same set of plans and specifications. For the bids to be accurate, your plans need to be complete and the specifications as precise as possible, call-ing out particular appliances, fixtures, floorings, roofing material, and so forth. (Some of these are specified in a stock-plan set; others are not.)

Call the contractors' references and ask about the quality of their work, their relationship with their clients, their promptness, and their readiness to follow up on problems. Visit former clients to check the contractor's work firsthand.

Be sure your final candidates are licensed, bonded, and insured for worker's compensation, public liability, and property damage. Also, try to determine how financially solvent they are (you can call their bank and credit references). Avoid contractors who are operating hand-to-mouth.

Don't automatically hire the contractor with the lowest bid if you don't think you'll get along well or if you have any doubts about the quality of the person's work. Instead, look for both the most reasonable bid and the contractor with the best credentials, references, terms, and compatibility with your family.

A word about bonds: You can request a performance bond that guarantees that your job will be finished by your contractor. If the job isn't completed, the bonding company will cover the cost of hiring another contractor to finish it. Bonds cost from 2 to 6 percent of the value of the project.

Your Building Contract

A building contract (see below) binds and protects both you and your contractor. It isn't just a legal document. It's also a list of the expectations of both parties. The best way to minimize the possibility of misunderstandings and costly changes later on is to write down every possible detail. Whether the contract is a standard form or one composed by you, have an attorney look it over before both you and the contractor sign it.

The contract should clearly specify all the work that needs to be done, including particular materials and work descriptions, the time schedule, and method of payment. It should be keyed to the working drawings.

A Sample Building Contract

Project and participants. Give a general description of the project, its address, and the names and addresses of both you and the builder.

Construction materials. Identify all construction materials by brand name, quality markings (species, grades, etc.), and model numbers where applicable. Avoid the clause "or equal," which allows the builder to substitute other materials for your choices. For materials you can't specify now, set down a budget figure.

Time schedule. Include both start and completion dates and specify that work will be "continuous." Although a contractor cannot be responsible for delays caused by strikes and material shortages, your builder should assume responsibility for completing the project within in a reasonable period of time.

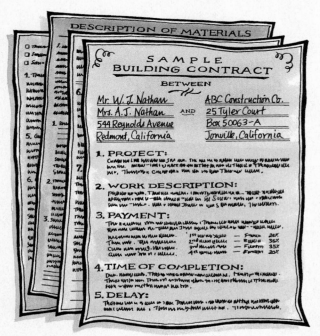

Work to be performed. State all work you expect the contractor to perform, from initial grading to finished painting.

Method and schedule of payment. Specify how and when payments are to be made. Typical agreements specify installment payments as particular phases of work are completed. Final payment is withheld until the job receives its final inspection and is cleared of all liens.

Waiver of liens. Protect yourself with a waiver of liens signed by the general contractor, the subcontractors, and all major suppliers. That way, subcontractors who are not paid for materials or services cannot place a lien on your property.

Personalizing Stock Plans

The beauty of buying stock plans for your new home is that they offer tested, well-conceived design at an affordable price. And stock plans dramatically reduce the time it takes to design a house, since the plans are ready when you are.

Because they were not created specifically for your family, stock plans may not reflect your personal taste. But it's not difficult to make revisions in stock plans that will turn your home into an expression of your family's personality. You'll surely want to add personal touches and choose your own finishes.

Ideally, the modifications you implement will be fairly minor. The more extensive the changes, the more expensive the plans. Major changes take valuable design time, and those that affect a house's structure may require a structural engineer's approval.

If you anticipate wholesale changes, such as moving a number of bearing walls or changing the roofline significantly, you may be better off selecting another plan. On the other hand, reconfiguring or changing the sizes of some rooms can probably be handled fairly easily.

Some structural changes may even be necessary to comply with local codes. Your area may have specific requirements for snow loads, energy codes, seismic or wind resistance, and so forth. Those types of modifications are likely to require the services of an architect or structural engineer.

Plan Modifications

Before you pencil in any changes, live with your plans for a while. Study them carefully—at your building site, if possible. Try to picture the finished house: how rooms will interrelate, where the sun will enter and at what angle, what the view will be from each window. Think about traffic patterns, access to rooms, room sizes, window and door locations, natural light, and kitchen and bathroom layouts.

Typical changes might involve adding windows or skylights to bring in natural light or capture a view. Or you may want to widen a hallway or doorway for roomier access, extend a room, eliminate doors, or change window and door sizes. Perhaps you'd like to shorten a room, stealing the gained space for a large closet. Look closely at the kitchen; it's not difficult to reconfigure the layout if it makes the space more convenient for you.

Above all, take your time—this is your home and it should reflect your taste and needs. Make your changes now, during the planning stage. Once construction begins, it will take crowbars, hammers, saws, new materials, and, most significantly, time to alter the plans. Because changes are not part of your building contract, you can count on them being expensive extras once construction begins.

Specifying Finishes

One way to personalize a house without changing its structure is to substitute your favorite finishes for those specified on the plan.

Would you prefer a stuccoed exterior rather than the wood siding shown on the plan? In most cases, this is a relatively easy change. Do you like the look of a wood shingle roof rather than the composition shingles shown on the plan? This, too, is easy. Perhaps you would like to change the windows from sliders to casements, or upgrade to high-efficiency glazing. No problem. Many of those kinds of changes can be worked out with your contractor.

Inside, you may want hardwood where vinyl flooring is shown. In fact, you can—and should—choose types, colors, and styles of floorings, wall coverings, tile, plumbing fixtures, door hardware, cabinetry, appliances, lighting fixtures, and other interior details, for it's these materials that will personalize your home. For help in making selections, consult an architect or interior designer (see page 8).

Each material you select should be spelled out clearly and precisely in your building contract.

Finishing touches can transform a house built from stock plans into an expression of your family's taste and style. Clockwise, from far left: Colorful tilework and custom cabinetry enliven a bathroom (Design: Osburn Design); highly organized closet system maximizes storage space (Architect: David Jeremiah Hurley); low-level deck expands living space to outdoor areas (Landscape architects: The Runa Group, Inc.); built-ins convert the corner of a guest room into a home office (Design: Lynn Williams of The French Connection); French country cabinetry lends style and old-world charm to a kitchen (Design: Garry Bishop/Showcase Kitchens).

WHAT OUR PLANS

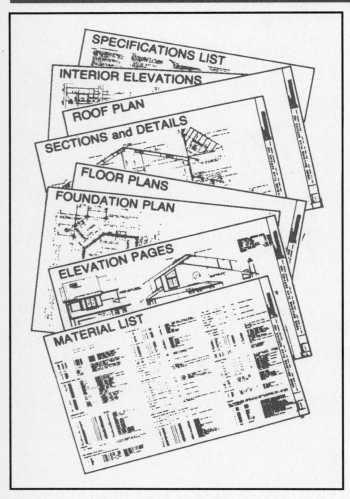

SPECIFICATIONS LIST
INTERIOR ELEVATIONS
ROOF PLAN
SECTIONS and DETAILS
FLOOR PLANS
FOUNDATION PLAN
ELEVATION PAGES
MATERIAL LIST

Our construction blueprints are detailed, clear and concise. All blueprints are designed by licensed architects or members of the American Institute of Building Design (AIBD), and all plans are designed to meet one of the recognized North American building codes (the Uniform Building Code, the Standard Building Code, the Basic Building Code or the National Building Code of Canada) in effect at the time and place they are drawn.

The blueprints for most home designs include the following elements, but the presentation of these elements may vary depending on the size and complexity of the home and the style of the individual designer:

Exterior Elevations

Exterior elevations show the front, rear and sides of the house, including exterior materials, details and measurements.

Foundation Plans

Foundation plans include drawings for a full, daylight or partial basement, crawlspace, slab, or pole foundation. All necessary notations and dimensions are included. (Foundation options will vary for each plan. If the home you want does not have the type of foundation you desire, a foundation conversion diagram is available.)

Detailed Floor Plans

Detailed floor plans show the placement of interior walls and the dimensions for rooms, doors, windows, stairways, etc., of each level of the house.

Cross Sections

Cross sections show details of the house as though it were cut in slices from the roof to the foundation. The cross sections specify the home's construction, insulation, flooring and roofing details.

Interior Elevations

Interior elevations show the specific details of cabinets (kitchen, bathroom and utility room), fireplaces, built-in units, and other special interior features, depending on the nature and complexity of the item.

Note: *To save money and to accommodate your own style and taste, we suggest contacting local cabinet and fireplace distributors for sizes and styles.*

PACKAGE

INCLUDE

Roof Details

Roof details show slope, pitch and location of dormers, gables and other roof elements, including clerestory windows and skylights. These details may be shown on the elevation sheet or on a separate diagram.

Note: *If trusses are used, we suggest using a local truss manufacturer to design your trusses to comply with your local codes and regulations.*

Electrical Layouts

Schematic electrical layouts show the suggested locations for switches, fixtures and outlets. These details may be shown on the floor plan or on a separate diagram.

General Specifications

General specifications provide general instructions and information regarding structure, excavating and grading, masonry and concrete work, carpentry and wood, thermal and moisture protection, and specifications about drywall, tile, flooring, glazing, caulking and sealants.

Note: *Due to regional variations, local availability of materials, local codes, methods of installation, and individual preferences, it is impossible to include much detail on heating, plumbing and electrical work on your plans. The duct work, venting and other details will vary depending on the type of heating and cooling system (forced air, hot water, electric, solar) and the type of energy (gas, oil, electricity, solar) that you use. These details and specifications are easily obtained from your builder, contractor and/or local suppliers.*

OTHER HELPFUL BUILDING AIDS

Every set of plans that you order will contain the details your builder needs. However, additional guides and information are also available as outlined below:

Reproducible Blueprint Set

Reproducible sets are useful if you will be making changes to the stock home plan you've chosen. This set consists of line drawings produced on erasable, reproducible paper for the purpose of modification. When alterations are complete, working copies can be made. *Bonus: Includes free working set

Mirror-Reversed Plans

Mirror-reversed plans are used when building the home in reverse of the illustrated floor plan. Reversed plans are available for an additional one-time surcharge. Since the lettering and dimensions will read backwards, we recommend that you order only one or two reversed sets in addition to the regular-reading sets.

Itemized List of Materials

An itemized list of materials details the quantity, type and size of materials needed to build your home. This list is helpful in acquiring an accurate construction estimate. An expanded material workbook is available for some plans. Call for details.

Description of Materials

A description of materials outlines the type and quality of materials suggested for the home. This form may be required for obtaining FHA or VA financing.

Typical "How-To" Diagrams

Plumbing, wiring, solar heating, and framing and foundation conversion diagrams are available. Each of these diagrams details the basic tools and techniques needed to plumb, wire, install a solar heating system, convert plans with 2x4 exterior walls to 2x6 (or vice versa), or adapt a plan for a basement, crawlspace or slab foundation.

Note: *These diagrams are general and not specific to any one plan.*

13

IMPORTANT ORDERING INFORMATION

ABOUT THE BLUEPRINTS

All of our plans are designed by licensed architects or members of the American Institute of Building Design (AIBD), and all plans are designed to meet one of the recognized North American building codes (the Uniform Building Code, the Standard Building Code, the Basic Building Code or the National Building Code of Canada) in effect at the time and place they are drawn.

BLUEPRINT PRICES

Our sales volume allows us to offer quality blueprints at a fraction of the cost it takes to develop them. Custom designs cost thousands of dollars, usually 5% to 15% of the cost of construction. Design costs for a $100,000 home, for example, can range from $5,000 to $15,000.

Our pricing schedule is based on total heated living space. Garages, porches, decks and basements are not included in the total square footage.

ARCHITECTURAL AND ENGINEERING SEALS

The increased concern over energy costs and safety has prompted many cities and states to require an architect or engineer to review and "seal" a blueprint prior to construction. There may be a fee for this service. Please contact your local lumberyard, municipal building department, builders association, or local chapter of the AIBD or the American Institute of Architects (AIA).

Please Note: *Plans for homes to be built in Nevada may have to be re-drawn and sealed by a Nevada-licensed design professional.*

EXCHANGE INFORMATION

Each set of blueprints is specially printed and shipped to you in response to your specific order; consequently, we cannot honor requests for refunds. If, for some reason, the blueprints that you ordered cannot be used, we will be pleased to exchange them within 30 days of the purchase date. Please note that a handling fee will be assessed for all exchanges. For more information, call us toll-free.

Please Note: *Reproducible sets cannot be exchanged for any reason.*

ESTIMATING BUILDING COSTS

Building costs vary widely depending on style, size, type of finishing materials you select, and the local rates for labor and building materials. A local average cost per square foot of construction can give you a rough estimate. To get the average cost per square foot in your area, you can call a local contractor, your state or local builders association, the National Association of Home Builders (NAHB), or the AIBD. A more accurate estimate will require a professional review of the working blueprints and the types of materials you will be using.

FOUNDATION OPTIONS AND EXTERIOR CONSTRUCTION

The most common foundation choices are slab, crawlspace or basement foundation; the exterior walls are typically constructed using 2x4s or 2x6s. Most professional contractors and builders can easily adapt a home to meet the foundation and exterior wall requirements that you desire.

If the home that you select does not offer the foundation or exterior wall requirements that you prefer, you may wish to purchase a typical foundation and framing conversion diagram.

Please Note: *These diagrams are not specific to any one plan.*

HOW MANY BLUEPRINTS SHOULD YOU ORDER?

A single set of blueprints is sufficient to study and review a home in greater detail. However, if you are planning to get cost estimates or are planning to build, you will need a minimum of 4 sets. If you will be modifying your home plan, we recommend ordering a reproducible set.

To help determine the number of sets you will need, see the chart below.

BLUEPRINT CHECKLIST

_____ **OWNER'S SET(S)**

_____ **BUILDER** (usually requires at least three sets; one for legal document, one for inspections and a minimum of one set for subcontractors)

_____ **BUILDING PERMIT DEPT.** (at least one set; check with your local governing body for number of sets required)

_____ **LENDING INSTITUTION** (usually one set for conventional mortgage; three sets for FHA or VA loans)

_____ **TOTAL NUMBER OF SETS**

REVISIONS, MODIFICATIONS AND CUSTOMIZATION

The tremendous variety of designs available from us allows you to choose the home that best suits your lifestyle, budget and building site. Through your choice of siding, roof, trim, decorating, color, etc., your home can be customized easily.

Minor changes and material substitutions can be made by any professional builder without the need for expensive blueprint revisions. However, if you will be making major changes, we strongly recommend that you order a reproducible set and seek the services of an architect or professional designer.

COMPLIANCE WITH CODES

Every state, county and municipality has its own codes, zoning requirements, ordinances and building regulations. Modifications may be necessary to comply with your specific requirements—snow loads, energy codes, seismic zones, etc. All of our plans are designed to meet the specifications of seismic zones I or II. We authorize the use of our blueprints expressly conditioned upon your obligation and agreement to strictly comply with all local building codes, ordinances, regulations and requirements—including permits and inspections at the time of construction.

LICENSE AGREEMENT, COPY RESTRICTIONS, COPYRIGHT

When you purchase a blueprint or reproducible set, we, as Licensor, grant you, as Licensee, the right to use these documents **to construct a single unit**. All of the plans in this publication are protected under the Federal Copyright Act, Title XVII of the United States Code and Chapter 37 of the Code of Federal Regulations. Each designer retains title and ownership of the original documents. The blueprints licensed to you cannot be resold or used by any other person, copied or reproduced by any means. When you purchase a reproducible set, you reserve the right to modify and reproduce the plan. Reproducible sets cannot be resold or used by any other person.

BLUEPRINT ORDER FORM

Ordering plans for your dream home is as easy as 1-2-3!

COMPLETE THIS ORDER FORM IN JUST 3 EASY STEPS, THEN MAIL IN YOUR ORDER, OR CALL 1-800-820-1283 FOR FASTER SERVICE!

Please read the ordering information below:

1 **BLUEPRINTS & ACCESSORIES**

Price Code	Study Set	4 Sets	8 Sets	12 Sets	Reproducible Set*
AAA	$284	$309	$349	$419	$484
AA	$324	$349	$389	$469	$524
A	$394	$419	$454	$529	$589
B	$429	$454	$494	$569	$629
C	$469	$494	$534	$609	$669
D	$539	$564	$609	$664	$704
E	$594	$619	$659	$739	$809
F	$634	$659	$699	$789	$854
G	$679	$704	$744	$829	$904
H	$719	$744	$789	$874	$949
I	$764	$789	$829	$914	$984

Prices subject to change

A Reproducible Set is produced on erasable paper for the purpose of modification. Only available for plans with these prefixes: A, ADI, AG, AGH, AHP, APS, AS, AX, B, BOD, BRF, C, CC, CDG[1], CH, CHP, CL, DBI, DCL, DD, DP, DW, E, EOF, FB, FI, G, GA, GL, GS, H, HDC, HDS, HFL, HOM, IDG, J, JWA, K, KD, KLF, KP, L, LM, LRD, LRK, LS, MIN, MWG, NBV, NW, OH, PH, PI, PIC[2], PW, RD, RDR, RJA, RN, RT, S, SDG, SG, SUL, SUN, THD, TS, UD, UDA, V, WGC, WH, Y

[1]*Not available for all plans. Please call before ordering.*
[2]*U.S. customers only*

Price Code	1 Set*	Price Code	1 Set*	Price Code	1 Set*
AAA	$60	C	$65	G	$75
AA	$60	D	$65	H	$75
A	$60	E	$70	I	$80
B	$60	F	$70		

Additional sets are available for $15 each.

2 **SHIPPING & HANDLING**

Add shipping and handling costs according to chart below:

	1-3 sets	4-7 sets	8 sets or more	Reproducible Set
U.S. Regular (5-6 working days)	$15.00	$17.50	$20.00	$20.00
U.S. Express (2-3 working days)	$30.00	$32.50	$35.00	$35.00
U.S. Next Day* (1 working day to most locations)	$45.00	$47.50	$50.00	$50.00
Canada Regular (5-7 working days)	$35.00	$40.00	$45.00	$45.00
Canada Express (2-4 working days)	$50.00	$55.00	$60.00	$60.00
International (7-10 working days)	$60.00	$70.00	$80.00	$80.00

Next-Day Delivery available for plans with the following prefixes: A, AGH, AX, B, BRF, CC, CL, DD[1], DP, E, EOF, FI, GA, GL[1], GLH, GS, H, HDC, HDS, HFL[1], HOM, J, JWB, KD, KLF, KP, L, LM, LRD, LRK, LS, MIN, PI, PIC, PW, Q, RD, RDR, RT, S, THD, TS, UD, Y

[1]*Not available for all plans. Please call before ordering.*

3 **PAYMENT INFORMATION**

Choose the method of payment you prefer. Send check, money order or credit card information along with name and address to:

COMPLETE THIS FORM

Plan Number: SS18–_____ **Price Code**_____

Foundation_____
(Carefully review the foundation option(s) available for your plan—basement, crawlspace, pole, pier or slab. If several options are offered, choose only one.)

1
☐ Study Set **(STAMPED "NOT FOR CONSTRUCTION")**
• RECOMMENDED FOR REVIEW/STUDY
☐ Four Sets
• RECOMMENDED FOR BIDDING
☐ Eight Sets   ➡ $_____
• RECOMMENDED FOR CONSTRUCTION   (See blueprint chart at left)
☐ Twelve Sets
• RECOMMENDED FOR MULTIPLE CONTRACTOR BIDS
☐ Reproducible Set
(Check for availability at left)
• RECOMMENDED FOR CONSTRUCTION/MODIFICATION. INCLUDES ONE FREE BLUEPRINT.

Additional Sets_____ **(Quantity)** $_____
Additional sets of the plan ordered are $50 each.   ($50 each)
Available on all plans. With minimum 4-set order only.

Mirror-Reversed Sets_____ **(Quantity)** $_____
From the total number of sets you ordered above, choose the   ($50 surcharge)
number of these that you want to be reversed. Pay only $50.
Note: All writing on mirror-reversed plans is backward. We recommend ordering one or two reversed sets in addition to the regular-reading sets.

Itemized List of Materials_____ **(Quantity)** $_____
Available for plans with these prefixes: A*, ADI*, AG*, AHP,   (See pricing chart at left)
APS*, AX*, B*, BOD*, C, CC*, CDG*, DBI, DD*, DW, E*, EOF*, FB[1], G, GLH, H, HDS*, HFL, HOM, I*, IDG, J*, K, L*, LM*, LMB*, LRD, NW*, P, PH, PIC, R*, RDR, RN, S*, SG*, SUL*, SUN, THD, UD*, UDA, VL, WGC*, WH, YS
*Not available on all plans. Please call before ordering.
[1]Expanded material workbook ($150) available for some plans.*

Description of Materials $_____
Sold only in sets of two for $60. For use in obtaining FHA or VA   ($60 for two sets)
financing. Available for plans with these prefixes: AHP, DW, H, K, P, PH, VL, Y, YS

Generic How-To Diagrams $_____
General guides on plumbing, wiring and solar heating, plus infor-   (Any one $20. Any two $30.
mation on how to convert from one foundation or exterior framing   Any three $40. All four only $45.)
to another. *Note: These diagrams are not specific to any one plan.*
☐ Plumbing   ☐ Wiring   ☐ Solar Heating   ☐ Framing & Foundation Conversion

2
SUBTOTAL $_____
SALES TAX* $_____
*MN residents add 6.5% sales tax
Attention Canadian customers: All sales are final, FOB St. Paul, Minnesota

3
SHIPPING/HANDLING $_____
(See chart at left)
GRAND TOTAL $_____

☐ Check/Money Order enclosed (in U.S. funds)
☐ VISA   ☐ MasterCard   ☐ AmEx   ☐ Discover
Credit Card #_____ **Exp. Date**_____

Name_____
Address_____
City_____ **State**_____ **Country**_____
ZIP_____ **Daytime Phone (____)**_____
Please check if you are a builder : ☐   **Home Phone (____)**_____

MAIL COUPON TO: HomeStyles.com, Dept. SS18
P.O. Box 75488
St. Paul, MN 55175-0488

Source Code SS18

OR FAX TO: (651) 602-5002

FOR FASTER SERVICE CALL 1-800-820-1283

Covered Porch Invites Visitors

- This nice home welcomes visitors with its covered front porch and its wide-open living areas.
- Detailed columns, railings and shutters decorate the front porch that guides guests to the central entry.
- Just off the entry, the bright living room merges with the dining room. The side wall is lined with glass, including a glass door that opens to the yard.
- The angled kitchen features a serving counter facing the dining room. A handry laundry closet and access to a storage area and the garage is nearby.
- An angled hall leads to the bedroom wing. The master suite offers a private bath, a walk-in closet and a dressing area with a vanity. Two additional bedrooms and another full bath are located down the hall.

Plan E-1217

Bedrooms: 3	Baths: 2

Living Area:	
Main floor	1,266 sq. ft.
Total Living Area:	**1,266 sq. ft.**
Garage and storage	550 sq. ft.
Exterior Wall Framing:	2x6

Foundation Options:
Crawlspace
Slab
(All plans can be built with your choice of foundation and framing. A generic conversion diagram is available. See order form.)

BLUEPRINT PRICE CODE:	A

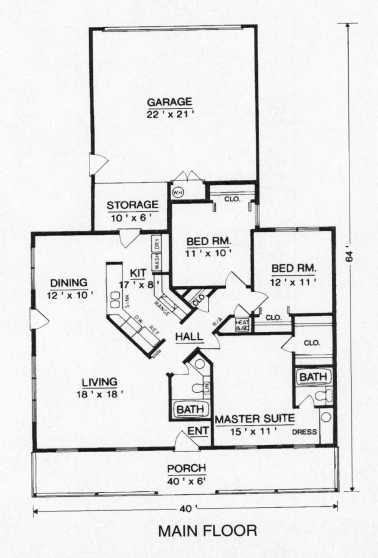

MAIN FLOOR

TO ORDER THIS BLUEPRINT, CALL TOLL-FREE 1-800-820-1283

Plan E-1217

PRICES AND DETAILS ON PAGES 12-15

Small Wonder

- This very affordable one-story home boasts an extremely efficient floor plan that maximizes the compact square footage. High ceilings in the shared living areas and in the master suite give the illusion of even more space.

- An elegant columned porch with gorgeous arched windows greets visitors and welcomes you home every day. Plenty of room is available here to sit and watch the day go by.

- The front entry opens directly into the good-sized living room, where you will enjoy years of memories in the making. A 10-ft. sloped ceiling soars above, while a warm fireplace flanked by decorative plant shelves serves as the room's comforting focal point.

- The tiled dining room and U-shaped kitchen nearby share a 10-ft. sloped ceiling. Easy access to the dining room will make family meals quick and easy. A patio provides a pleasing setting to enjoy a glass of fresh lemonade.

- The secluded master bedroom features a 10-ft. sloped ceiling and a private bath.

Plan DD-1100-B

Bedrooms: 3	Baths: 2
Living Area:	
Main floor	1,100 sq. ft.
Total Living Area:	**1,100 sq. ft.**
Garage	416 sq. ft.
Exterior Wall Framing:	2x4

Foundation Options:

Crawlspace

Slab

(All plans can be built with your choice of foundation and framing. A generic conversion diagram is available. See order form.)

BLUEPRINT PRICE CODE:	A

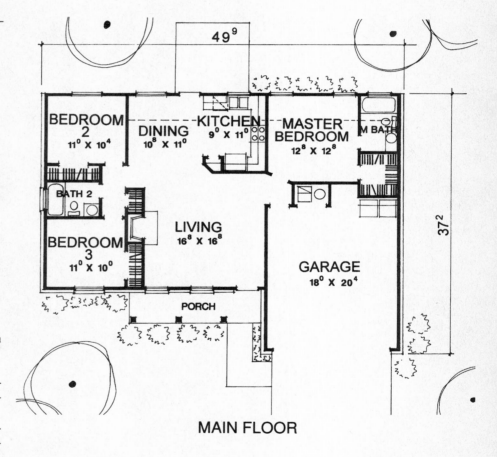

MAIN FLOOR

Stylish Exterior, Open Floor Plan

- With its simple yet stylish exterior, this modest-sized design is suitable for country or urban settings.
- A covered front porch and a gabled roof extension accent the facade while providing plenty of sheltered space for outdoor relaxation.
- Inside, the open floor plan puts available space to efficient use.
- The living room, which offers an inviting fireplace, is expanded by a cathedral ceiling. The adjoining dining area is open to the island kitchen, and all three rooms combine to create one huge gathering place.
- The master suite features a private bath and a large walk-in closet.
- Two more good-sized bedrooms share a second full bath.
- A convenient utility area leads to the carport, which incorporates extra storage space.

Plan J-86155

Bedrooms: 3	Baths: 2
Living Area:	
Main floor	1,385 sq. ft.
Total Living Area:	**1,385 sq. ft.**
Standard basement	1,385 sq. ft.
Carport	380 sq. ft.
Exterior Wall Framing:	2x4

Foundation Options:

Standard basement

Crawlspace

Slab

(All plans can be built with your choice of foundation and framing. A generic conversion diagram is available. See order form.)

BLUEPRINT PRICE CODE:	A

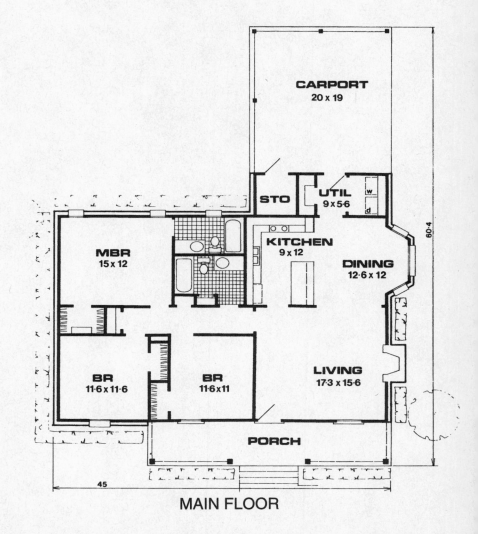

MAIN FLOOR

Plan J-86155

PRICES AND DETAILS ON PAGES 12-15

Appealing Farmhouse

- This appealing farmhouse design features a shady and inviting front porch with decorative railings.
- Inside, 14-ft. vaulted ceilings expand the living and dining rooms.
- This large area is brightened by bay windows and warmed by a unique two-way fireplace. Sliding glass doors lead to a sunny backyard patio.
- The functional kitchen includes a pantry closet, plenty of cabinet space and a serving bar to the dining room.
- The master bedroom boasts a mirrored dressing area, a private bath and abundant closet space.
- Two additional bedrooms share another full bath. The third bedroom includes a cozy window seat.

Plan NW-521

Bedrooms: 3	Baths: 2
Living Area:	
Main floor	1,187 sq. ft.
Total Living Area:	**1,187 sq. ft.**
Garage	448 sq. ft.
Exterior Wall Framing:	2x6

Foundation Options:

Crawlspace
(All plans can be built with your choice of foundation and framing. A generic conversion diagram is available. See order form.)

BLUEPRINT PRICE CODE: A

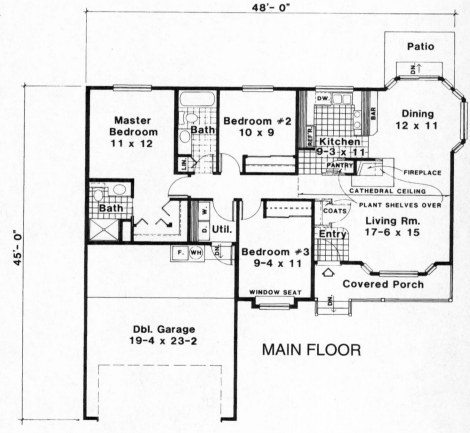

MAIN FLOOR

Distinctive Inside and Out

- A decorative columned entry, shuttered windows and a facade of stucco and stone offer a distinct look to this economical one-story home.
- The focal point of the interior is the huge, central family room. The room is enhanced by a dramatic corner fireplace, a 15-ft.-high vaulted ceiling and a neat serving bar that extends from the kitchen and includes a wet bar.
- A decorative plant shelf adorns the entrance to the adjoining breakfast room, which features a lovely bay window. The kitchen offers a pantry and a pass-through to the family room.
- The formal dining room is easy to reach from both the kitchen and the family room, and is set off with columned arches and a raised ceiling.
- The secluded master suite boasts a vaulted private bath with dual sinks, an oval garden tub, a separate toilet room and a large walk-in closet.
- Two more bedrooms share a second bath at the other end of the home.

Plan FB-5001-SAVA

Bedrooms: 3	Baths: 2
Living Area:	
Main floor	1,429 sq. ft.
Total Living Area:	**1,429 sq. ft.**
Daylight basement	1,429 sq. ft.
Garage and storage	436 sq. ft.
Exterior Wall Framing:	2x4

Foundation Options:

Daylight basement
Crawlspace
Slab

(All plans can be built with your choice of foundation and framing. A generic conversion diagram is available. See order form.)

BLUEPRINT PRICE CODE:	A

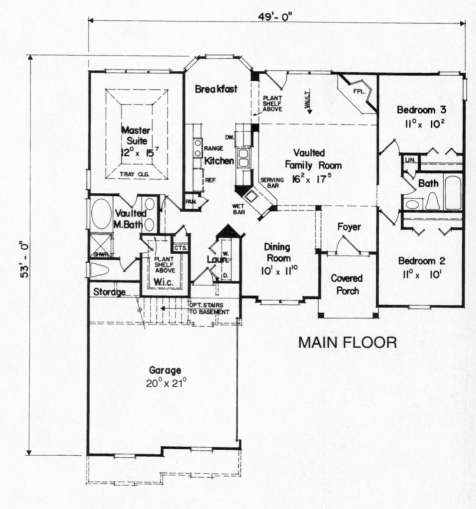

MAIN FLOOR

TO ORDER THIS BLUEPRINT, CALL TOLL-FREE 1-800-820-1283

Plan FB-5001-SAVA

PRICES AND DETAILS ON PAGES 12-15

Rustic Ranch-Style Design

- This ranch-style home offers a rustic facade that is warm and inviting. The railed front porch and stone accents are especially appealing.
- The interior is warm as well, with the focal point being the attractive living room. Features here include an eye-catching fireplace, patio access and a dramatic 14-ft. sloped ceiling with exposed beams.
- The open dining room lies off the foyer and adjoins the efficient U-shaped kitchen, which includes a pantry and a broom closet.
- The master suite features a large walk-in closet and a roomy master bath.
- At the other end of the home, two secondary bedrooms with abundant closet space share another full bath.

Plan E-1410

Bedrooms: 3	Baths: 2
Living Area:	
Main floor	1,418 sq. ft.
Total Living Area:	**1,418 sq. ft.**
Garage	484 sq. ft.
Storage	38 sq. ft.
Exterior Wall Framing:	2x4

Foundation Options:

Crawlspace

Slab

(All plans can be built with your choice of foundation and framing. A generic conversion diagram is available. See order form.)

BLUEPRINT PRICE CODE: **A**

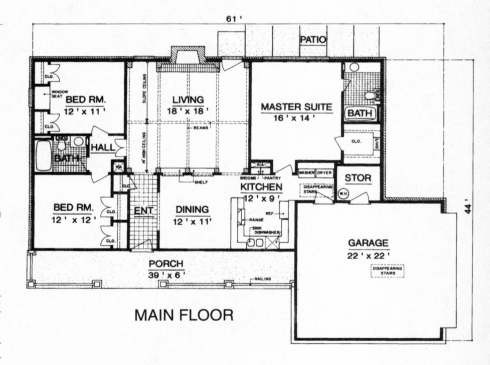

MAIN FLOOR

High-Profile Contemporary

- This design does away with wasted space, putting the emphasis on quality rather than on size.
- The angled floor plan minimizes hall space and creates smooth traffic flow while adding architectural appeal. The roof framing is square, however, to allow for economical construction.
- The spectacular living and dining rooms share a 16-ft. cathedral ceiling and a fireplace. Both rooms have lots of glass overlooking an angled rear terrace.
- The dining room includes a glass-filled alcove and sliding patio doors topped by transom windows. Tall windows frame the living room fireplace and trace the slope of the ceiling.
- A pass-through joins the dining room to the combination kitchen and family room, which features a snack bar and a clerestory window.
- The sleeping wing provides a super master suite, which boasts a skylighted dressing area and a luxurious bath. The optional den, or third bedroom, shares a second full bath with another bedroom that offers a 14-ft. sloped ceiling.

Plan K-688-D

Bedrooms: 2+	Baths: 2½
Living Area:	
Main floor	1,340 sq. ft.
Total Living Area:	**1,340 sq. ft.**
Standard basement	1,235 sq. ft.
Garage	484 sq. ft.
Exterior Wall Framing:	2x4 or 2x6

Foundation Options:

Standard basement

Slab

(All plans can be built with your choice of foundation and framing. A generic conversion diagram is available. See order form.)

BLUEPRINT PRICE CODE:	A

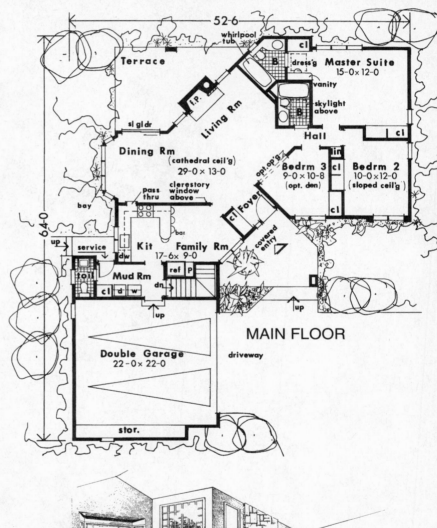

MAIN FLOOR

VIEW INTO DINING ROOM AND LIVING ROOM

Plan K-688-D

PRICES AND DETAILS ON PAGES 12-15

Active Living Made Easy

- This home is perfect for active living. Its rectangular design allows the use of truss roof framing, which makes construction easy and economical.
- The galley-style kitchen and the sunny dining area are kept open to the living room, forming one huge activity space. Two sets of sliding glass doors expand the living area to the large deck.

- The secluded master bedroom offers a private bath, while the remaining bedrooms share a hall bath.
- The two baths, the laundry facilities and the kitchen are clustered to allow common plumbing walls.
- Plan H-921-1A has a standard crawlspace foundation and an optional solar-heating system. Plan H-921-2A has a Plen-Wood system, which utilizes the sealed crawlspace as a chamber for distributing heated or cooled air. Both versions of the design call for energy-efficient 2x6 exterior walls.

Plans H-921-1A & -2A	
Bedrooms: 3	**Baths:** 2
Living Area:	
Main floor	1,164 sq. ft.
Total Living Area:	**1,164 sq. ft.**
Exterior Wall Framing:	2x6
Foundation Options:	**Plan #**
Crawlspace	H-921-1A
Plen-Wood crawlspace	H-921-2A
(All plans can be built with your choice of foundation and framing. A generic conversion diagram is available. See order form.)	
BLUEPRINT PRICE CODE:	**A**

Main Floor

42'-0" 8'-0"

30'-0"

BEDROOM 11'-6" x 13'-6"

BATH

w d LAUNDRY

DINING

CLOSET

KITCHEN 9'-7" x 8'-2"

BATH

wh

LIVING RM 12'-0" x 23'-0"

DECK

CLOS CLOS

LINEN

ENTRY

CLOSET

BEDROOM 11'-6" x 10'-3"

BEDROOM 10'-9" x 10'-0"

CLOSET

MAIN FLOOR

Family-Style Leisure Living

- This handsome ranch-style home features a floor plan that is great for family living and entertaining.
- In from the quaint covered porch, the spacious formal areas flow together for a dramatic impact. The living room is enhanced by a fireplace and a sloped ceiling. A patio door in the dining room extends activities to the outdoors.
- The efficient U-shaped kitchen opens to the dining room and offers a pantry, a window above the sink and abundant counter space.
- A good-sized utility room with convenient laundry facilities opens to the carport. This area also includes a large storage room and disappearing stairs to even more storage space.
- Three bedrooms and two baths occupy the sleeping wing. The master suite features a large walk-in closet and a private bath.
- The two remaining bedrooms are well proportioned and share a hall bath. Storage space is well accounted for here as well, with two linen closets and a coat closet in the bedroom hall.

Plan E-1308

Bedrooms: 3	Baths: 2
Living Area:	
Main floor	1,375 sq. ft.
Total Living Area:	**1,375 sq. ft.**
Carport	430 sq. ft.
Storage	95 sq. ft.
Exterior Wall Framing:	2x4

Foundation Options:

Crawlspace
Slab
(All plans can be built with your choice of foundation and framing. A generic conversion diagram is available. See order form.)

BLUEPRINT PRICE CODE: A

MAIN FLOOR

TO ORDER THIS BLUEPRINT, CALL TOLL-FREE 1-800-820-1283 Plan E-1308 *PRICES AND DETAILS ON PAGES 12-15*

Affordable Pleasures

- This compact home comes with an affordable price tag and plenty of amenities usually found only in much larger, and more costly, homes.
- An elegant porch with stately columns framing an oversized Palladian window will impress guests and passersby.
- Inside, the foyer looks into the living room at the rear of the home. A corner fireplace adds a comforting glow to all gatherings, while a counter provides a handy place to serve snacks.
- The walk-through kitchen is located between the dining room and the casual morning room. A cheery bay embraces the morning room; a beautiful French door opens to a backyard patio.
- An incredible master bath with a dual-sink vanity, two walk-in closets and a separate tub and shower highlights the master suite nearby.
- All of the rooms mentioned above have 10-ft. ceilings.
- Across the home, two spacious bedrooms with ample closet space share a full hall bath.

Plan DD-1382	
Bedrooms: 3	**Baths: 2**
Living Area:	
Main floor	1,388 sq. ft.
Total Living Area:	**1,388 sq. ft.**
Garage	449 sq. ft.
Exterior Wall Framing:	2x4
Foundation Options:	
Crawlspace	
Slab	

(All plans can be built with your choice of foundation and framing. A generic conversion diagram is available. See order form.)

BLUEPRINT PRICE CODE:	**A**

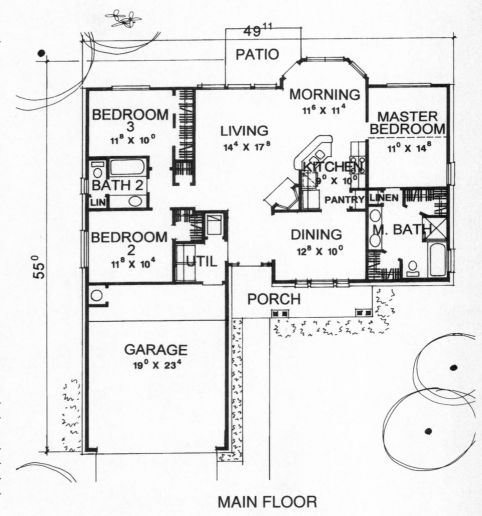

MAIN FLOOR

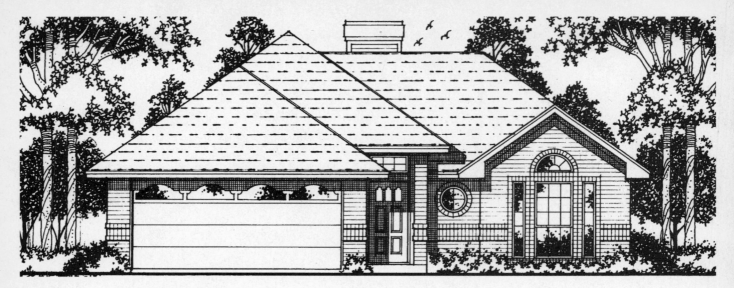

Free and Clear

- This home's central living areas flow together under the glow of natural light.
- In the living room, a warm fireplace and built-in cabinets attract the eye. A tidy backyard patio beckons from beyond.
- A boxed-out window brightens the dining room, which swings easily between formal and casual occasions. The galley-style kitchen flaunts every desirable amenity, and welcomes sleepy-eyed children to its breakfast bar for their hot cereal and orange juice.
- The master bedroom is designed with peace and quiet in mind. A true retreat, the suite boasts a private bath with an opulent garden tub, a separate shower and walk-in closets for Mom and Dad. A dual-sink vanity nicely rounds out the room's amenities.
- There's plenty of room for growing kids in the two other bedrooms. The foremost bedroom has a breathtaking window treatment with a glorious half-round at its crown.
- A full bath near the home's front entry serves the kids' rooms and comes in handy when guests arrive after a long road trip!

Plan KD-1322

Bedrooms: 3	Baths: 2
Living Area:	
Main floor	1,322 sq. ft.
Total Living Area:	**1,322 sq. ft.**
Garage and storage	432 sq. ft.
Exterior Wall Framing:	2x4

Foundation Options:

Slab

(All plans can be built with your choice of foundation and framing. A generic conversion diagram is available. See order form.)

BLUEPRINT PRICE CODE:	A

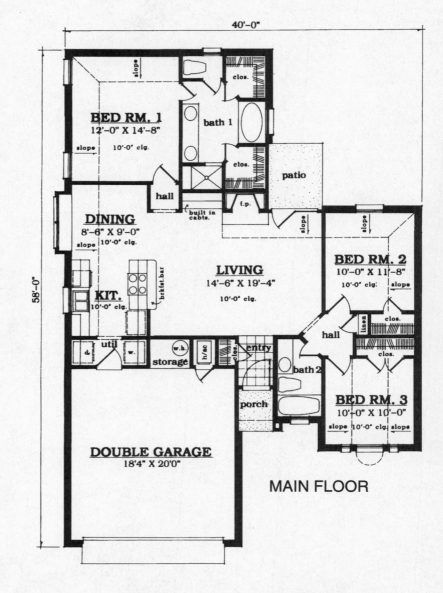

MAIN FLOOR

One-Story with Impact

- Striking gables, a brick facade and an elegant sidelighted entry give this one-story plenty of impact.
- The impressive interior spaces begin with an 11-ft., 8-in. raised ceiling in the foyer. To the left of the foyer, decorative columns and a large picture window grace the dining room.
- The wonderful living spaces center around a huge family room, which features a 14-ft.-high vaulted ceiling and another pair of columns that separate it from the hall. A stunning fireplace is framed by a window and a beautiful French door.
- The open kitchen and breakfast area features a built-in desk, a pantry closet and a pass-through above the sink.
- An elegant 10-ft. tray ceiling is featured in the master suite, which also boasts a 13-ft. vaulted bath with a garden spa tub, a separate shower, a big walk-in closet and an attractive plant shelf.

Plan FB-1553

Bedrooms: 3	Baths: 2
Living Area:	
Main floor	1,553 sq. ft.
Total Living Area:	**1,553 sq. ft.**
Daylight basement	1,553 sq. ft.
Garage	410 sq. ft.
Exterior Wall Framing:	2x4

Foundation Options:
Daylight basement
Crawlspace
Slab
(All plans can be built with your choice of foundation and framing. A generic conversion diagram is available. See order form.)

BLUEPRINT PRICE CODE: B

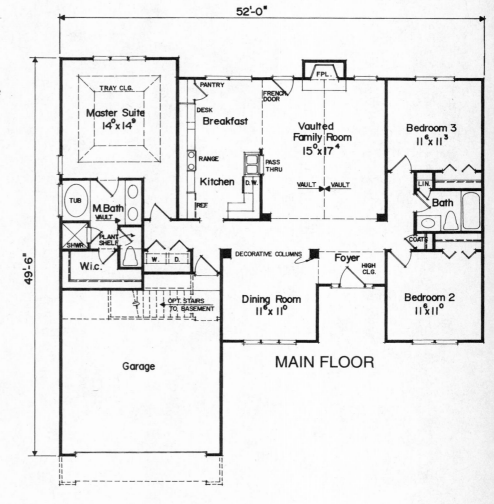

MAIN FLOOR

Inviting Country Porch

- A columned porch with double doors invites you into the rustic living areas of this ranch-style home.
- Inside, the entry allows views back to the expansive, central living room and the backyard beyond.
- The living room boasts an exposed-beam ceiling and a massive fireplace with a wide stone hearth, a wood box and built-in bookshelves. A sunny patio offers additional entertaining space.
- The dining room and the efficient kitchen combine for easy meal service, with a serving bar separating the two.
- The main hallway leads to the sleeping wing, which offers a large master bedroom with a walk-in closet and a private bath.
- Two additional bedrooms share another full bath, and a laundry closet is easily accessible to the entire bedroom wing.

Plan E-1304

Bedrooms: 3	**Baths:** 2

Living Area:	
Main floor	1,395 sq. ft.
Total Living Area:	**1,395 sq. ft.**
Garage and storage	481 sq. ft.
Exterior Wall Framing:	2x4

Foundation Options:
Crawlspace
Slab
(All plans can be built with your choice of foundation and framing. A generic conversion diagram is available. See order form.)

BLUEPRINT PRICE CODE:	**A**

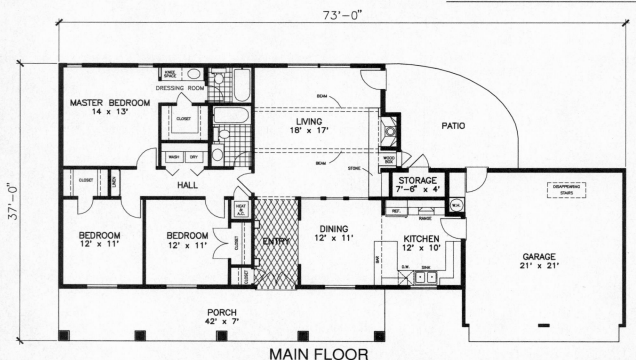

MAIN FLOOR

Plan E-1304

PRICES AND DETAILS ON PAGES 12-15

All in One!

- This plan puts today's most luxurious home-design features into one attractive, economical package.
- The covered front porch and the gabled roofline, accented by an arched window and a round louver vent, give the exterior a homey yet stylish appeal.
- Just inside the front door, the ceiling rises to 11 ft., offering an impressive greeting. The spacious living room is flooded with light through a central skylight and a pair of French doors that frame the smart fireplace.
- The living room flows into the nice-sized dining room, also with an 11-ft. ceiling. The adjoining kitchen offers a handy laundry closet, lots of counter space and a sunny dinette that opens to an expansive backyard terrace.
- The bedroom wing includes a wonderful master suite with a sizable sleeping room and an adjacent dressing area with two closets. Glass blocks above the dual-sink vanity in the master bath let in light yet maintain privacy. A whirlpool tub and a separate shower complete the suite.
- The larger of the two remaining bedrooms boasts an 11-ft.-high ceiling and an arched window.

Plan HFL-1680-FL

Bedrooms: 3	Baths: 2
Living Area:	
Main floor	1,367 sq. ft.
Total Living Area:	**1,367 sq. ft.**
Standard basement	1,367 sq. ft.
Garage	431 sq. ft.
Exterior Wall Framing:	2x6

Foundation Options:

Standard basement
(All plans can be built with your choice of foundation and framing. A generic conversion diagram is available. See order form.)

BLUEPRINT PRICE CODE: **A**

VIEW INTO LIVING ROOM

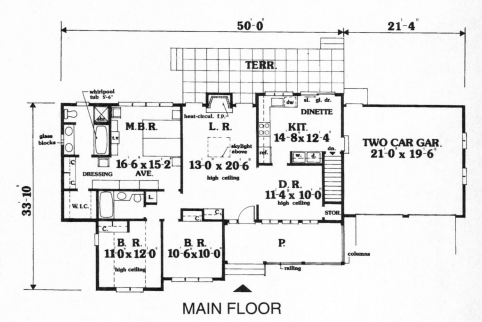

MAIN FLOOR

Elegant Touch

- A stunning exterior of brick, siding and copper flashing adds an elegant touch to this feature-filled one-story home.
- The recessed sidelighted entry opens directly into the bright and airy family room, which boasts a 12-ft. ceiling and a striking window-flanked fireplace.
- The adjacent formal dining room features a 9-ft. tray ceiling and includes a French door to a backyard patio.
- Designed with the gourmet in mind, the spacious kitchen offers a pantry, an angled eating bar and a sunny breakfast area. A French door accesses a covered back porch.
- Enhanced by a 14-ft. vaulted ceiling and decorative plant shelves, the master suite unfolds to a sitting area and a roomy walk-in closet. The vaulted master bath showcases a garden tub, a separate shower and a functional dual-sink vanity with knee space.
- On the opposite side of the home, two additional bedrooms are serviced by a second full bath.
- A laundry room is conveniently located between the entry and the garage.

Plan APS-1516

Bedrooms: 3	Baths: 2
Living Area:	
Main floor	1,593 sq. ft.
Total Living Area:	**1,593 sq. ft.**
Garage	482 sq. ft.
Exterior Wall Framing:	2x4

Foundation Options:

Slab

(All plans can be built with your choice of foundation and framing. A generic conversion diagram is available. See order form.)

BLUEPRINT PRICE CODE:	B

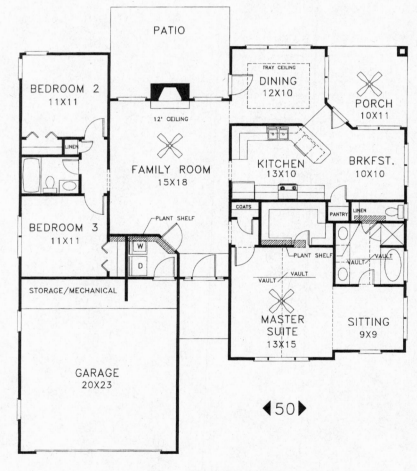

MAIN FLOOR

Plan APS-1516

PRICES AND DETAILS ON PAGES 12-15

Exciting Great Room Featured

- A brick and wood exterior accented by multiple gables and ornate windows gives this smart-looking one-story home lots of curb appeal.
- The amenity-filled interior is just as exciting. The 17-ft. vaulted foyer leads immediately into the spacious Great Room that also features a 17-ft.-high vaulted ceiling and a handsome fireplace flanked by windows.
- The adjoining dining room flows nicely into the breakfast area and the kitchen. The impressive kitchen offers an angled serving bar and a convenient pantry, while the sunny breakfast area has a French door to the backyard.
- The master suite boasts a 10-ft. tray ceiling and a walk-in closet with a plant shelf. The vaulted master bath features a garden tub and a dual-sink vanity.
- The two remaining bedrooms are serviced by another full bath.

Plan FB-1359

Bedrooms: 3	Baths: 2
Living Area:	
Main floor	1,359 sq. ft.
Total Living Area:	**1,359 sq. ft.**
Garage	407 sq. ft.
Exterior Wall Framing:	2x4

Foundation Options:

Crawlspace

Slab

(All plans can be built with your choice of foundation and framing. A generic conversion diagram is available. See order form.)

BLUEPRINT PRICE CODE:	**A**

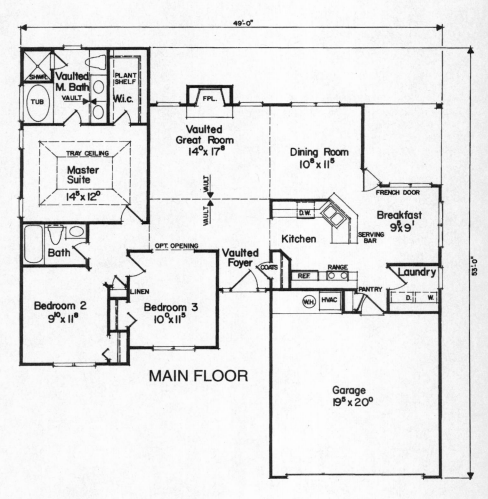

MAIN FLOOR

Comfortable Ranch Design

- This affordable ranch design offers numerous amenities and is ideally structured for comfortable living, both indoors and out.
- A tiled reception hall leads into the spacious living and dining rooms, which feature a handsome brick fireplace, an 11-ft. sloped ceiling and two sets of sliding glass doors to access a lovely backyard terrace.
- The adjacent family room, designed for privacy, showcases a large boxed-out window with a built-in seat. The kitchen features an efficient U-shaped counter, an eating bar and a pantry.
- The master suite has its own terrace and private bath with a whirlpool tub.
- Two additional bedrooms share a second full bath.
- The garage has two separate storage areas—one accessible from the interior and the other from the backyard.

VIEW INTO LIVING ROOM AND DINING ROOM

Plan K-518-A

Bedrooms: 3	**Baths:** 2

Living Area:

Main floor	1,276 sq. ft.
Total Living Area:	**1,276 sq. ft.**
Standard basement	1,247 sq. ft.
Garage and storage	579 sq. ft.
Exterior Wall Framing:	2x4 or 2x6

Foundation Options:

Standard basement
Slab
(All plans can be built with your choice of foundation and framing. A generic conversion diagram is available. See order form.)

BLUEPRINT PRICE CODE:	**A**

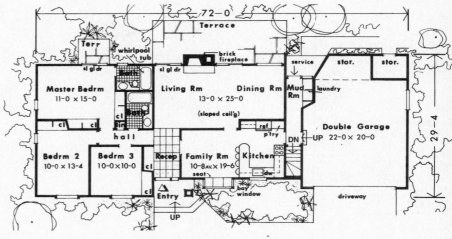

MAIN FLOOR

Plan K-518-A

Extra-Special Ranch-Style

- Repeating gables, wood siding and brick adorn this ranch-style home, which offers numerous amenities in its compact interior.
- The entry leads directly into a spectacular 21-ft.-high vaulted family room, an ideal entertainment area accented by a corner fireplace and a French door to the backyard.
- A serving bar connects the family room with the efficient kitchen, which has a handy pantry, ample counter space and a sunny breakfast room.
- The luxurious master suite boasts a 10½-ft. tray ceiling, a large bank of windows and a walk-in closet. The master bath features a garden tub.
- Two more bedrooms, one with a 14½-ft. vaulted ceiling, share another full bath.
- The two-car garage provides convenient access to the kitchen and laundry area.

Plan FB-1104

Bedrooms: 3	Baths: 2
Living Area:	
Main floor	1,104 sq. ft.
Total Living Area:	**1,104 sq. ft.**
Daylight basement	1,104 sq. ft.
Garage	400 sq. ft.
Exterior Wall Framing:	2x4

Foundation Options:

Daylight basement

Crawlspace

(All plans can be built with your choice of foundation and framing. A generic conversion diagram is available. See order form.)

BLUEPRINT PRICE CODE:	A

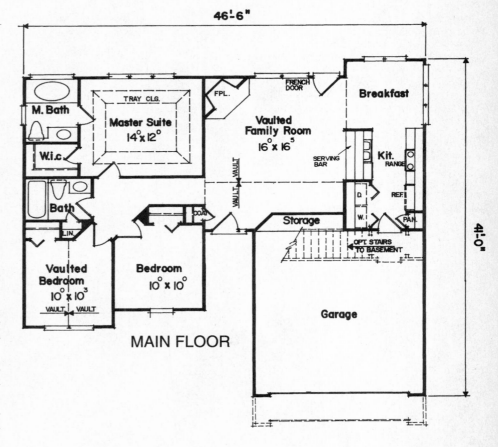

MAIN FLOOR

Bold New Economic Plan

- The inviting entry of this economical three-bedroom ranch flows directly into the spacious living room.
- Warmed by a fireplace, the living room is easily served from the kitchen's angled snack counter. The adjoining dining area enjoys access to a covered backyard patio.
- The charming master bedroom offers a private bath, a dressing area and a roomy walk-in closet.
- Two additional bedrooms boast walk-in closets and are served by a nearby hallway bath.
- The convenient laundry/utility room accesses the two-car garage, which includes extra storage space.
- At only 46 ft. wide, this design would be suitable for a narrow lot.

Plan SDG-81115

Bedrooms: 3	Baths: 2
Living Area:	
Main floor	1,296 sq. ft.
Total Living Area:	**1,296 sq. ft.**
Garage	400 sq. ft.
Exterior Wall Framing:	2x4

Foundation Options:

Slab

(All plans can be built with your choice of foundation and framing. A generic conversion diagram is available. See order form.)

BLUEPRINT PRICE CODE: A

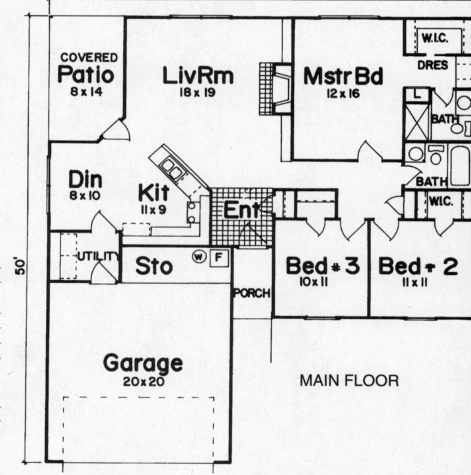

MAIN FLOOR

Plan SDG-81115

PRICES AND DETAILS ON PAGES 12-15

Eye-Catching Details

- This eye-catching home features a handsome exterior and an exciting floor plan that maximizes square footage.
- The covered porch leads into a vaulted foyer with an angled coat closet. Straight ahead, the 16½-ft.-high vaulted Great Room combines with the dining room and kitchen to create one expansive living and entertaining area.
- The Great Room offers a fireplace and access to the backyard. The galley-style kitchen has a 16½-ft.-high ceiling and is bordered by the vaulted dining room on one side and a breakfast area with a laundry closet on the other.
- The master suite boasts a 15-ft., 8-in. tray ceiling. The 13-ft.-high vaulted bath has a garden tub, a separate shower and a vanity with knee space.
- The two remaining bedrooms are located on the opposite side of the home and share a full bath. A plant shelf is an attention-getting detail found here.

Plan FB-1289

Bedrooms: 3	Baths: 2
Living Area:	
Main floor	1,289 sq. ft.
Total Living Area:	**1,289 sq. ft.**
Daylight basement	1,289 sq. ft.
Garage	430 sq. ft.
Exterior Wall Framing:	2x4

Foundation Options:
Daylight basement
Crawlspace
Slab
(All plans can be built with your choice of foundation and framing. A generic conversion diagram is available. See order form.)

BLUEPRINT PRICE CODE: A

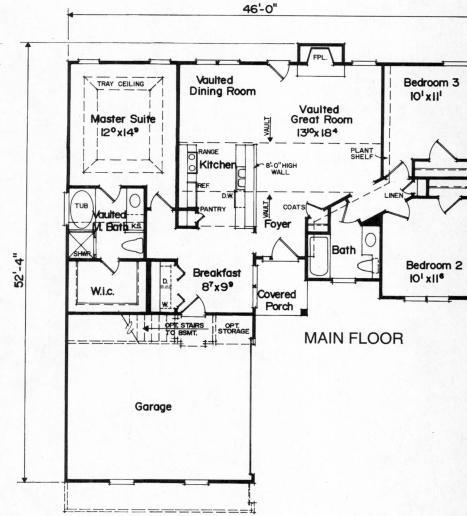

MAIN FLOOR

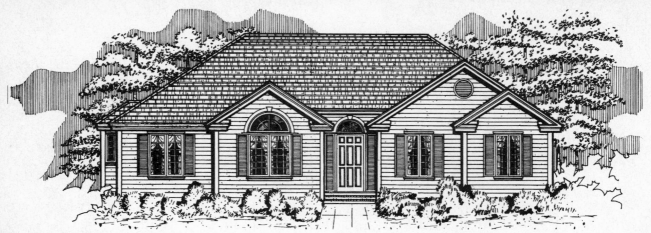

Relax in a Sun Room Porch

- Classic styling is captured in this home's elegant exterior, accented with half-round windows.
- The graceful foyer has a sloped ceiling and flows into a huge entertaining space. The living and dining rooms share a fireplace and a view of the adjoining patio through exciting rear glass walls.
- A large casual living space is created with a sunny eating area and large kitchen. The addition of a sun room porch provides extra space for relaxing or entertaining.
- At the opposite end of the home, the master suite is the perfect quiet retreat. The bedroom features a tray ceiling and a private patio. A large walk-in closet and a personal bath are also included.
- Two secondary bedrooms and another full bath complete the floor plan.

Plan AHP-9370

Bedrooms: 3	Baths: 2
Living Area:	
Main floor	1,248 sq. ft.
Sunroom porch	125 sq. ft.
Total Living Area:	**1,373 sq. ft.**
Standard basement	1,248 sq. ft.
Garage and storage	507 sq. ft.
Exterior Wall Framing:	2x4 or 2x6

Foundation Options:
Standard basement
Crawlspace
Slab
(Typical foundation & framing conversion diagram available—see order form.)

BLUEPRINT PRICE CODE:	A

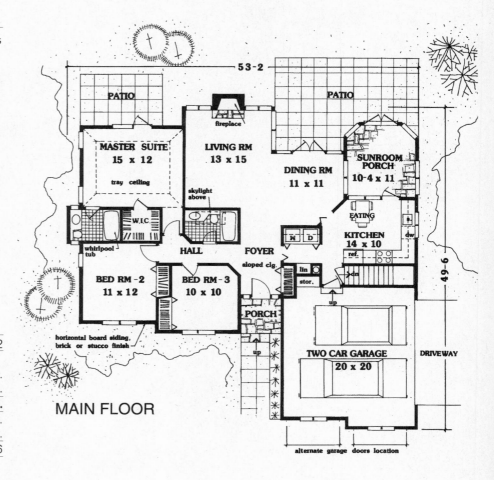

MAIN FLOOR

TO ORDER THIS BLUEPRINT, CALL TOLL-FREE 1-800-820-1283

Plan AHP-9370

PRICES AND DETAILS ON PAGES 12-15

Economical Three-Bedroom

- A striking covered entry with stately columns adds a distinguished look to this economical one-story home.
- Inside, a spacious living and dining room combination easily and elegantly accommodates formal occasions.
- The large family room is open to the kitchen, which offers an oversized snack bar and a pantry closet. A bright

eating area overlooks a lovely outdoor patio. A pocket door closes off the kitchen from the formal dining room.
- The laundry room is conveniently located near the kitchen and the carport with extra storage space.
- The sleeping wing houses a large master bedroom with a private bath, two linen closets, a walk-in closet and a separate dressing area set off with wood spindles.
- The two extra bedrooms have walk-in closets and share another full bath across the hall.

Plan E-1300	
Bedrooms: 3	**Baths:** 2
Living Area:	
Main floor	1,366 sq. ft.
Total Living Area:	**1,366 sq. ft.**
Carport and storage	470 sq. ft.
Exterior Wall Framing:	2x4
Foundation Options:	

Crawlspace
Slab
(All plans can be built with your choice of foundation and framing. A generic conversion diagram is available. See order form.)

BLUEPRINT PRICE CODE:	A

MAIN FLOOR

Charming
Simplicity

- This home features a covered front porch and a simple floor plan, each enhancing the home's charming appeal.
- In the living room, the cozy fireplace offers warmth and drama. Built-in bookcases are featured on either side.
- The adjoining dining room flows into the bright island kitchen and opens to the backyard. Laundry facilities and a carport entrance are nearby.
- The secluded master bedroom features a sloped ceiling, a corner window, a walk-in closet, a dressing area and a separate bath.
- Two nice-sized bedrooms share a full bath at the opposite end of the home.

Plan J-8670

Bedrooms: 3	Baths: 2
Living Area:	
Main floor	1,522 sq. ft.
Total Living Area:	**1,522 sq. ft.**
Standard basement	1,522 sq. ft.
Carport and storage	436 sq. ft.
Exterior Wall Framing:	2x4

Foundation Options:

Standard basement
Crawlspace
Slab

(All plans can be built with your choice of foundation and framing. A generic conversion diagram is available. See order form.)

BLUEPRINT PRICE CODE:	B

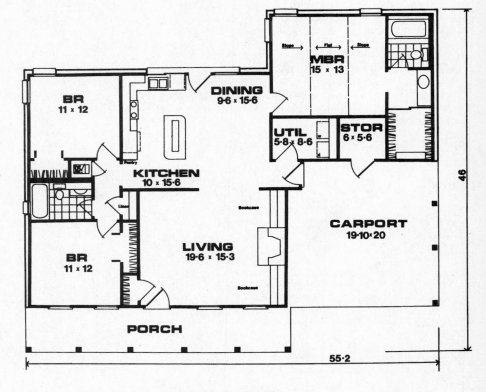

MAIN FLOOR

Plan J-8670

PRICES AND DETAILS
ON PAGES 12-15

Living Is Easy!

- Filled with popular features but affordably sized, this charming country home is a great choice for a new family.
- Past the inviting covered front porch and beyond a decorative open railing, the spacious living room is brightened by a lovely bay window with a built-in seat. A handsome fireplace adds warmth to the area.

- The efficient U-shaped kitchen offers a stylish eating bar and a windowed sink.
- The adjoining dining room is large enough for any occasion, and offers handy sliding glass doors to a sunny backyard patio.
- In the sleeping wing of the home, the good-sized master bedroom features two closets and a private bath.
- The two secondary bedrooms share a nice full bath, which includes a handy laundry closet.

Plan AX-98602	
Bedrooms: 3	**Baths:** 2
Living Area:	
Main floor	1,253 sq. ft.
Total Living Area:	**1,253 sq. ft.**
Basement	1,253 sq. ft.
Garage	368 sq. ft.
Exterior Wall Framing:	2x4

Foundation Options:
Daylight basement
Standard basement
Crawlspace
Slab
(All plans can be built with your choice of foundation and framing. A generic conversion diagram is available. See order form.)

BLUEPRINT PRICE CODE:	**A**

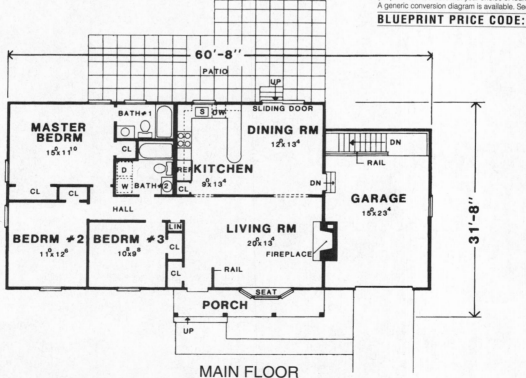

MAIN FLOOR

Economical and Functional

- Economically structured and architecturally refined, this four-bedroom ranch home offers lots of light-filled spaces.
- The entry area is brightened by optional skylights. Guests proceed into the large living and dining rooms, which are further expanded by a sloped ceiling. Other features include a bay window, a brick fireplace and sliders to a rear terrace.
- A cozy family room, dinette and kitchen boast a peninsula serving bar and a nearby half-bath and laundry area.
- The master suite offers a private bath with whirlpool tub and sliding glass doors to a secluded terrace.
- The three remaining bedrooms share a full bath with a dual-sink vanity.

Plan K-659-U

Bedrooms: 4	Baths: 2½

Living Area:	
Main floor	1,580 sq. ft.

Total Living Area:	**1,580 sq. ft.**
Standard basement	1,512 sq. ft.
Garage and storage	439 sq. ft.

Exterior Wall Framing:	2x4 or 2x6

Foundation Options:
Standard basement
Slab
(Typical foundation & framing conversion diagram available—see order form.)

BLUEPRINT PRICE CODE:	**B**

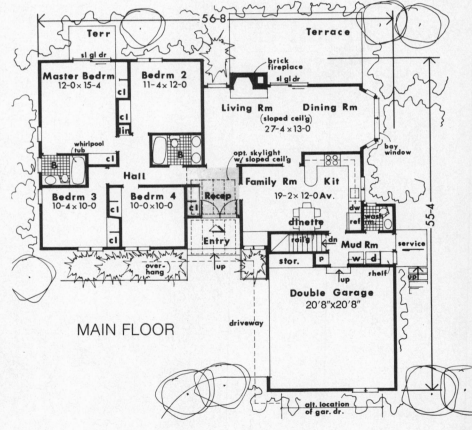

MAIN FLOOR

Designed for Today's Family

- Compact and affordable, this home is designed for today's young families.
- The Great Room features corner windows, an impressive fireplace and a 12-ft.-high vaulted ceiling.
- The kitchen/dining room combination offers space for two people to share food preparation and clean-up chores.
- The master suite is impressive for a home of this size, and includes a cozy window seat, a large walk-in closet and a private bath.
- Another full bath serves the remainder of the main floor. The optional third bedroom could be used as a den or as an expanded dining area.

Plan B-8317

Bedrooms: 2+	**Baths:** 2

Living Area:

Main floor	1,016 sq. ft.
Total Living Area:	**1,016 sq. ft.**
Exterior Wall Framing:	2×4

Foundation Options:

Slab
(All plans can be built with your choice of foundation and framing. A generic conversion diagram is available. See order form.)

BLUEPRINT PRICE CODE: A

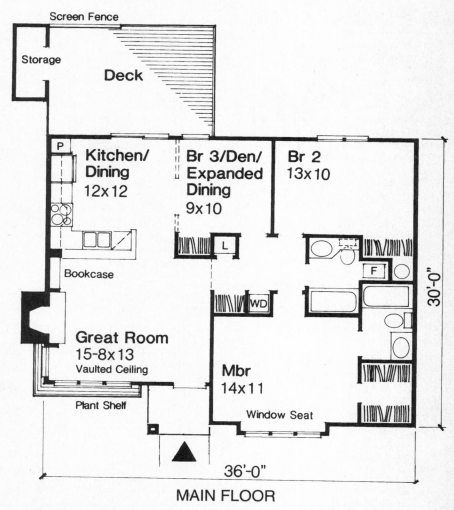

MAIN FLOOR

Maximum Livability

- Compact and easy to build, this appealing ranch-style home is big on charm and livability.
- The entry of the home opens to a dramatic 13-ft. vaulted living room with exposed beams, a handsome fireplace and access to a backyard patio.
- Wood post dividers set off the large raised dining room, which is brightened by a stunning window wall.
- The adjoining kitchen offers a spacious snack bar and easy access to the utility room and the two-car garage. A nice storage area is also included.
- Three bedrooms and two baths occupy the sleeping wing. One of the baths is private to the master suite, which features a walk-in closet and a dressing area with a sit-down make-up table. The two remaining bedrooms also have walk-in closets.

Plan E-1305

Bedrooms: 3	Baths: 2
Living Area:	
Main floor	1,346 sq. ft.
Total Living Area:	**1,346 sq. ft.**
Garage	441 sq. ft.
Storage	44 sq. ft.
Exterior Wall Framing:	2x4

Foundation Options:

Crawlspace

Slab

(All plans can be built with your choice of foundation and framing. A generic conversion diagram is available. See order form.)

BLUEPRINT PRICE CODE: A

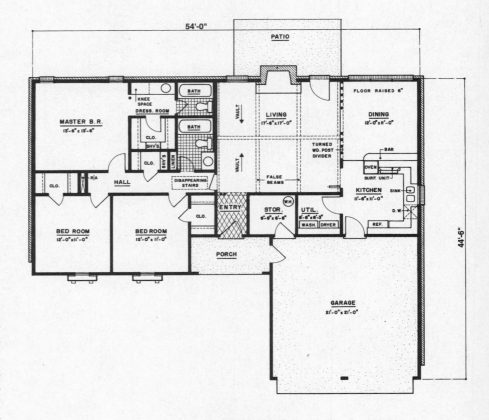

MAIN FLOOR

Striking One-Story Home

- Eye-catching angles, both inside and out, are the keynotes of this luxurious one-story home.
- The striking double-door entry is illuminated by a skylight. The foyer is just as impressive, with its cathedral ceiling and skylight.
- The sunken living room also features a cathedral ceiling, and a bay-window alcove faces the front.
- A low partition separates the living room from the formal dining room. Here, too, a cathedral ceiling and bay windows add interesting angles and spaciousness to the room.
- The open family room, breakfast room and kitchen offer plenty of space for casual family living. The family room includes a corner fireplace with adjacent built-in shelves. The bayed breakfast area boasts a cathedral ceiling and French doors to the backyard. An angled snack counter faces the U-shaped kitchen.
- The master bedroom also has a bay window facing the backyard, plus a large walk-in closet. Also included is a private bath with a whirlpool tub.
- Two more bedrooms, another full bath and a utility area complete the design.

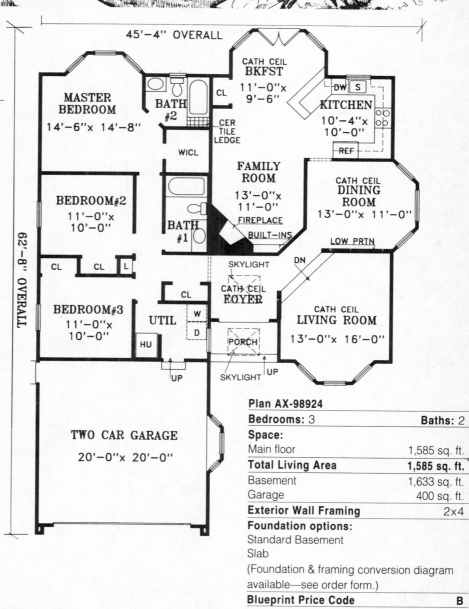

Plan AX-98924	
Bedrooms: 3	**Baths:** 2
Space:	
Main floor	1,585 sq. ft.
Total Living Area	**1,585 sq. ft.**
Basement	1,633 sq. ft.
Garage	400 sq. ft.
Exterior Wall Framing	2x4
Foundation options:	
Standard Basement	
Slab	
(Foundation & framing conversion diagram available—see order form.)	
Blueprint Price Code	B

ALTERNATE MASTER BATH

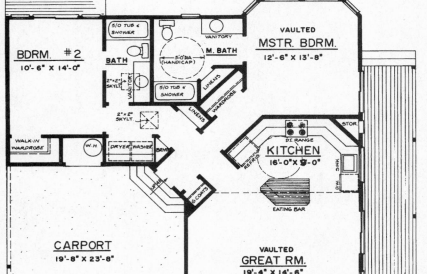

MAIN FLOOR

Enchanting Island Design

- Designed for a scenic waterfront site, this home captures the enchantment of the tropics.
- A wide veranda embraces two sides of the home, while a deck faces the rear. The low-slung roof, sturdy columns and the gabled, arched entryway give the home a relaxed, inviting look.
- Inside, a large, vaulted Great Room takes advantage of the home's modest square footage. A large eating bar connects the Great Room to the efficient galley-style kitchen.
- The master bedroom features a bayed window wall, a vaulted ceiling and a private bath. A skylight brightens the hall that leads to another bathroom and to the laundry area. The second bedroom enjoys private access to a deck and to the bath.
- The interior spaces are designed for wheelchair accessiblity, with 3½-ft.-wide hall openings and a 5-ft. turning radius in the kitchen and the master bath. Also note the abundant storage space throughout.

Plan LMB-1185-CD

Bedrooms: 2	Baths: 2
Living Area:	
Main floor	1,111 sq. ft.
Total Living Area:	**1,111 sq. ft.**
Carport	465 sq. ft.
Exterior Wall Framing:	2x4
Foundation Options:	
Crawlspace	
(Typical foundation & framing conversion diagram available—see order form.)	
BLUEPRINT PRICE CODE:	A

Plan LMB-1185-CD

PRICES AND DETAILS
ON PAGES 12-15

Love at First Sight!

- Upon seeing its covered front porch and stylish brick-accented exterior, it's easy to fall in love with this adorable home.
- Past the ornate and inviting entry, the spacious family room's dramatic window-flanked fireplace is an impressive introduction to the home's interior. A high plant shelf and a 12-ft. vaulted ceiling add to the ambience.
- The adjoining dining room is great for casual or formal occasions. The sliding glass doors that access the backyard may be built into a sunny window bay for a more dramatic effect.
- The efficient galley-style kitchen offers a pantry, an attached laundry room and a door to the garage.
- Three bedrooms occupy the sleeping wing. The master bedroom includes a roomy walk-in closet. The private master bath features a 12-ft. vaulted ceiling, a garden tub, a separate shower and a dual-sink vanity.
- A second full bath services the secondary bedrooms, one of which may be expanded by a 12-ft. vaulted ceiling.

Plan APS-1103

Bedrooms: 3	Baths: 2
Living Area:	
Main floor	1,197 sq. ft.
Total Living Area:	**1,197 sq. ft.**
Garage	380 sq. ft.
Exterior Wall Framing:	2x4
Foundation Options:	
Slab	

(All plans can be built with your choice of foundation and framing. A generic conversion diagram is available. See order form.)

BLUEPRINT PRICE CODE: A

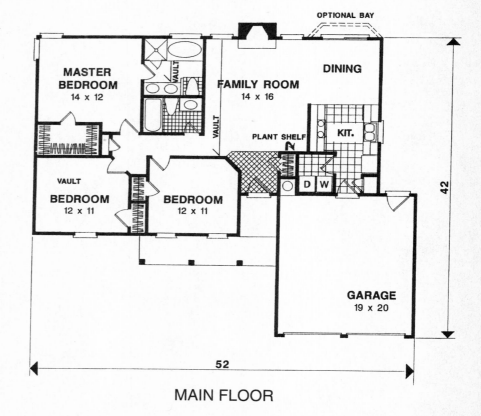

MAIN FLOOR

Designed for Easy Living

- A covered porch and an open foyer welcome guests to this stylish home.
- The spacious living and dining rooms merge together for a large activity or entertaining expanse. A bay window at one end and sliding glass doors at the other brighten the area, while a stone fireplace sets a comfortable mood.
- The kitchen's handy snack bar makes the dining room suitable for casual dining as well as formal entertaining. The patio is perfect for outdoor events.
- Three bedrooms make up the sleeping wing, removed from the rest of the home. The two secondary bedrooms share a hall bath. The master bedroom has its own bath, in addition to a large walk-in closet.
- An oversized laundry room is located near the garage access.

Plan LMB-2203-T

Bedrooms: 3	Baths: 2
Living Area:	
Main floor	1,248 sq. ft.
Total Living Area:	**1,248 sq. ft.**
Garage	484 sq. ft.
Exterior Wall Framing:	2x6

Foundation Options:

Crawlspace
(All plans can be built with your choice of foundation and framing. A generic conversion diagram is available. See order form.)

BLUEPRINT PRICE CODE:	**A**

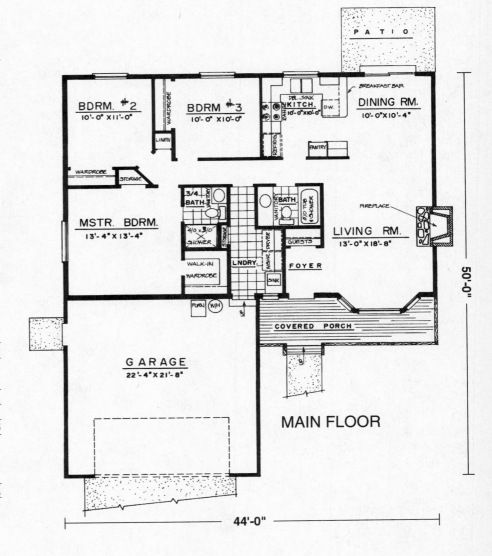

MAIN FLOOR

Plan LMB-2203-T

Country Highlights

- This nice home has country highlights, with shuttered windows, lap siding and a quaint covered porch.
- The foyer flows into the spacious living room, which offers a 9-ft.-high ceiling, a warm fireplace and tall windows that give views to the front porch. French doors open from the adjoining dining room to a backyard terrace.
- The kitchen features a sunny dinette that accesses the terrace, plus an angled pass-through to the dining room. A nifty mudroom with laundry facilities accesses the garage and the terrace.
- The master bedroom boasts a large walk-in closet and a private bath with a dual-sink vanity, a whirlpool tub and a separate shower.
- Across the home, two secondary bedrooms share another full bath.
- Dormered windows brighten the unfinished upper floor, which provides for future expansion possibilities.

Plan HFL-1700-SR

Bedrooms: 3+	Baths: 2
Living Area:	
Main floor	1,567 sq. ft.
Total Living Area:	**1,567 sq. ft.**
Upper floor (unfinished)	338 sq. ft.
Standard basement	1,567 sq. ft.
Garage	504 sq. ft.
Exterior Wall Framing:	2x6
Foundation Options:	
Standard basement	
Slab	

(All plans can be built with your choice of foundation and framing. A generic conversion diagram is available. See order form.)

BLUEPRINT PRICE CODE:	B

VIEW INTO LIVING ROOM

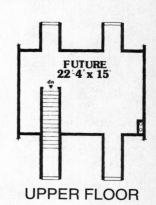

FUTURE
22'-4" x 15'

UPPER FLOOR

MAIN FLOOR

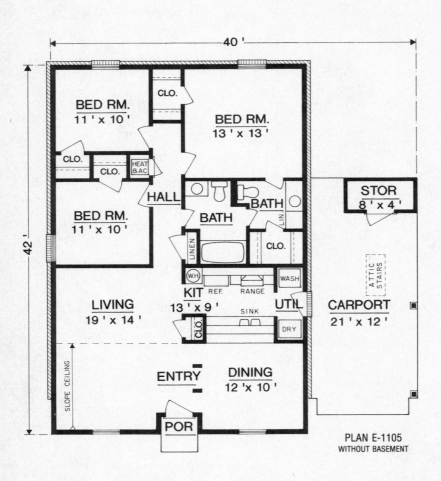

BED RM.
11' x 10'

CLO.

BED RM.
13' x 13'

CLO.

CLO.

HEAT & AC

HALL

BATH

BATH

LINEN

CLO.

BED RM.
11' x 10'

40'

42'

STOR
8' x 4'

ATTIC STAIRS

W.H.

KIT
13' x 9'

REF.

RANGE

WASH

UTIL

CARPORT
21' x 12'

SINK

DRY

LIVING
19' x 14'

SLOPE CEILING

CLO.

ENTRY

DINING
12' x 10'

POR

PLAN E-1105
WITHOUT BASEMENT

Simple, Economical to Build

AREAS
Living .... 1168 sq. ft.
Carport, Storage,
 Stoops .... 316 sq. ft.
Total .... 1484 sq. ft.

Exterior walls are 2x6 construction.
Specify crawlspace or slab foundation.

**TO ORDER THIS BLUEPRINT,
CALL TOLL-FREE 1-800-820-1283**

Blueprint Price Code A
Plan E-1105

**PRICES AND DETAILS
ON PAGES 12-15**

Extra Sparkle

- A lovely front porch with a cameo front door, decorative posts, bay windows and dormers give this country-style home extra sparkle.
- The Great Room is at the center of the floor plan, where it merges with the dining room and the screened porch. The Great Room features a 10-ft. tray ceiling, a fireplace, a built-in wet bar and a wall of windows to the patio.
- The eat-in kitchen has a half-wall that keeps it open to the Great Room and hallway. The dining room offers a half-wall facing the foyer and a bay window overlooking the front porch.
- The delectable master suite is isolated from the other bedrooms and includes a charming bay window, a 10-ft. tray ceiling and a luxurious private bath.
- The two smaller bedrooms are off the main foyer and separated by a full bath.
- A mudroom with a washer and dryer is accessible from the two-car garage.

Plan AX-91312

Bedrooms: 3	Baths: 2
Space:	
Main floor	1,595 sq. ft.
Total Living Area	**1,595 sq. ft.**
Screened Porch	178 sq. ft.
Basement	1,595 sq. ft.
Garage, Storage and Utility	508 sq. ft.
Exterior Wall Framing	2x4

Foundation Options:

Daylight basement
Standard basement
Slab
(All plans can be built with your choice of foundation and framing. A generic conversion diagram is available. See order form.)

Blueprint Price Code	B

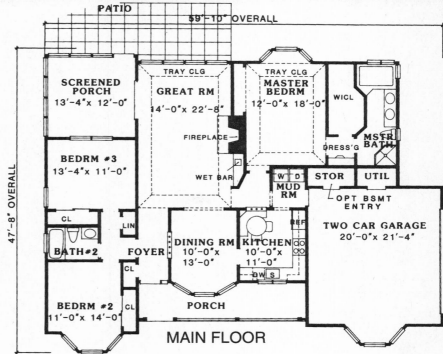

MAIN FLOOR

VIEW INTO GREAT ROOM

Comfortable L-Shaped Ranch

- From the covered entry to the beautiful and spacious family gathering areas, this comfortable ranch-style home puts many extras into a compact space.
- Straight off the central foyer, an inviting fireplace and a bright bay window highlight the living and dining area, while sliding glass doors open to a wide backyard terrace.
- The combination kitchen/family room features a large eating bar. The nearby mudroom offers a service entrance, laundry facilities, access to the garage and room for a half-bath.
- In the isolated sleeping wing, the master bedroom boasts a private bath and plenty of closet space. Two additional bedrooms share another full bath.

Plan K-276-R

Bedrooms: 3	Baths: 2+
Living Area:	
Main floor	1,245 sq. ft.
Total Living Area:	**1,245 sq. ft.**
Standard basement	1,245 sq. ft.
Garage	499 sq. ft.
Exterior Wall Framing:	2x4 or 2x6

Foundation Options:

Standard basement
Crawlspace
Slab

(All plans can be built with your choice of foundation and framing. A generic conversion diagram is available. See order form.)

BLUEPRINT PRICE CODE:	**A**

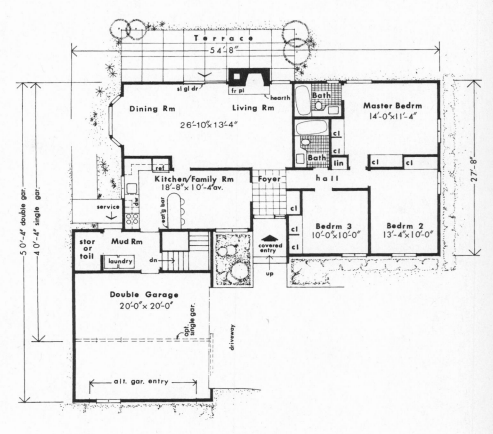

MAIN FLOOR

Luxury in a Small Package

- The elegant exterior of this design sets the tone for the luxurious spaces within.
- The foyer opens to the centrally located living room, which features a 15-ft. cathedral ceiling, a two-way fireplace and access to a lovely rear terrace.
- The unusual kitchen design includes an angled snack bar that lies between the bayed breakfast den and the formal dining room. Sliding glass doors open to another terrace.
- The master suite is a dream come true, with its romantic fireplace, built-in desk and 9-ft.-high tray ceiling. The private bath includes a whirlpool tub and a dual-sink vanity.
- Another full bath serves the remaining two bedrooms, one of which boasts a cathedral ceiling and a tall arched window.

Plan AHP-9300

Bedrooms: 3	Baths: 2
Living Area:	
Main floor	1,513 sq. ft.
Total Living Area:	**1,513 sq. ft.**
Standard basement	1,360 sq. ft.
Garage	400 sq. ft.
Exterior Wall Framing:	2x4 or 2x6

Foundation Options:

Standard basement
Crawlspace
Slab
(All plans can be built with your choice of foundation and framing. A generic conversion diagram is available. See order form.)

BLUEPRINT PRICE CODE:	B

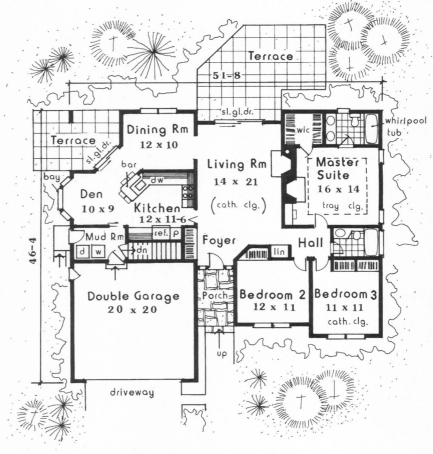

MAIN FLOOR

Cozy, Rustic Country Home

- This cozy, rustic home offers a modern, open interior that efficiently maximizes the square footage.
- The large living room features a 13-ft. sloped ceiling accented by rustic beams and an eye-catching corner fireplace.
- The living room flows into the adjoining dining room and the efficient U-shaped kitchen for a spacious, open feel.
- The master and secondary bedrooms are separated by the activity areas. The master suite includes a private bath and a separate dressing area with a dual-sink vanity.
- The secondary bedrooms share another full bath.

Plan E-1109

Bedrooms: 3	Baths: 2
Living Area:	
Main floor	1,191 sq. ft.
Total Living Area:	**1,191 sq. ft.**
Garage	462 sq. ft.
Storage & utility	55 sq. ft.
Exterior Wall Framing:	2x6

Foundation Options:
Crawlspace
Slab
(All plans can be built with your choice of foundation and framing. A generic conversion diagram is available. See order form.)

BLUEPRINT PRICE CODE:	**A**

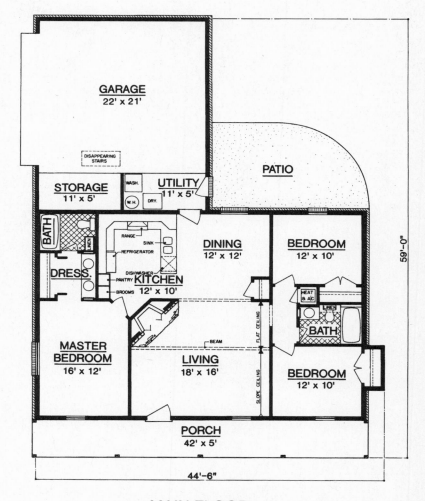

MAIN FLOOR

Plan E-1109

PRICES AND DETAILS ON PAGES 12-15

Adorable and Affordable

- This charming one-story home has much to offer, despite its modest size and economical bent.
- The lovely full-width porch has old-fashioned detailing, such as the round columns, decorative railings and ornamental molding.
- An open floor plan maximizes the home's square footage. The front door opens to the living room, where a railing creates a hallway effect while using very little space.
- Straight ahead, the dining room adjoins the island kitchen, while offering a compact laundry closet and sliding glass doors to a large rear patio.
- Focusing on quality, the home also offers features such as a 10-ft. tray ceiling in the living room and a 9-ft. stepped ceiling in the dining room.
- The three bedrooms are well proportioned. The master bedroom includes a private bathroom, while the two smaller bedrooms share another full bath. Note that the fixtures are arranged to reduce plumbing runs.

Plan AX-91316

Bedrooms: 3	Baths: 2
Living Area:	
Main floor	1,097 sq. ft.
Total Living Area:	**1,097 sq. ft.**
Basement	1,097 sq. ft.
Garage	461 sq. ft.
Exterior Wall Framing:	2x4

Foundation Options:

Daylight basement

Standard basement

Slab

(All plans can be built with your choice of foundation and framing. A generic conversion diagram is available. See order form.)

BLUEPRINT PRICE CODE:	A

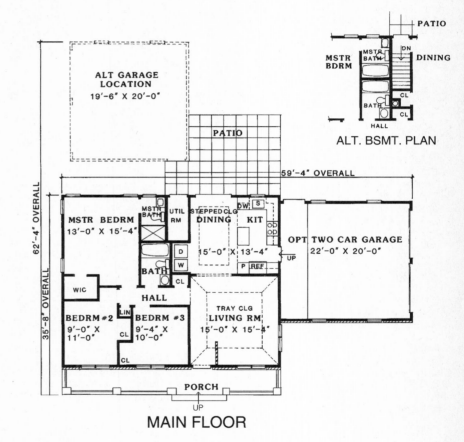

MAIN FLOOR

VIEW INTO LIVING ROOM AND DINING ROOM

Charming Traditional

- The attractive facade of this traditional home features decorative fretwork and louvers in the gables, plus eye-catching window and door treatments.
- The entry area features a commanding view of the living room, which boasts a 12½-ft. ceiling and a corner fireplace. A rear porch and patio are visible through French doors.
- The bayed dining room shares an eating bar with the U-shaped kitchen. The nearby utility room includes a pantry and laundry facilities.
- The quiet master suite includes a big walk-in closet and a private bath with a dual-sink vanity.
- On the other side of the home, double doors close off the two secondary bedrooms from the living areas. A full bath services this wing.

Plan E-1428

Bedrooms: 3	Baths: 2

Living Area:

Main floor	1,415 sq. ft.
Total Living Area:	**1,415 sq. ft.**
Garage	484 sq. ft.
Storage	60 sq. ft.
Exterior Wall Framing:	**2x6**

Foundation Options:
Crawlspace
Slab
(All plans can be built with your choice of foundation and framing. A generic conversion diagram is available. See order form.)

BLUEPRINT PRICE CODE: A

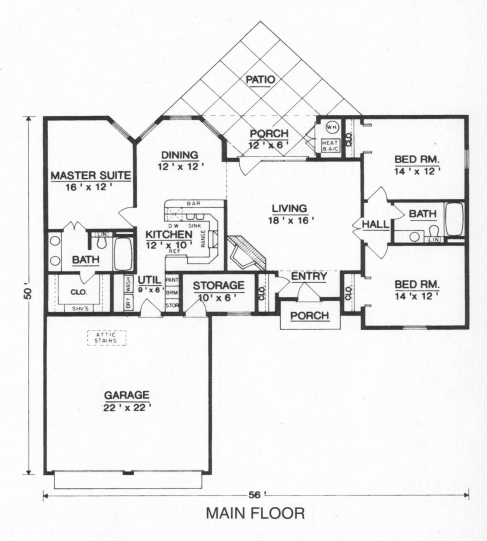

MAIN FLOOR

Plan E-1428

PRICES AND DETAILS ON PAGES 12-15

Inviting Windows

- This comfortable home presents an impressive facade, with its large and inviting front window arrangement.
- A step down from the front entry, the Great Room boasts a 12-ft. vaulted ceiling with a barrel-vaulted area that outlines the half-round front window. The striking angled fireplace can be enjoyed from the adjoining dining area.
- The galley-style kitchen hosts a half-round cutout above the sink and a breakfast area that accesses a backyard deck and patio. The kitchen, breakfast area and dining area also are enhanced by 12-ft. vaulted ceilings.
- The master bedroom features a boxed-out window, a walk-in closet and a ceiling that vaults to 12 feet. The private bath includes a garden tub, a separate shower and a private toilet compartment.
- Another full bath serves the two remaining bedrooms, one of which has sliding glass doors to the deck and would make an ideal den.

Plan B-902

Bedrooms: 2+	Baths: 2
Living Area:	
Main floor	1,368 sq. ft.
Total Living Area:	**1,368 sq. ft.**
Standard basement	1,368 sq. ft.
Garage	412 sq. ft.
Exterior Wall Framing:	2x4

Foundation Options:

Standard basement

(All plans can be built with your choice of foundation and framing. A generic conversion diagram is available. See order form.)

BLUEPRINT PRICE CODE: **A**

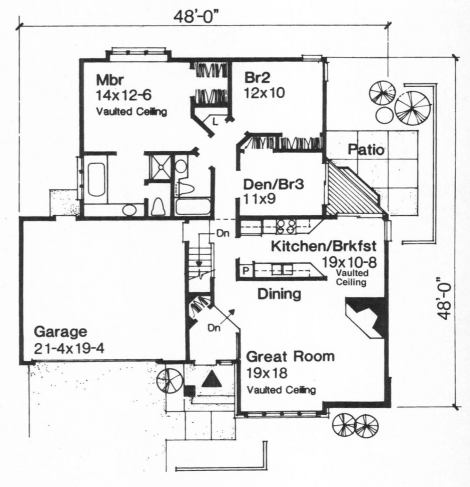

MAIN FLOOR

Quality Details Inside and Out

- A sparkling stucco finish, an eye-catching roofline and elegant window treatments hint at the quality features found inside this exquisite home.
- The airy entry opens to a large, central living room, which is embellished with a 10-ft. ceiling and a dramatic fireplace.
- The living room flows into a nice-sized dining area. A covered side porch expands the entertaining area.
- A functional eating bar and pantry are featured in the adjoining U-shaped kitchen. The nearby hallway to the garage neatly stores a washer, a dryer and a laundry sink.
- Secluded to the back of the home is a private master suite with a romantic sitting area and a large walk-in closet. The master bath offers dual sinks and an exciting oval tub.
- Two secondary bedrooms and another bath are located on the other side of the living room and entry.

Plan E-1435

Bedrooms: 3	Baths: 2
Living Area:	
Main floor	1,442 sq. ft.
Total Living Area:	**1,442 sq. ft.**
Garage and storage	516 sq. ft.
Exterior Wall Framing:	2x4

Foundation Options:

Crawlspace

Slab

(All plans can be built with your choice of foundation and framing. A generic conversion diagram is available. See order form.)

BLUEPRINT PRICE CODE:	**A**

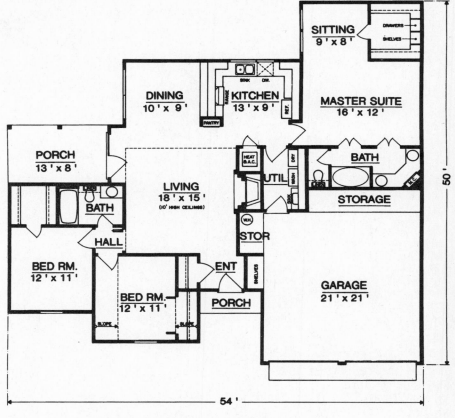

MAIN FLOOR

Plan E-1435

PRICES AND DETAILS ON PAGES 12-15

Outstanding One-Story

- Vaulted living spaces add to the spacious feel of this outstanding home, which would be ideal for a narrow lot.
- The focal point is the spacious Great Room and dining room area, enhanced by a 13½-ft. vaulted ceiling and a large fireplace flanked by windows to overlook the lovely patio and backyard.
- The dining room offers access to a secluded side courtyard.
- A beautiful bay window in the adjoining kitchen brightens the room and overlooks a front garden. A 10½-ft. vaulted ceiling and a functional snack bar are also featured.
- The master suite offers a sitting room with sliding glass doors to the patio. A private bath and a walk-in closet are also included.
- The two remaining bedrooms share the hall bath.

Plans P-6588-2A & -2D

Bedrooms: 3	**Baths:** 2

Living Area:	
Main floor (crawlspace version)	1,362 sq. ft.
Main floor (basement version)	1,403 sq. ft.

Total Living Area:	**1,362/1,403 sq. ft.**
Daylight basement	1,303 sq. ft.
Garage	427 sq. ft.

Exterior Wall Framing:	**2x6**
Foundation Options:	**Plan #**
Daylight basement	P-6588-2D
Crawlspace	P-6588-2A

(All plans can be built with your choice of foundation and framing. A generic conversion diagram is available. See order form.)

BLUEPRINT PRICE CODE:	**A**

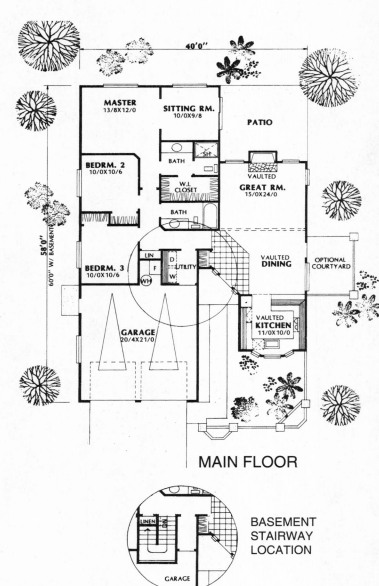

MAIN FLOOR

BASEMENT STAIRWAY LOCATION

Wide Angles
Add Style

- The comfortably-sized living areas of this gorgeous home are stylishly enhanced by wide, interesting angles.
- Past the covered front porch, the sidelighted front door brightens the living room just ahead.
- The spacious living room is warmed by a dramatic corner fireplace and opens to an angled, covered back porch.
- A stunning bayed dining room merges with the kitchen and its functional angled snack bar. Laundry facilities and access to the garage are nearby.
- The master suite is removed from the secondary bedrooms and features double doors to a deluxe private bath with an angled spa tub, a dual-sink vanity and a large walk-in closet.
- Another full bath serves the two additional bedrooms at the opposite end of the home.

Plan E-1426

Bedrooms: 3	Baths: 2
Living Area:	
Main floor	1,420 sq. ft.
Total Living Area:	**1,420 sq. ft.**
Garage and storage	540 sq. ft.
Exterior Wall Framing:	2x6

Foundation Options:

Crawlspace
Slab
(All plans can be built with your choice of foundation and framing. A generic conversion diagram is available. See order form.)

BLUEPRINT PRICE CODE: A

MAIN FLOOR

Plan E-1426
PRICES AND DETAILS ON PAGES 12-15

A Perfect Fit

- This country-style home will fit anywhere. Its charming character and narrow width make it ideal for those who value vintage styling along with plenty of yard space.
- The quaint covered front porch opens into the living room, which boasts a 12-ft., 8-in. cathedral ceiling and an inviting fireplace.
- The adjacent bay-windowed dining area features a 9-ft.-high vaulted ceiling and easy access to the efficient, galley-style kitchen.
- Off the kitchen, a handy laundry/utility room is convenient to the back entrance. The carport can accommodate two cars and includes a lockable storage area.
- The master bedroom suite offers a roomy walk-in closet, a private bath and sliding glass doors to a rear patio.
- Another full bath is centrally located for easy service to the rest of the home. Two more nice-sized bedrooms complete the plan.

Plan J-86119

Bedrooms: 3	Baths: 2
Living Area:	
Main floor	1,346 sq. ft.
Total Living Area:	**1,346 sq. ft.**
Standard basement	1,346 sq. ft.
Carport	400 sq. ft.
Exterior Wall Framing:	2x4

Foundation Options:

Standard basement
Crawlspace
Slab

(All plans can be built with your choice of foundation and framing. A generic conversion diagram is available. See order form.)

BLUEPRINT PRICE CODE:	**A**

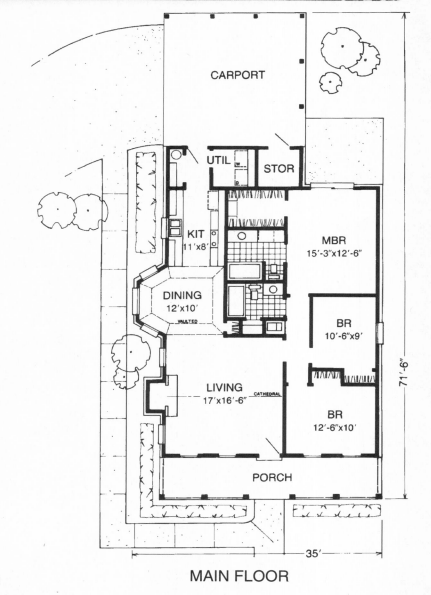

MAIN FLOOR

Garden Home

- This thoroughly modern plan exhibits beautiful traditional touches in its exterior design.
- A garden area leads visitors to a side door with a vaulted entry.
- A delightful kitchen/nook area is just to the right of the entry, and includes a convenient snack bar, a pantry and a nearby laundry room. The bayed breakfast nook overlooks the front yard.
- The living and dining areas share a 12½-ft.-high vaulted ceiling, making an impressive space for entertaining and family living. The stone fireplace and patio view add to the dramatic atmosphere.
- The master suite boasts a large closet and a private bath.
- Two more bedrooms share another bath off the hall.

Plans P-6598-2A & -2D

Bedrooms: 3	Baths: 2
Living Area:	
Main floor (with crawlspace)	1,375 sq. ft.
Main floor (with basement)	1,470 sq. ft.
Total Living Area:	**1,375/1,470 sq. ft.**
Daylight basement	1,470 sq. ft.
Garage	435 sq. ft.
Exterior Wall Framing:	2x4
Foundation Options:	**Plan #**
Daylight basement	P-6598-2D
Crawlspace	P-6598-2A

(All plans can be built with your choice of foundation and framing. A generic conversion diagram is available. See order form.)

BLUEPRINT PRICE CODE:	**A**

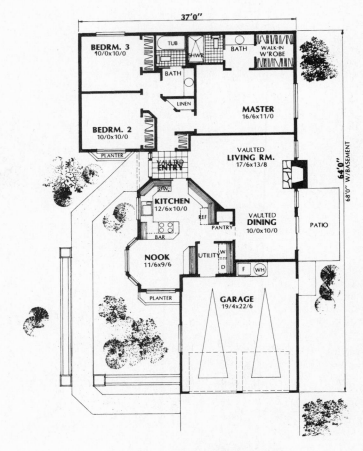

MAIN FLOOR

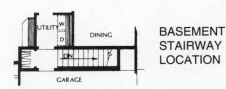

BASEMENT STAIRWAY LOCATION

Plans P-6598-2A & -2D

PRICES AND DETAILS ON PAGES 12-15

Street Privacy

- If privacy from street traffic or noise is a concern, this unique home design will fit the bill. The views are oriented to the rear, leaving the front of the home quiet and protected.
- The covered entry porch opens to a spacious living room that overlooks a back porch and patio area. A dramatic corner fireplace is an inviting feature.
- A functional snack bar separates the kitchen from the adjoining dining room, which boasts a lovely bay window.
- Just off the kitchen, a deluxe utility room doubles as a mudroom. The area includes a pantry, a broom closet, a storage closet and laundry facilities.
- The private master suite has an angled window wall, a large walk-in closet and a nice-sized bath with twin sinks.
- Two more bedrooms share another full bath on the opposite end of the home.

Plan E-1424

Bedrooms: 3	Baths: 2
Living Area:	
Main floor	1,415 sq. ft.
Total Living Area:	**1,415 sq. ft.**
Garage	484 sq. ft.
Storage	60 sq. ft.
Exterior Wall Framing:	2x6

Foundation Options:

Crawlspace
Slab
(All plans can be built with your choice of foundation and framing. A generic conversion diagram is available. See order form.)

BLUEPRINT PRICE CODE:	**A**

MAIN FLOOR

Easy to Build

- This compact vacation or retirement home is economical and easy to build. As versatile as it is affordable, this home is suitable for a scenic, sloping or narrow lot.
- The main entrance is located on the side of the home, near the carport, which includes two storage areas.
- An impressive 12-ft., 4-in. sloped ceiling presides over the open living and dining rooms. A corner fireplace warms the entire area, while sliding glass doors provide access to a fabulous railed, wraparound deck.

- The efficient kitchen includes an 11-ft. sloped ceiling, a convenient laundry closet and deck access.
- Down the hall, the two front bedrooms feature high, triangular windows on the street side. The master bedroom boasts a 12-ft., 4-in. ceiling, two wardrobe closets and a private bath with an oversized, sit-down shower.
- The two secondary bedrooms are expanded by 11½-ft. ceilings and share the hall bath. Both baths have 11-ft. sloped ceilings.
- The optional daylight basement offers space for a recreation room that opens to the backyard.

Plans H-18 & -18-A		
Bedrooms: 3		**Baths:** 2
Living Area:		
Main floor (crawlspace version)		1,056 sq. ft.
Main floor (basement version)		1,104 sq. ft.
Total Living Area:		**1,056/1,104 sq. ft.**
Daylight basement		1,104 sq. ft.
Carport and storage		320 sq. ft.
Exterior Wall Framing:		2x4
Foundation Options:		**Plan #**
Daylight basement		H-18
Crawlspace		H-18-A
(All plans can be built with your choice of foundation and framing. A generic conversion diagram is available. See order form.)		
BLUEPRINT PRICE CODE:		A

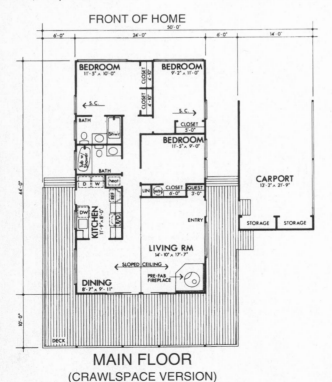

MAIN FLOOR
(CRAWLSPACE VERSION)

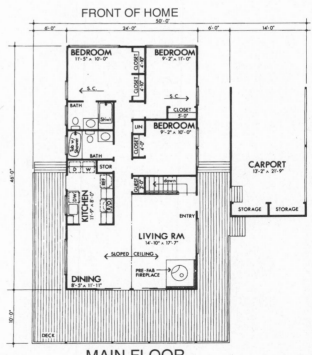

MAIN FLOOR
(BASEMENT VERSION)

TO ORDER THIS BLUEPRINT, CALL TOLL-FREE 1-800-820-1283   Plans H-18 & -18-A   *PRICES AND DETAILS ON PAGES 12-15*

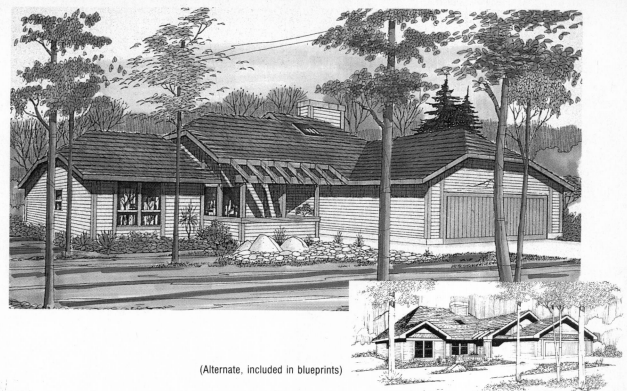

(Alternate, included in blueprints)

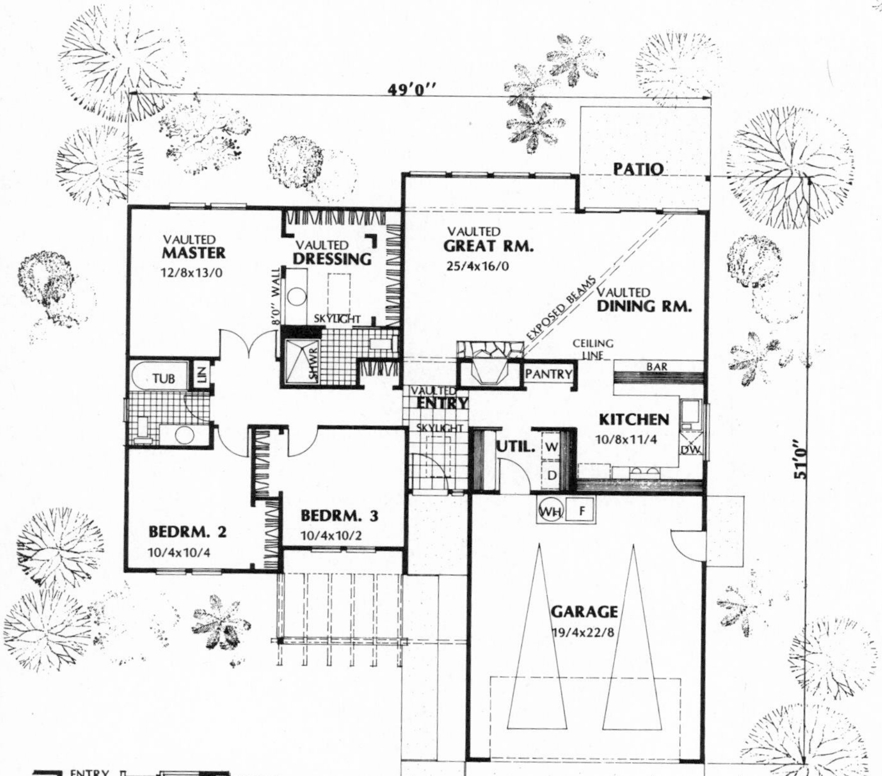

49'0"
PATIO
VAULTED
MASTER
12/8x13/0
VAULTED
DRESSING
8'0" WALL
SKYLIGHT
SHWR
TUB
LIN
VAULTED
GREAT RM.
25/4x16/0
EXPOSED BEAMS
VAULTED
DINING RM.
CEILING
LINE
BAR
PANTRY
VAULTED
ENTRY
SKYLIGHT
UTIL.
W
D
KITCHEN
10/8x11/4
DW
WH
F
BEDRM. 2
10/4x10/4
BEDRM. 3
10/4x10/2
GARAGE
19/4x22/8
51'0"

PLAN P-6584-4A
WITHOUT BASEMENT

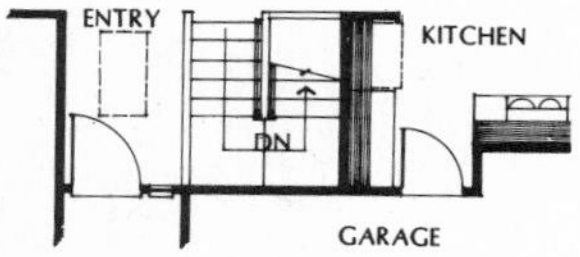

ENTRY
KITCHEN
DN
GARAGE

PLAN P-6584-4D
WITH DAYLIGHT BASEMENT

Main floor	1,458 sq. ft.
Lower floor	1,413 sq. ft.

Total living area: 1,415 sq. ft.
(Not counting garage)

Distinctive Contemporary Offers Two Exterior Designs

An open-arbor entry porch, boxed chimney, horizontal board siding and semihipped rooflines lend a custom look to the exterior of this contemporary ranch home. And the home's 1,415 sq. ft. interior is equally distinctive.

The front entry hall, which separates the spacious, open living area from the comfortably sized bedroom wing, has a vaulted ceiling with skylight for a dramatic first impression. The great room also has a vaulted ceiling, plus a long window wall (with sliding-glass door off the dining area opening onto a partly covered patio) and large fireplace.

There's an efficient U-shaped kitchen with pantry storage and an adjacent utility room. (In the daylight basement version, the utility room is replaced by stairs, and the entry to the garage is relocated.) A large master bedroom suite also has a vaulted ceiling with a skylight in the wardrobe/dressing area.

Blueprint Price Code A

TO ORDER THIS BLUEPRINT, CALL TOLL-FREE 1-800-820-1283

Plans P-6584-4A & 4D

PRICES AND DETAILS ON PAGES 12-15

Photo courtesy of Barclay Home Designs

Light-Filled, Flowing Spaces

- A beautiful bay window in the living room and an open, light-filled floor plan distinguish this stylish home.
- The large combined living and dining area—equally suitable for family gatherings or for more formal entertaining—features a fireplace and a view of a covered patio.
- The sunny, bayed breakfast nook accesses the patio, while the efficient kitchen includes a sizable pantry.
- Double doors open to the spacious master suite, which features a private bath and a walk-in closet.
- The two remaining bedrooms have large windows overlooking the backyard and share a full bath. One of the bedrooms is conveniently located off the breakfast nook, and could be used as a TV room, study or guest bedroom.
- Nice laundry facilities are located near the entrance to the two-car garage.

Plan R-1028

Bedrooms: 2+	Baths: 2
Living Area:	
Main floor	1,305 sq. ft.
Total Living Area:	**1,305 sq. ft.**
Garage	429 sq. ft.
Exterior Wall Framing:	2x6

Foundation Options:

Crawlspace
(All plans can be built with your choice of foundation and framing. A generic conversion diagram is available. See order form.)

BLUEPRINT PRICE CODE: **A**

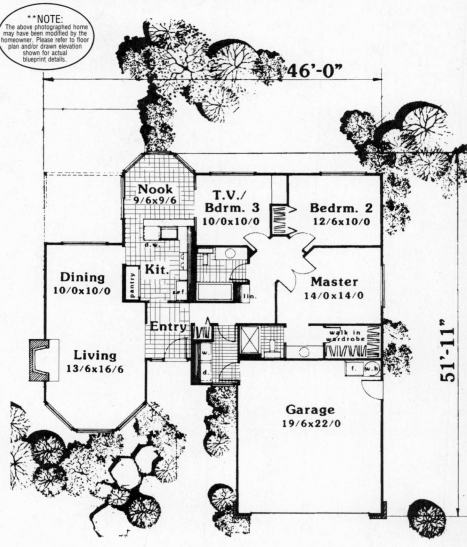

NOTE:
The above photographed home may have been modified by the homeowner. Please refer to floor plan and/or drawn elevation shown for actual blueprint details.

46'-0"

51'-11"

Nook 9/6x9/6

T.V./ Bdrm. 3 10/0x10/0

Bedrm. 2 12/6x10/0

Dining 10/0x10/0

Kit.

pantry

Master 14/0x14/0

Entry

Living 13/6x16/6

walk in wardrobe

Garage 19/6x22/0

MAIN FLOOR

Plan R-1028

PRICES AND DETAILS
ON PAGES 12-15

Rustic Appeal

- Stone and wood combine with high angled windows to give this rustic home an appealing facade.
- The entry opens directly from a wide front deck to the majestic living room, which is accented by a 15-ft. cathedral ceiling with exposed beams. A massive central stone fireplace is the focal point of the room, while tall windows overlook the deck.
- Behind the fireplace, the cathedral ceiling continues into the adjoining

dining room, which offers ample space for formal occasions.
- The galley-style kitchen features a sunny sink and easy service to the dining room. Just a step away, a pantry, a laundry closet and access to the carport are also available.
- The master suite boasts a walk-in closet, a private master bath and sliding glass doors to the deck.
- Across the home, two additional bedrooms share another full bath.
- Two handy storage areas are attached to the carport.

Plan C-7360	
Bedrooms: 3	**Baths:** 2
Living Area:	
Main floor	1,454 sq. ft.
Total Living Area:	**1,454 sq. ft.**
Daylight basement	1,454 sq. ft.
Carport	400 sq. ft.
Storage	120 sq. ft.
Exterior Wall Framing:	2x4
Foundation Options:	

Daylight basement
Crawlspace
Slab
(All plans can be built with your choice of foundation and framing. A generic conversion diagram is available. See order form.)

BLUEPRINT PRICE CODE:	A

MAIN FLOOR

67'-0"

34'-10"

- CARPORT 20'-0"x20'-0"
- STORAGE
- STORAGE
- W / D
- KITCHEN 15'-2"x8'-8"
- LIN.
- P.
- BATH
- CL.
- DINING 15'-0"x12'-0"
- BEDROOM 15'-2"x11'-0"
- BATH
- CL.
- M. BEDROOM 15'-2"x13'-6"
- CATHEDRAL CEILING
- CL.
- CL.
- BEDROOM 12'-8"x11'-0"
- LIVING 15'-0"x21'-10"
- DECK

Easy, Open Floor Plan

- This attractive home flaunts a mixture of vertical and horizontal wood siding, and the wide-open floor plan permits easy traffic flow.

- A large, central living room merges with a dining area at the back of the home. The skylighted living room features a 10-ft. ceiling, a handsome fireplace and a patio door to a covered side porch.

- The roomy U-shaped kitchen includes a pantry and a convenient eating bar. Nearby, a utility room offers garage access and extra freezer space.

- The isolated master suite boasts a sunny sitting area and a large walk-in closet. The private master bath has two sets of double doors and offers an exciting oval tub, a separate toilet room and his-and-hers sinks in a long, angled vanity.

- Two more bedrooms and another full bath are at the other end of the home.

Plan E-1430

Bedrooms: 3	Baths: 2
Living Area:	
Main floor	1,430 sq. ft.
Total Living Area:	**1,430 sq. ft.**
Garage and storage	465 sq. ft.
Exterior Wall Framing:	2x4

Foundation Options:

Crawlspace

Slab

(All plans can be built with your choice of foundation and framing. A generic conversion diagram is available. See order form.)

BLUEPRINT PRICE CODE: **A**

MAIN FLOOR

Plan E-1430

PRICES AND DETAILS ON PAGES 12-15

One-Story with Dimension

- An eye-catching front window and half-hipped roofs add dimension to this feature-filled one-story.
- The covered entry opens to a tiled foyer, where the living and dining rooms merge to the left.
- The living room showcases a lovely window seat set into a 10-ft.-high vaulted alcove that is topped by a half-round transom. The dining room includes an angled china niche.
- The open kitchen faces a sunny nook with a bay window and access to a backyard patio. The cooktop island has a snack bar that easily services the adjoining family room, where a corner woodstove warms the entire area.
- Double doors open to the elegant master suite, which boasts a split bath with a skylighted dressing area.
- A second full bath serves the two remaining bedrooms.

Plan R-1063

Bedrooms: 3	Baths: 2
Living Area:	
Main floor	1,585 sq. ft.
Total Living Area:	**1,585 sq. ft.**
Garage	408 sq. ft.
Exterior Wall Framing:	2x6

Foundation Options:

Crawlspace
(All plans can be built with your choice of foundation and framing. A generic conversion diagram is available. See order form.)

BLUEPRINT PRICE CODE: B

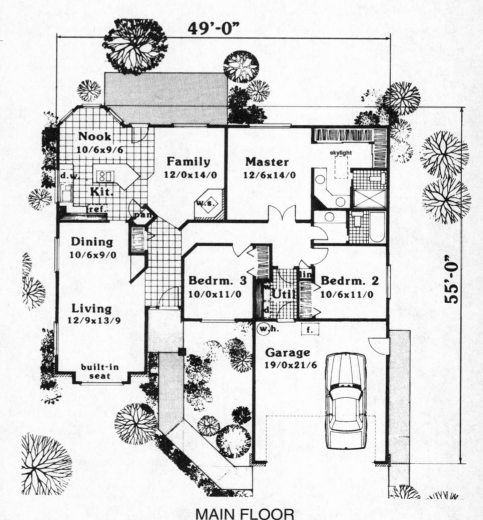

MAIN FLOOR

Easy-Living One-Story

- Low-maintenance brick adds style and durability to this easy-living one-story.
- The friendly porch welcomes guests inside. The entry offers a view through the living room to the backyard.
- With its massive brick fireplace, rustic beams and high 13-ft. cathedral ceiling, the living room is cozy, yet dramatic! A French door alongside the fireplace provides access to a nice patio.
- The living room is set off from the dining room by decorative wood posts. The bright dining room is also distinguished by its raised floor.
- The U-shaped kitchen is equipped with a convenient snack bar, plenty of counter space and a sunny windowed sink. Easy access to the laundry room and to the two-car garage is also a plus.
- Walk-in closets are included in each of the three bedrooms. The master suite also boasts a private bath and a separate dressing area with knee space.

Plan E-1307

Bedrooms: 3	Baths: 2
Living Area:	
Main floor	1,346 sq. ft.
Total Living Area:	**1,346 sq. ft.**
Garage	441 sq. ft.
Storage	44 sq. ft.
Exterior Wall Framing:	2x4

Foundation Options:

Crawlspace

Slab

(All plans can be built with your choice of foundation and framing. A generic conversion diagram is available. See order form.)

BLUEPRINT PRICE CODE: A

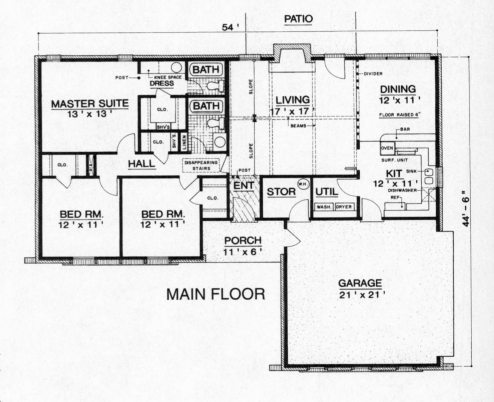

MAIN FLOOR

Plan E-1307

PRICES AND DETAILS ON PAGES 12-15

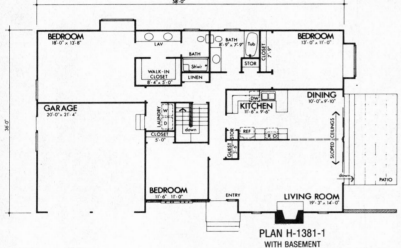

PLAN H-1381-1
WITH BASEMENT

Total living area: 1,596 sq. ft.
(Not counting basement or garage)

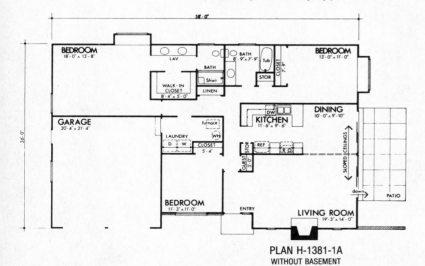

PLAN H-1381-1A
WITHOUT BASEMENT
(CRAWLSPACE FOUNDATION)

Total living area: 1,587 sq. ft.
(Not counting garage)

Popular Contemporary

This low-slung contemporary design contains a lot more space than is apparent from the outside. Oriented towards the outdoor sideyard, it features a pair of sliding glass doors offering outside access from both the living and dining room.

Effective zoning is the rule here: Bedrooms are secluded on one side to the rear; living areas and active kitchen space are grouped on the opposite side of the home.

All of these rooms are easily reached from a central hallway that provides excellent traffic flow, precluding unnecessary cross-room traffic.

Note the convenient location of the laundry room and staircase to the basement. Access to the garage is also available from the interior of the home. A generous assortment of plumbing facilities is grouped at the rear of the home. One bath serves the master bedroom privately. Another complete unit serves the balance of the house.

The attractive low silhouette is embellished with architectural touches such as the interesting window seats, the extension of the masonry wall that shields the side patio, and the low pitched roof.

Overall width of the home is 58' and greatest depth measures 36'. Exterior walls are 2x6 construction.

Blueprint Price Code B

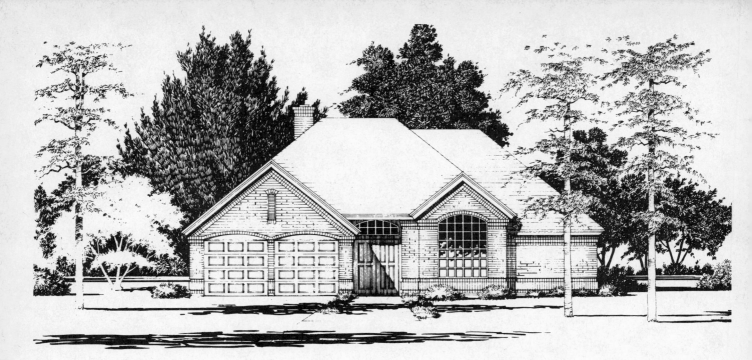

Compact Home Big on Style

- While compact in size, this stylish one-story offers lots of room and little wasted space.
- Staggered rooflines, brick accents and beautiful arched windows smarten the exterior.
- The interior offers a large central living room with a 10-ft. ceiling, a warming fireplace flanked by windows and an adjoining patio.
- The spacious breakfast area merges with the living room and the walk-through kitchen. The formal dining room is located on the opposite end of the kitchen.
- Separated from the other two bedrooms, the master suite is both private and spacious. It offers its own garden bath with twin vanities and walk-in closets, plus a separate tub and shower.

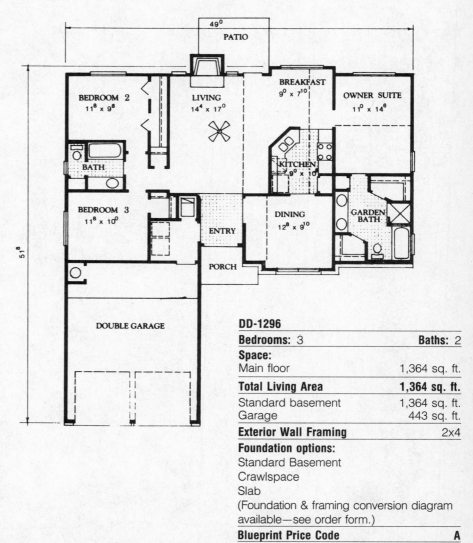

DD-1296

Bedrooms: 3	**Baths:** 2

Space:	
Main floor	1,364 sq. ft.
Total Living Area	**1,364 sq. ft.**
Standard basement	1,364 sq. ft.
Garage	443 sq. ft.
Exterior Wall Framing	2x4

Foundation options:
Standard Basement
Crawlspace
Slab
(Foundation & framing conversion diagram available—see order form.)

Blueprint Price Code	A

Plan DD-1296

Compact Design Offers Secluded Entry

- This efficient and economical design offers a stylish exterior and an interior that provides for comfortable living.
- The living and dining area is huge for a home of this size, and the corner fireplace is a real eye-catcher.
- The efficient U-shaped kitchen is open to the dining room and includes a floor-to-ceiling pantry as well as abundant cabinet space.
- The master suite boasts a private bath and a large walk-in closet. Two other bedrooms share another full bath.
- A small side porch accesses the dining room as well as a large utility and storage area.

Plan E-1214

Bedrooms: 3	Baths: 2
Space:	
Main floor	1,200 sq. ft.
Total Living Area	**1,200 sq. ft.**
Porches	60 sq. ft.
Utility & Storage	100 sq. ft.
Exterior Wall Framing	2x6
Foundation options:	

Crawlspace
Slab
(Foundation & framing conversion diagram available—see order form.)

Blueprint Price Code	**A**

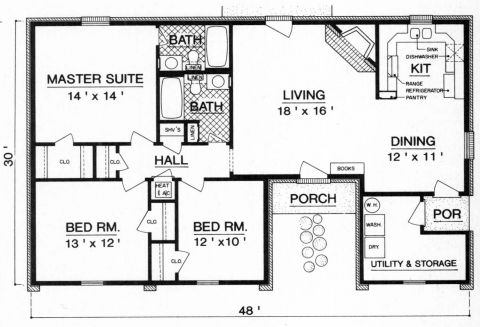

High Ceilings, Large Spaces!

- This affordable home is filled with large spaces that are further enhanced by high ceilings and lots of windows.
- The charming exterior is complemented by a combination of lap siding and brick, along with a columned front porch and a sidelighted entry door.
- Inside, the first area to come into view is the huge family room, which features a 15½-ft. vaulted ceiling and an efficient corner fireplace. Sliding glass doors open up the room to the backyard.

- The family room flows into the spacious breakfast room and kitchen. A picture window or an optional bay window brightens the breakfast room, while the kitchen offers a window above the sink and a convenient laundry closet that hides the clutter.
- The master suite leaves out nothing. An 11-ft. tray ceiling in the sleeping area gives way to the vaulted master bath, which is accented with a plant shelf above the entrance. A roomy walk-in closet is also included. The two smaller bedrooms share a hall bath.
- The optional basement doubles the home's size, providing ample expansion space.

Plan FB-1070

Bedrooms: 3	**Baths:** 2

Living Area:	
Main floor	1,070 sq. ft.
Total Living Area:	**1,070 sq. ft.**
Daylight basement	1,070 sq. ft.
Garage	484 sq. ft.
Exterior Wall Framing:	2x4

Foundation Options:
Daylight basement
Crawlspace
Slab
(All plans can be built with your choice of foundation and framing. A generic conversion diagram is available. See order form.)

BLUEPRINT PRICE CODE:	A

48'-0"

36'-0"

OPT. BAY WINDOW

D.
D.W.
Kitchen
REF.
W.
Stor.

Breakfast

OPT. STAIRS TO BSMT.

Vaulted Family Room
13³x20¹⁰

VAULT

FPL.

TUB

Vaulted M. Bath

W.i.c.

PLANT SHELF

TRAY CLG.

Master Suite
14⁶x12⁰

W.H.

Garage

COATS

Covered Porch

Bedroom 2
10⁰x10⁰

LIN.

Bedroom 3
11'x10⁰

MAIN FLOOR

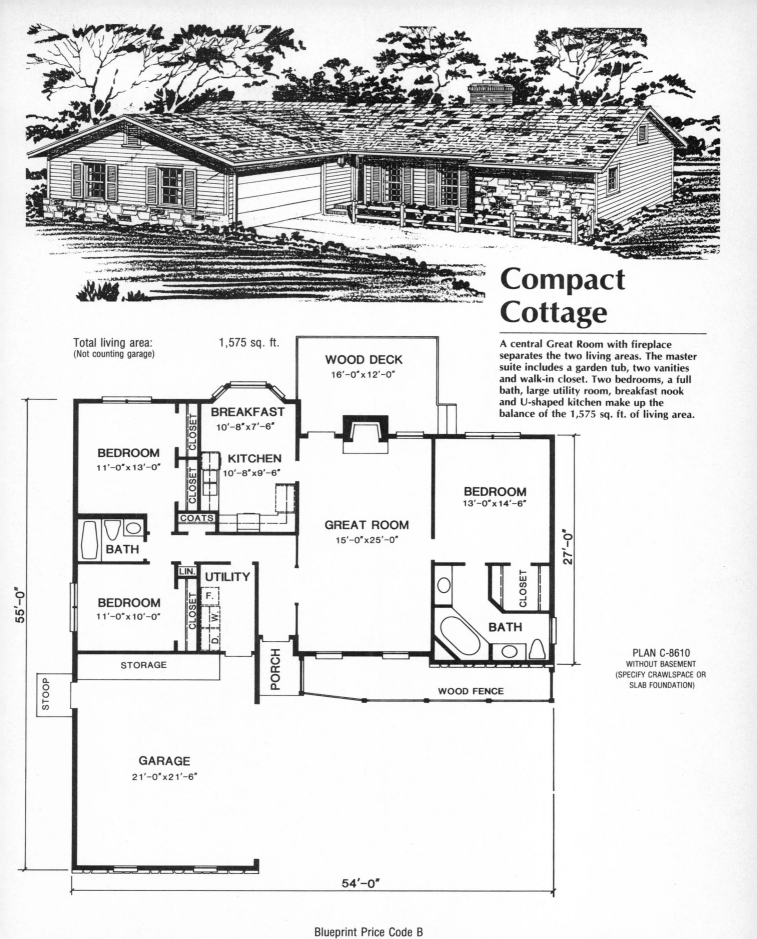

Compact Cottage

A central Great Room with fireplace separates the two living areas. The master suite includes a garden tub, two vanities and walk-in closet. Two bedrooms, a full bath, large utility room, breakfast nook and U-shaped kitchen make up the balance of the 1,575 sq. ft. of living area.

Total living area: 1,575 sq. ft.
(Not counting garage)

WOOD DECK
16'-0" x 12'-0"

BREAKFAST
10'-8" x 7'-6"

CLOSET

BEDROOM
11'-0" x 13'-0"

CLOSET

KITCHEN
10'-8" x 9'-6"

COATS

BATH

BEDROOM
13'-0" x 14'-6"

GREAT ROOM
15'-0" x 25'-0"

27'-0"

LIN.

UTILITY

CLOSET

F.

BEDROOM
11'-0" x 10'-0"

CLOSET

D. W.

BATH

CLOSET

55'-0"

STORAGE

PORCH

STOOP

WOOD FENCE

GARAGE
21'-0" x 21'-6"

PLAN C-8610
WITHOUT BASEMENT
(SPECIFY CRAWLSPACE OR
SLAB FOUNDATION)

54'-0"

Blueprint Price Code B

Plan C-8610

Sleek One-Story

- Steep, sleek rooflines and a trio of French doors with half-round transoms give this one-story a look of distinction.
- The covered front porch opens to the spacious living room, where a central fireplace cleverly incorporates a wet bar, bookshelves and a coat closet.
- Behind the fireplace, the adjoining dining room offers views to the backyard through an arched window arrangement. The two rooms are expanded by 11-ft. ceilings and a covered back porch.
- A snack bar connects the dining room to the U-shaped kitchen, which offers a pantry closet and large windows over the sink. Laundry facilities are nearby.
- The secluded master suite features a large walk-in closet and a private bath. Across the home, the secondary bedrooms each have a walk-in closet and share another full bath.

Plan E-1427

Bedrooms: 3	Baths: 2
Living Area:	
Main floor	1,444 sq. ft.
Total Living Area:	**1,444 sq. ft.**
Garage and storage	540 sq. ft.
Exterior Wall Framing:	2x4

Foundation Options:

Crawlspace

Slab

(All plans can be built with your choice of foundation and framing. A generic conversion diagram is available. See order form.)

BLUEPRINT PRICE CODE: **A**

MAIN FLOOR

Plan E-1427

Rustic Exterior, Refined Interior

- This home offers lots of opportunities for enjoying the outdoors, with its lavish use of glass, large patio and wood deck or optional greenhouse.
- The rustic exterior sports vertical cedar siding contrasted with stone veneer. The home's tuck-under garage and rear-view orientation make it perfect for scenic lots on a slope.
- The large living room includes such extras as built-in shelves, a bay window and a fireplace.
- The two dining areas and the central kitchen all face the rear deck. Plenty of glass in each room offers great views of the outdoors. Converting the deck into a greenhouse adds 168 sq. ft. of space.
- The two bathrooms and the foyer are arranged to help buffer the bedrooms from the main living areas.
- The lower level is a self-sufficient unit, making it a perfect suite for guests, elderly parents or college-aged children. In addition to a full bath and a large bedroom, it includes a family room with a fireplace, a built-in kitchenette and a pair of sliding glass doors to the patio.

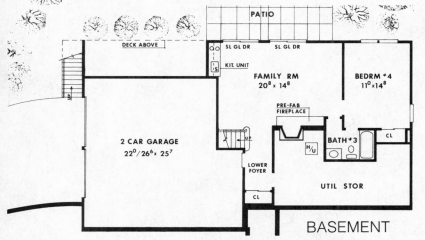

MAIN FLOOR

BASEMENT

Plan AX-98483	
Bedrooms: 3-4	**Baths:** 2-3
Living Area:	
Main floor	1,528 sq. ft.
Daylight basement (finished portion)	504 sq. ft.
Total Living Area:	**1,528/2,032 sq. ft.**
Storage and utility	243 sq. ft.
Garage	619 sq. ft.
Exterior Wall Framing:	2x4
Foundation Options:	
Daylight basement	
Crawlspace	
(Typical foundation & framing conversion diagram available—see order form.)	
BLUEPRINT PRICE CODE:	B/C

Inviting Full-Width Porch

AREAS

Living	1365 sq. ft.
Storage	87 sq. ft.
Carport	441 sq. ft.
Porch	255 sq. ft.
Total	2148 sq. ft.

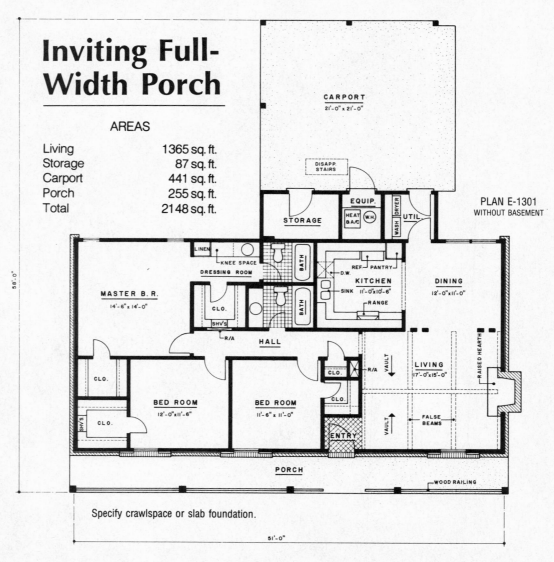

PLAN E-1301
WITHOUT BASEMENT

Specify crawlspace or slab foundation.

Blueprint Price Code A
Plan E-1301

PRICES AND DETAILS
ON PAGES 12-15

Large on Looks

- A handsome hipped roof with deep overhangs gives this design a big look, even though it has a modest 1,160 sq ft. of living space. The covered front porch with graceful arches and posts adds to the home's curb appeal.
- A decorative railing separates the large living room from the foyer, which includes two hall closets. The living room is open to the dining room, offering views to the patio through sliding glass doors.

- The sunny eat-in kitchen overlooks the patio and adjoins a mudroom that includes a pantry, a laundry area and additional closet space. More storage is located at the rear of the garage, accessible from the patio.
- The spacious master bedroom has a private bath and dual closets. Another full bath is convenient to the secondary bedrooms as well as to the living areas.
- All of the essentials and the amenities are included on one level, making this a great retirement home. For growing families, the optional basement provides expansion possibilities.

Plan HFL-1410-TN

Bedrooms: 3	**Baths:** 2

Living Area:	
Main floor	1,243 sq. ft.
Total Living Area:	**1,243 sq. ft.**
Standard basement	1,103 sq. ft.
Garage	380 sq. ft.
Storage	92 sq. ft.
Exterior Wall Framing:	2x4

Foundation Options:
Standard basement
Slab
(Typical foundation & framing conversion diagram available—see order form.)

BLUEPRINT PRICE CODE:	A

MAIN FLOOR

Floor plan details: 66'-4" wide, 30'-4" deep

- PATIO
- BED RM 11'-0" x 11'-0"
- BED RM 10'-0" x 10'-0"
- DINING RM 12'-4" x 10'-0"
- KITCHEN 11'-0" x 10'-0"
- MUD RM / laundry
- STORAGE
- HALL
- BATH
- MASTER BED RM 14'-0" x 11'-4"
- LIVING RM 21'-4" x 12'10"
- space divider
- TWO CAR GARAGE 20'-0" x 19'-0"
- BATH
- PORTICO
- htr. flue
- pantry
- service
- sl. gl. dr.
- dw, s., range, ref
- dn, stor.

Plan HFL-1410-TN

PRICES AND DETAILS ON PAGES 12-15

Cozy and Compact

- Quality and comfort are the keynotes of this compact home.
- The spacious living room includes a vaulted, beamed ceiling, built-in book cases and a corner hearth with a woodstove.
- The dining room adjoins the living room to create a great space for entertaining large groups.
- The walk-through kitchen includes a pantry and adjoins a handy utility room.
- The master suite offers two closets, a dressing area and a deluxe bath.
- Two secondary bedrooms also feature large closets and share a second full bath.

Plan E-1402

Bedrooms: 3	Baths: 2
Living Area:	
Main floor	1,400 sq. ft.
Total Living Area:	**1,400 sq. ft.**
Carport	440 sq. ft.
Exterior Wall Framing:	2x4

Foundation Options:
Crawlspace
Slab
(Typical foundation & framing conversion diagram available—see order form.)

BLUEPRINT PRICE CODE:	A

MAIN FLOOR

Compact Plan for Small Lot

- Luxury is not forgotten in this compact one-story home, which is perfect for a small or narrow lot.
- Off the entry, the living room boasts a 13-ft.-high vaulted ceiling and a boxed-out window. The adjoining dining area features a half-wall opening to the hall.
- The kitchen is separated from the family room by a functional eating bar. The family room is brightened by sliding glass doors that open to a patio.
- The master bedroom offers generous closet space and a private bath with a dual-sink vanity. Two additional bedrooms share another full bath.

Plans P-7699-2A & -2D

Bedrooms: 3	Baths: 2
Living Area:	
Main floor (crawlspace version)	1,460 sq. ft.
Main floor (basement version)	1,509 sq. ft.
Total Living Area:	**1,460/1,509 sq. ft.**
Daylight basement	1,530 sq. ft.
Garage	383 sq. ft.
Exterior Wall Framing:	2x4
Foundation Options:	**Plan #**
Daylight basement	P-7699-2D
Crawlspace	P-7699-2A

(All plans can be built with your choice of foundation and framing. A generic conversion diagram is available. See order form.)

BLUEPRINT PRICE CODE:	A/B

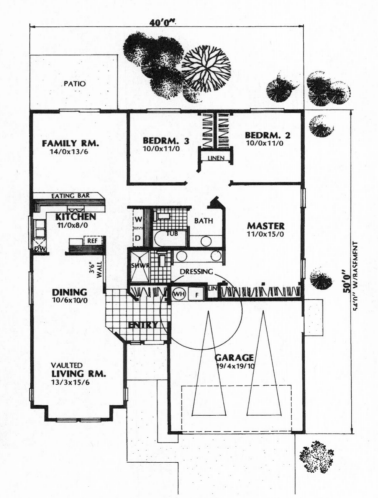

MAIN FLOOR

BASEMENT STAIRWAY LOCATION

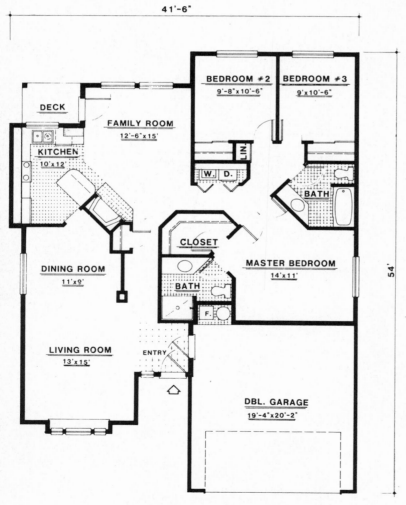

41'-6"

DECK

FAMILY ROOM
12'-6"x15'

BEDROOM #2
9'-8"x10'-6"

BEDROOM #3
9'x10'-6"

KITCHEN
10'x12'

LIN.

W. D.

BATH

CLOSET

DINING ROOM
11'x9'

MASTER BEDROOM
14'x11'

BATH

F.

LIVING ROOM
13'x15'

ENTRY

54'

DBL. GARAGE
19'-4"x20'-2"

Angles Add Interior Excitement

- Eye-catching exterior leads into exciting interior.
- You'll find cathedral ceilings throughout the living and dining area.
- Angular kitchen includes eating bar, plenty of cabinet and counter space.
- Master suite includes angled double-door entry, private bath and large walk-in closet.
- Family room and kitchen join together to make large casual family area.
- Main bathroom continues the angled motif, and the washer and dryer are conveniently located in the bedroom hallway.

Plan NW-864

Bedrooms: 3	Baths: 2
Total living area:	1,449 sq. ft.
Garage:	390 sq. ft.
Exterior Wall Framing:	2x6

Foundation options:
 Crawlspace only.
(Foundation & framing conversion diagram available — see order form.)

| **Blueprint Price Code:** | A |

Plan NW-864

Charming Accents

- Traditional accents add warmth and charm to the facade of this affordable one-story home.
- Decorative, beveled oval glass adorns the elegant entry, which is flanked by sidelights.
- The tiled foyer introduces the spacious family room, which is enhanced by a 12-ft. vaulted ceiling and a nice fireplace. A French door provides easy access to the backyard.
- The galley-style kitchen flows into the sunny dining area, which can be extended with an optional bay window.
- The secluded master bedroom features plenty of closet space. The private master bath boasts a corner garden tub, a separate shower and two sinks. The bath may be expanded with a 13-ft. vaulted ceiling.
- Two additional bedrooms share a hall bath in the opposite wing. A nice-sized laundry room is centrally located.

Plan APS-1205

Bedrooms: 3	Baths: 2
Living Area:	
Main floor	1,296 sq. ft.
Total Living Area:	**1,296 sq. ft.**
Garage	380 sq. ft.
Exterior Wall Framing:	2x4

Foundation Options:

Crawlspace

Slab

(All plans can be built with your choice of foundation and framing. A generic conversion diagram is available. See order form.)

BLUEPRINT PRICE CODE:　　　　**A**

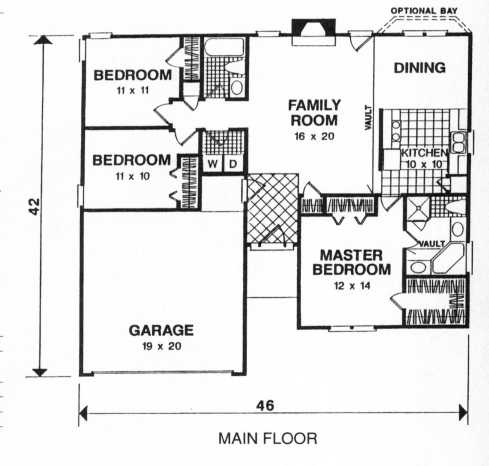

MAIN FLOOR

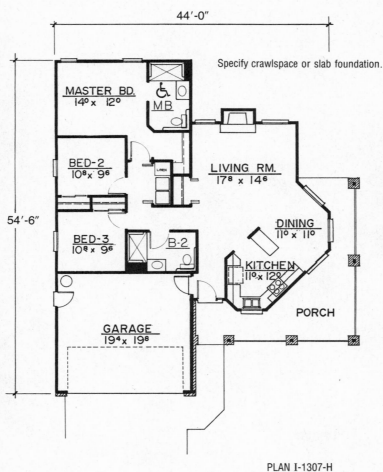

44'-0"

Specify crawlspace or slab foundation.

MASTER BD.
14^0 x 12^0

MB

BED-2
10^8 x 9^6

LIVING RM.
17^8 x 14^6

54'-6"

LINEN

DINING
11^0 x 11^0

BED-3
10^8 x 9^6

B-2

KITCHEN
11^0 x 12^0

PORCH

GARAGE
19^4 x 19^8

Compact Design Features Innovative Floor Plan

PLAN I-1307-H
WITHOUT BASEMENT

Total living area: 1,307 sq. ft.
(Not counting garage)

Blueprint Price Code A

Plan I-1307-H

TO ORDER THIS BLUEPRINT,
CALL TOLL-FREE 1-800-820-1283

PRICES AND DETAILS
ON PAGES 12-15

Oriented for Scenic Rear View

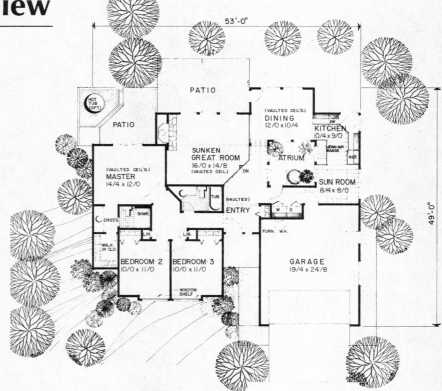

PLAN P-6533-2D
WITH DAYLIGHT BASEMENT

Main floor: 1,484 sq. ft.
(Not counting garage)
Basement level: 1,484 sq. ft.

PLAN P-6533-2A
WITHOUT BASEMENT
(CRAWLSPACE FOUNDATION)

Total living area: 1,399 sq. ft.
(Not counting garage)

Blueprint Price Code A

Plans P-6533-2A & -2D

Compact Home with Rustic Look

- While it may resemble a hunting lodge on the outside, this home is cozy and modern inside.
- The spacious living room offers sloped ceilings, a great fireplace and hearth and a view through the open dining room to the rear of the home.
- The kitchen is designed for convenience, featuring a broom closet and a double pantry.
- The master suite is luxurious for a compact home, with its large closet, compartmentalized bath and dressing room with double vanity.
- Two secondary bedrooms are on the opposite side of the home for privacy and share another full bath.
- Note the unusual wrap-around arrangement of the utility/storage area and garage.

Plan E-1106

Bedrooms: 3	Baths: 2

Space:	
Main floor	1,187 sq. ft.

Total Living Area	**1,187 sq. ft.**
Garage	440 sq. ft.
Utility & Storage	108 sq. ft.
Porch	99 sq. ft.

Exterior Wall Framing	2x6

Foundation options:
Crawlspace
Slab
(Foundation & framing conversion diagram available—see order form.)

Blueprint Price Code	**A**

Floor Plan Labels

UTILITY & STORAGE 18'-0" x 6'-0"
DRY
WASH
BED ROOM 12'-0" x 10'-0"
CLO.
DINING 14'-0" x 10'-3"
BAR
W.H.
D.W.
RANGE
KITCHEN 14'-0" x 8'-5"
SINK
REF.
BATH
DISAPPEARING STAIRS
GARAGE 22'-0" x 20'-0"
HEAT & A/C
LINEN
BATH
HALL
CLO.
PHONE NICHE
BROOMS PANTRY
DRESS. ROOM
CLO.
BEAMS
LIVING 18'-0" x 14'-0"
MASTER B.R. 15'-0" x 12'-0"
BED ROOM 12'-0" x 10'-0"
SLOPE
FLAT CEILING
SLOPE
PORCH 18'-4" x 6'-0"
40'-0"
62'-0"

Plan E-1106

PRICES AND DETAILS ON PAGES 12-15

At One with the Sun

- This two-bedroom ranch home combines an open floor plan with large expanses of glass to get the most out of the sun.
- The vaulted kitchen faces a cheerful sun porch on one side and opens to the dining and living rooms on the other.
- The dining and living rooms are combined to create one huge area, which is enhanced by vaulted ceilings and views of the large rear deck. A corner fireplace radiates warmth to the entire living area.
- The master bedroom has twin walk-in closets and a private bath. Another full bath, a laundry closet and a den or second bedroom complete the efficient plan.
- The full basement offers more potential living space.

Plan B-91012

Bedrooms: 2	Baths: 2
Space:	
Main floor	1,421 sq. ft.
Total Living Area	**1,421 sq. ft.**
Basement	1,421 sq. ft.
Garage	440 sq. ft.
Exterior Wall Framing	**2x4**

Foundation options:

Standard Basement

(Foundation & framing conversion diagram available—see order form.)

Blueprint Price Code	**A**

REAR VIEW

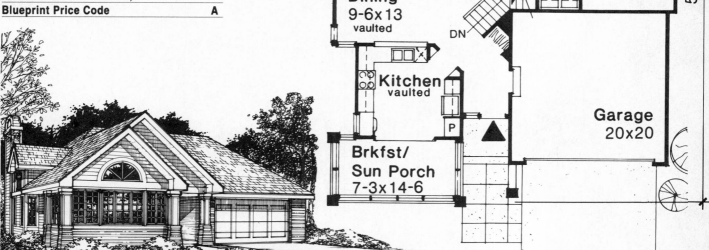

FRONT VIEW · MAIN FLOOR

43'-0"

56'-8"

MBr 14x16 vaulted

Deck

Living Rm 17-6x12 vaulted

Br 2/ Den 11-4x10

Dining 9-6x13 vaulted

W D

DN

Kitchen vaulted

Garage 20x20

Brkfst/ Sun Porch 7-3x14-6

P

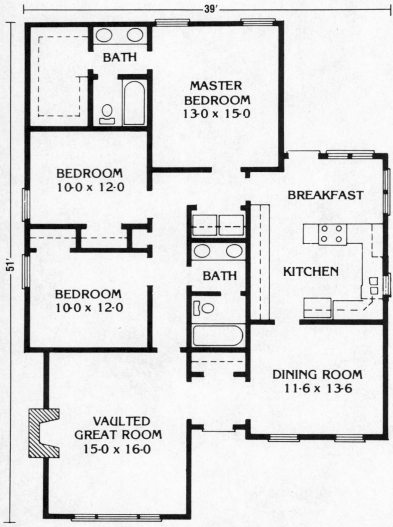

BATH

MASTER
BEDROOM
13·0 x 15·0

BEDROOM
10·0 x 12·0

BREAKFAST

BATH

KITCHEN

BEDROOM
10·0 x 12·0

DINING ROOM
11·6 x 13·6

VAULTED
GREAT ROOM
15·0 x 16·0

39'

51'

Appealing French Details

Authentic French details adorn the facade of this appealing one-story design. The slightly recessed doorway, arched windows, and curved shutters all add interest to this beautifully proportioned residence.

The vaulted ceiling of the Great Room makes this room appear much larger than its dimensions state. An oversized Palladian window creates a dramatic focal point and floods the room with natural light. The kitchen contains an unusual amount of cabinets and counter space.

Abundant closet space is provided for the inhabitants of the master bedroom. Also, note the convenient location of the laundry center, handy to both kitchen and bedroom areas.

PLAN V-1586
WITHOUT BASEMENT
(CRAWLSPACE FOUNDATION)

Total living area: 1,586 sq. ft.

9'-0" CEILINGS THROUGHOUT

Blueprint Price Code B

Plan V-1586

FRONT VIEW

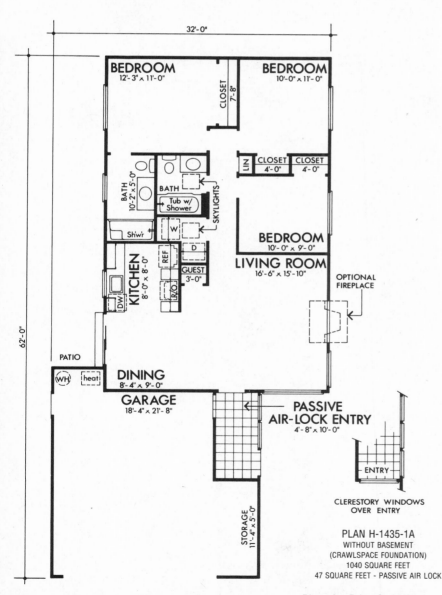

32'-0"

BEDROOM
12'-3" x 11'-0"

BEDROOM
10'-0" x 11'-0"

CLOSET
7'-8"

BATH
10'-2" x 5'-0"

BATH

Tub w/
Shower

SKYLIGHTS

LIN

CLOSET
4'-0"

CLOSET
4'-0"

Sh'wr

W

KITCHEN
8'-0" x 8'-0"

REF

D

GUEST
3'-0"

BEDROOM
10'-0" x 9'-0"

LIVING ROOM
16'-6" x 15'-10"

OPTIONAL
FIREPLACE

DW

62'-0"

PATIO

WH

heat

DINING
8'-4" x 9'-0"

GARAGE
18'-4" x 21'-8"

PASSIVE
AIR-LOCK ENTRY
4'-8" x 10'-0"

ENTRY

STORAGE
11'-4" x 5'-0"

CLERESTORY WINDOWS
OVER ENTRY

PLAN H-1435-1A
WITHOUT BASEMENT
(CRAWLSPACE FOUNDATION)
1040 SQUARE FEET
47 SQUARE FEET - PASSIVE AIR LOCK

Affordable First Home

The prime consideration in the design of this home is to provide affordable housing especially for those venturing into home ownership for the first time. Though the main building contains only 1,040 sq. ft., it is so carefully planned that it boasts two separate bathrooms and inside laundry facilities.

Bedrooms, though modest in size, are more than adequate, and each is equipped with at least 4' of closet space behind handsome sliding doors. The inside bath and laundry facilities are illuminated by overhead skylights, which also make a modest contribution toward heating each space with natural sun glow.

A parallel kitchen arrangement adjoins the dining space, and nearby sliding glass doors facilitate outdoor living and dining on the patio. The 16'-6" by almost 16' living room is deceptively large, containing nearly 264 sq. ft., the same as the 13' x 20' living room one finds in many larger homes.

A passive air-lock entry almost entirely surrounded by glass not only provides a private access space, but also contributes to the heating by collecting and storing the sun's natural heat whenever available. Direct access to the attached double garage is a bonus not found in many similar small homes.

With land costs soaring, the shape of this home provides initial savings because it is suitable for a lot width of less than 50'.

Total living area: 1,040 sq. ft.
(Not counting garage)
Air lock entry: 47 sq. ft.

Blueprint Price Code A

Plan H-1435-1A

Refined One-Story

- A symmetrical roofline and a stucco facade with corner quoins and keystone accents add a refined look to this elegant one-story.
- The eye-catching entry leads into a surprisingly spacious interior, beginning with a family room that features an 11-ft., 8-in.-high ceiling and a handsome window-flanked fireplace.
- The kitchen showcases an angled serving bar that faces the sunny breakfast room. A French door between the breakfast room and the formal dining room opens to a covered patio for more dining and entertaining space.
- The fantastic master suite features an elegant 10-ft. tray ceiling. The superb private bath boasts a 13-ft. vaulted ceiling, an overhead plant shelf, a garden tub and a walk-in closet.
- The two front-facing bedrooms share a hall bath that includes a vanity with knee space.

Plan FB-1531

Bedrooms: 3	Baths: 2
Living Area:	
Main floor	1,531 sq. ft.
Total Living Area:	**1,531 sq. ft.**
Garage	440 sq. ft.
Exterior Wall Framing:	2x4

Foundation Options:

Crawlspace

Slab

(All plans can be built with your choice of foundation and framing. A generic conversion diagram is available. See order form.)

BLUEPRINT PRICE CODE:	**B**

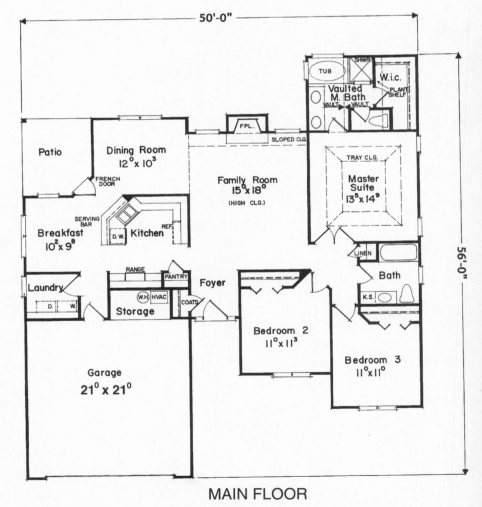

MAIN FLOOR

Plan FB-1531

ELEVATION A

ELEVATION B

ELEVATION C

Plan HDS-90-821

Bedrooms: 3	**Baths:** 2

Space:
Total living area: 1,280 sq. ft.
Garage: approx. 360 sq. ft.

Exterior Wall Framing: concrete block

Foundation options:
Slab.
(Foundation & framing conversion diagram available — see order form.)

Blueprint Price Code: A

Striking, Sunny Master Suite

- This striking Mediterranean opens to a vaulted combination living/dining room with a view to the rear of the home and glass sliders opening to the covered patio.
- A pass-thru and eating bar separate the Great Room from the kitchen, which offers plenty of space, plus an attached breakfast area.
- Convenient laundry facilities lie close to the master bedroom and bath.
- The elegantly vaulted master suite offers his and her closets and a lovely bay window; the bath has private toilet.
- The secondary bedrooms also display vaulted ceilings.
- NOTE: All three elevation choices and plan options are included in the plans.

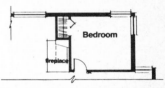

OPTION "A" W/ FIREPLACE

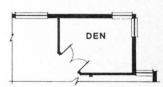

OPTION "B" W/ DEN

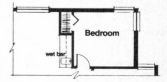

OPTION "C" W/ WET BAR

MASTER BATH W/ TUB OPTION

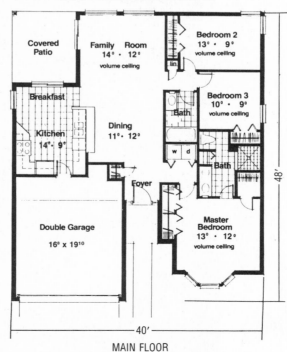

MAIN FLOOR

Dynamite Detailing

- Fine detailing, both inside and out, drenches this diminutive two-bedroom home in style, function and charm.
- The multi-gabled roofline combined with the recessed, double-door entry makes a strong statement on the outside.
- The reception hall is brightened by a clerestory window in its sloped ceiling. The huge living and dining area is expanded by a cathedral ceiling and complemented by a bay window, a built-in china niche, skylights and a fireplace. A sliding glass door opens to a terrace for easy outdoor entertaining.
- A pass-through links the living/dining area to the eat-in kitchen, which is given added dimension by a bumped-out window and an angled wall.
- The main hall leads to a full bath and a den or second bedroom. The blueprints include details for completely framing in the second bedroom, or creating an opening to the living room that can be closed off by folding doors.
- The roomy master suite includes a private terrace, a large walk-in closet and a full bath.

Plan K-677-R

Bedrooms: 1-2	Baths: 2
Living Area:	
Main floor	1,094 sq. ft.
Total Living Area:	**1,094 sq. ft.**
Standard basement	1,045 sq. ft.
Garage	400 sq. ft.
Exterior Wall Framing:	2x4 or 2x6

Foundation Options:
Standard basement
Slab
(Typical foundation & framing conversion diagram available—see order form.)

BLUEPRINT PRICE CODE: A

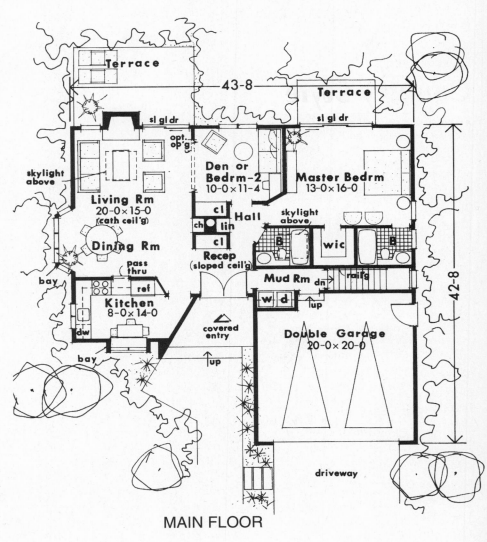

MAIN FLOOR

Plan K-677-R

PRICES AND DETAILS ON PAGES 12-15

Classic Country-Style

- The classic covered front porch with decorative railings and columns make this home reminiscent of an early 20th-century farmhouse.
- Dormers give the home the appearance of a two-story, even though it is designed for single-level living.
- The huge living room features a ceiling that slopes up to 13 feet. A corner fireplace radiates warmth to both the living room and the dining room.
- The dining room overlooks a backyard patio and shares a versatile serving bar with the open kitchen. A large utility room is just steps away.
- The master bedroom boasts a roomy bath with a dual-sink vanity. The two smaller bedrooms at the other end of the home share a full bath.

Plan E-1412

Bedrooms: 3	**Baths: 2**
Living Area:	
Main floor	1,484 sq. ft.
Total Living Area:	**1,484 sq. ft.**
Garage	440 sq. ft.
Exterior Wall Framing:	2x6

Foundation Options:

Crawlspace
Slab

(All plans can be built with your choice of foundation and framing. A generic conversion diagram is available. See order form.)

BLUEPRINT PRICE CODE: **A**

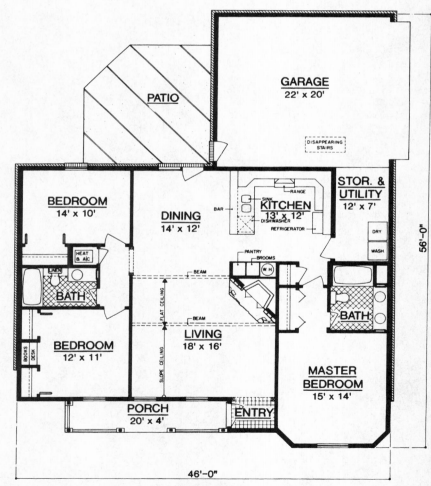

MAIN FLOOR

FRONT VIEW

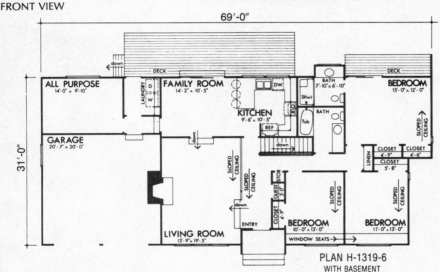

69'-0"

ALL PURPOSE
14'-0" x 9'-10"

FAMILY ROOM
14'-2" x 10'-5"

LAUNDRY

DECK

BEDROOM
15'-0" x 12'-0"

DECK

KITCHEN
9'-6" x 10'-5"

BATH
7'-10" x 6'-10"

BATH

GARAGE
20'-7" x 20'-0"

31'-0"

SLOPED CEILING

SLOPED CEILING

LINEN

CLOSET
4'-9"

CLOSET
4'-6"

CLOSET
5'-8"

ENTRY

LIVING ROOM
13'-9" x 19'-5"

GUEST CLOSET
3'-0"

CLOSET
4'-9"

BEDROOM
10'-0" x 13'-5"

BEDROOM
11'-0" x 13'-0"

SLOPED CEILING

SLOPED CEILING

WINDOW SEATS

PLAN H-1319-6
WITH BASEMENT

Total living area: 1,402 sq. ft.
(Not counting basement or garage)

Garage: 651 sq. ft.

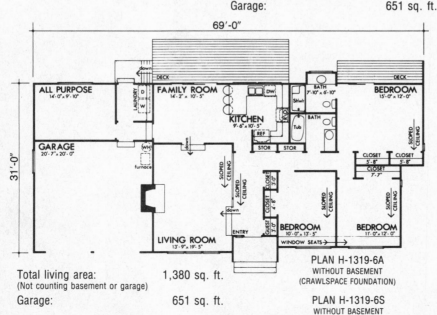

69'-0"

ALL PURPOSE
14'-0" x 9'-10"

FAMILY ROOM
14'-2" x 10'-5"

LAUNDRY

DECK

BEDROOM
15'-0" x 12'-0"

DECK

KITCHEN
9'-6" x 10'-5"

BATH
7'-10" x 6'-10"

BATH

GARAGE
20'-7" x 20'-0"

31'-0"

WH

furnace

STOR

STOR

SLOPED CEILING

SLOPED CEILING

CLOSET
5'-8"

CLOSET
5'-8"

CLOSET
7'-7"

ENTRY

LIVING ROOM
13'-9" x 19'-5"

GUEST CLOSET
3'-0"

CLOSET
4'-8"

BEDROOM
10'-0" x 13'-5"

BEDROOM
11'-0" x 12'-0"

SLOPED CEILING

SLOPED CEILING

WINDOW SEATS

PLAN H-1319-6A
WITHOUT BASEMENT
(CRAWLSPACE FOUNDATION)

PLAN H-1319-6S
WITHOUT BASEMENT
(SLAB FOUNDATION)

Total living area: 1,380 sq. ft.
(Not counting basement or garage)

Garage: 651 sq. ft.

Modest-Sized Plan Includes Large-Home Amenities

This home combines a smart outside structure with a functional inside setting in a practical and economical way. The main entrance opens to the entry half flanked by an elegant sunken living room. Massive fireplace, dashing vaulted ceiling and open railing decorate the interior. One step up leads to the family room which can serve as dining room for formal entertaining or as a nook with breakfast bar for fast and informal get-togethers. Sliding glass doors open to a spacious outside deck.

A main focal point is the fully equipped kitchen with generous counter space and cabinetry.

The extra-duty laundry room includes a closet and overhead cabinetry. Outside access is through a door which opens to the rear of the home, and a second door which opens to a double car garage. A practical all-purpose room, next to the laundry room, is an ideal place for extra storage or studio space.

Closets are abundant throughout — two in main entry hall, two sets of storage and linen closets at the central hallway, dual wardrobe units in the master bedroom, and single units in the other bedrooms. Plan H-1319-6 (with basement) takes some of the closet space for the stairway, so the linen closet is relocated.

The master bedroom is served by a private bathroom and an exclusive sun deck reached through sliding glass doors. The other two bedrooms are detailed with attractive bay windows and vaulted ceiling.

Skillful planning, elimination of wasted space, and overall comfort are the main features in this home.

Blueprint Price Code A

Exciting Exterior Options

ELEVATION A

ELEVATION B

- Two exciting elevations are available with this striking stucco design. (Both are included with blueprint purchase.)
- The stately, covered front entry and elegant window treatments are just the beginning of the excitement. Inside is a huge formal living area with volume ceilings.
- The adjoining family room offers built-in shelving and provisions for an optional corner fireplace or media center. Triple sliders open to the rear covered patio.
- The eat-in country kitchen overlooks the family room and features a handy serving counter, a pantry and a laundry closet.
- Separated from the two secondary bedrooms, the master bedroom is a quiet retreat. It offers patio access and an oversized private bath with a huge walk-in closet, a big corner tub and separate vanities that flank a sitting area.

Plan HDS-99-140	
Bedrooms: 3	**Baths:** 2
Living Area:	
Main floor	1,550 sq. ft.
Total Living Area:	**1,550 sq. ft.**
Garage	475 sq. ft.
Exterior Wall Framing:	2x4
Foundation Options:	
Slab	
(Typical foundation & framing conversion diagram available—see order form.)	
BLUEPRINT PRICE CODE:	B

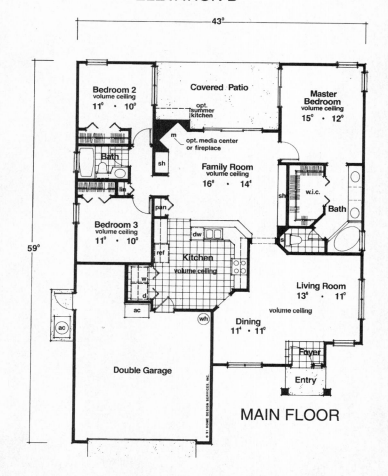

MAIN FLOOR

REAR VIEW

Angled Solar Efficiency

- Dramatically angled to maximize the benefits of passive-solar technology, this compact one-story home can be adapted to many sites and orientations.
- South-facing rooms, including the combination sun room and den, absorb and store heat energy in thermal floors for nighttime radiation.
- Heavy insulation in exterior walls and ceilings, plus double glazing in windows, keep heat loss to a minimum. During the summer, heat is expelled through an operable clerestory window and through an automatic vent in the sun room.
- The entrance vestibule provides an immediate view of the sun room and the outdoors beyond.
- The living lounge boasts a warm fireplace, a bright bay window and a 14-ft. vaulted ceiling.
- The kitchen features an eating bar, while the attached dining area opens to a large rear terrace.
- The bedrooms are isolated for total privacy. The master suite features a private bath and a large walk-in closet.

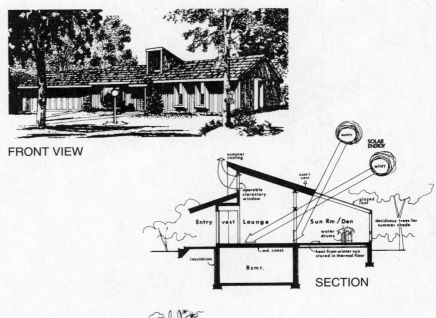

FRONT VIEW

SECTION

Plan K-505-R

Bedrooms: 3	Baths: 2
Living Area:	
Main floor	1,261 sq. ft.
Sun room	164 sq. ft.
Total Living Area:	**1,425 sq. ft.**
Standard basement	1,030 sq. ft.
Garage	466 sq. ft.
Exterior Wall Framing:	2x4 or 2x6

Foundation Options:

Standard basement

Slab

(All plans can be built with your choice of foundation and framing. A generic conversion diagram is available. See order form.)

BLUEPRINT PRICE CODE: A

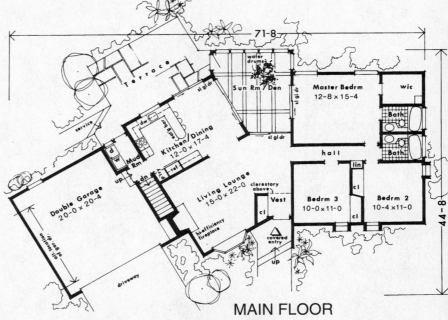

MAIN FLOOR

TO ORDER THIS BLUEPRINT, CALL TOLL-FREE 1-800-820-1283   Plan K-505-R   *PRICES AND DETAILS ON PAGES 12-15*

FRONT VIEW

Total living area: 1,231 sq. ft.
(Not counting basement or garage)

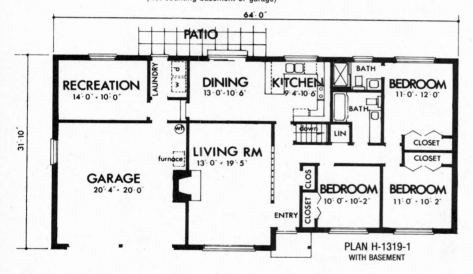

PLAN H-1319-1
WITH BASEMENT

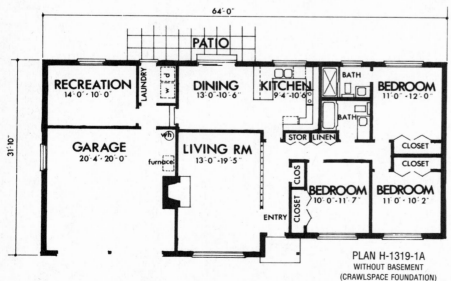

PLAN H-1319-1A
WITHOUT BASEMENT
(CRAWLSPACE FOUNDATION)

Ever-Popular Brick Rambler

The simple rectangular shape and small square footage of this design make it a good choice for first-home buyers or for retirees. But this home is more than the basic rambler. The low-slung roof is staggered to form two levels and is capped with a modified hip roof — sometimes known as a "Tahitian roof" — for a look of refinement. The exterior walls are covered with 4" thick brick veneer, with corbeled brick used to trim the windows.

The interior hosts all the features today's homeowners are looking for while keeping the total living area under 1,250 sq. ft. The main entry provides a warm reception area for guests. To the left is the living room and fireplace, sectioned off from the hallway by a 9' wide half-wall with turned posts extending to the ceiling. The main hall has a guest closet and intersects with the hallways leading to the kitchen and the bedrooms.

The U-shaped kitchen features a breakfast bar that provides seating space for four people. The refrigerator, drop-in range and sink are positioned in a step-saving triangle, with plenty of counter space in between. The adjacent dining room has sliding glass doors opening onto the backyard patio.

Another rear entrance leads into the laundry room, which is also accessible from the garage. The laundry and recreation rooms are a step down from the main part of the house and can be closed off from the dining room.

All three bedrooms are equipped with 2' x 7' closets, with more storage space outside the main bath. The master bedroom features a bath of its own.

The optional basement includes a family room with a fireplace, plus a bathroom, fourth bedroom and a general-use area.

TO ORDER THIS BLUEPRINT,
CALL TOLL-FREE 1-800-820-1283

Blueprint Price Code A
Plans H-1319-1 & -1A

PRICES AND DETAILS
ON PAGES 12-15

95

Angled Solar One-Story

- Captivating angles, solar efficiency and an open floor plan highlight this contemporary home.
- A covered entry leads into the reception area, which is dramatically brightened by a clerestory window.
- The spacious living room features a majestic sloped ceiling, an inviting high-efficiency fireplace and sliding glass doors to a backyard terrace.
- Glazed roof panels in the dining room capture the sun's warmth for winter heating, and adjustable shades promote summertime cooling.
- The kitchen features a generous angled counter, a skylight, a full pantry and a dinette area for family dining.
- The expansive master suite has its own private terrace and whirlpool bath.
- Two additional bedrooms share a second full bath.

Plan K-523-C	
Bedrooms: 3	**Baths:** 2
Living Area:	
Main floor	1,285 sq. ft.
Total Living Area:	**1,285 sq. ft.**
Standard basement	1,264 sq. ft.
Garage and storage	477 sq. ft.
Exterior Wall Framing:	2x4 or 2x6
Foundation Options:	
Standard basement	
Slab	

(All plans can be built with your choice of foundation and framing. A generic conversion diagram is available. See order form.)

BLUEPRINT PRICE CODE:	A

MAIN FLOOR

Plan K-523-C

PRICES AND DETAILS ON PAGES 12-15

Luxury in a Compact Design

• Stucco exterior and diamond-grill windows accent the cozy cottage look.
• Vaulted living room ceiling.
• Interesting kitchen design, with adjoining laundry area.
• Living/dining areas join for spacious area for parties or family gatherings.

Plan E-901

Bedrooms: 2	Baths: 2
Total living area:	984 sq. ft.
Unheated area:	113 sq. ft.
Exterior Wall Framing:	2x4

Foundation options:
Crawlspace.
Slab.
(Foundation & framing conversion diagram available — see order form.)

Blueprint Price Code	AA

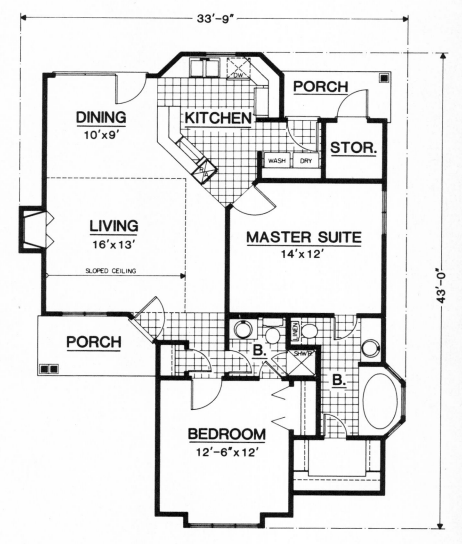

FRONT VIEW

Designed Around Step-Saving Floor Plan

This compact design utilizes a basic floor plan formerly found mostly in large

homes. The entry hall is the focal center of the traffic plan. It connects with all the rooms to save steps and provide floor space for storage closets and additional plumbing.

Even though the home is only 1,357 sq. ft., it still includes three bedrooms. Note that the master bedroom includes a private bath as well as a large walk-in closet.

There is no shortage of functional kitchen cabinetry and appliance installations. The kitchen is combined with the open planning of the family room for multi-purpose use.

Total living area: 1,357 sq. ft.
(Not counting garage)

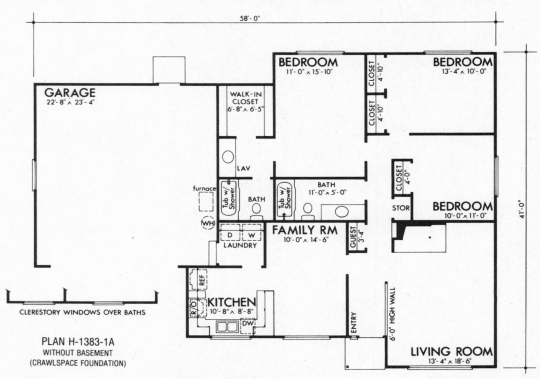

PLAN H-1383-1A
WITHOUT BASEMENT
(CRAWLSPACE FOUNDATION)

Blueprint Price Code A

Plan H-1383-1A

PRICES AND DETAILS ON PAGES 12-15

Extraordinary Split-Level

- This design boasts a striking arched window in an inviting facade that introduces an extraordinary split-level floor plan.
- The recessed entry opens into the expansive living room, with its fabulous windows, nice fireplace and breathtaking 12-ft. vaulted ceiling.
- The dining room, which features a 14-ft. vaulted ceiling, expands the open living area and lends an air of spaciousness to the entire main floor.
- The kitchen is a gourmet's dream, offering a wraparound counter, a double sink and a pass-through to the dining room. A 12-ft. vaulted ceiling is shared with the sunny breakfast room, which shows off a built-in desk and sliding-door access to a backyard deck.
- The sizable master bedroom, a second bedroom and a shared bath are several steps up from the main level, creating a sense of privacy.
- The third bedroom makes a great den, playroom, office or guest room.

Plan B-87112	
Bedrooms: 2+	**Baths: 2**
Living Area:	
Main floor	1,452 sq. ft.
Total Living Area:	**1,452 sq. ft.**
Standard basement	1,452 sq. ft.
Garage	448 sq. ft.
Exterior Wall Framing:	2x4
Foundation Options:	
Standard basement	

(All plans can be built with your choice of foundation and framing. A generic conversion diagram is available. See order form.)

BLUEPRINT PRICE CODE: A

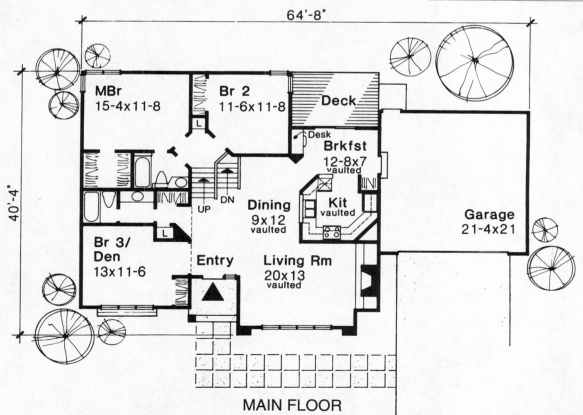

64'-8"

40'-4"

MBr
15-4x11-8

Br 2
11-6x11-8

Deck

Desk

Brkfst
12-8x7
vaulted

Dining
9x12
vaulted

Kit
vaulted

Br 3/
Den
13x11-6

Entry

Living Rm
20x13
vaulted

Garage
21-4x21

DN

UP

MAIN FLOOR

Traditional Heritage

- A distinctive roofline and a covered wraparound porch reflect this charming home's traditional heritage.
- The roomy entry flows directly into the spacious, open living area. Enhanced by a cathedral ceiling, the living room is warmed by a fireplace and offers a French door to a backyard patio. A good-sized laundry room is nearby.

- The adjoining dining area shares porch access with the stylish gourmet kitchen, which includes an eating bar and a garden window over the sink.
- The master bedroom suite features a lavish private bath with a garden spa tub, a separate shower, a dual-sink vanity and a big walk-in closet.
- A second full bath, located at the end of the bedroom hallway, is convenient to the two remaining bedrooms.
- The double carport includes a separate lockable storage area.

Plan J-86142	
Bedrooms: 3	**Baths:** 2
Living Area:	
Main floor	1,536 sq. ft.
Total Living Area:	**1,536 sq. ft.**
Standard basement	1,536 sq. ft.
Carport and storage	520 sq. ft.
Exterior Wall Framing:	2x4

Foundation Options:

Standard basement
Crawlspace
Slab
(All plans can be built with your choice of foundation and framing. A generic conversion diagram is available. See order form.)

BLUEPRINT PRICE CODE:	B

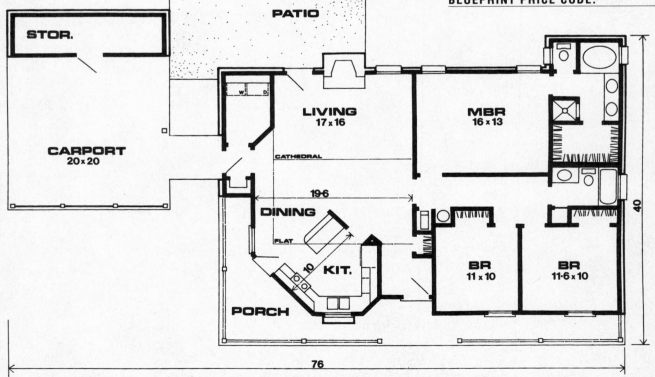

MAIN FLOOR

Plan J-86142

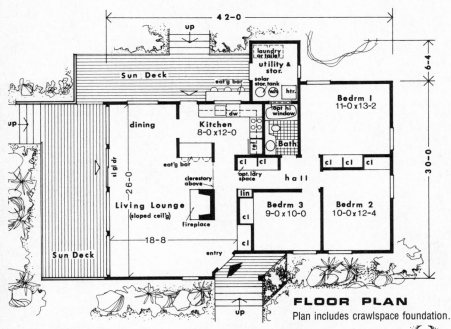

FLOOR PLAN
Plan includes crawlspace foundation.

42-0

up

Sun Deck

up

dining

Kitchen
8-0 x 12-0

eat'g bar

26-0

Living Lounge
(sloped ceil'g)

18-8

Sun Deck

eat'g bar

clerestory
above

fireplace

opt. ldry
space

laundry
or toilet

utility &
stor.

solar
stor. tank

opt hi
window

htr.

dw

ref

Bath

cl cl

cl

cl cl cl

hall

lin

Bedrm 1
11-0 x 13-2

Bedrm 3
9-0 x 10-0

Bedrm 2
10-0 x 12-4

cl

cl

entry

up

6-4

30-0

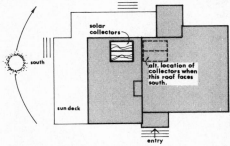

ORIENTATION FEASIBILITY
mirror plan also possible
home may be built without solar system

south

solar
collectors

alt. location of
collectors when
this roof faces
south.

sun deck

entry

Living With Sunpower

Angled wood siding accentuates the architectural geometry of this flexible leisure home. The house is designed to exploit sun power and conserve energy. Focal point of the plan is an outsized living lounge that has pitched ceiling and overall dimensions of 18'-8" by 26'-0". Note the glass wall that leads to the spacious sun deck. A roomy kitchen is accessible from another sun deck and serves two eating bars as well as the dining room. The three bedrooms are well isolated from noise and traffic. Adjacent to the kitchen is the utility-storage room that can accommodate laundry facilities.

As an option, two solar collectors can be installed on the roof, either over the living lounge, or on the opposite roof, depending on the southern exposure. Solar equipment may be installed now or in the future.

Total living area: 1,077 sq. ft.

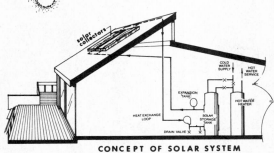

CONCEPT OF SOLAR SYSTEM
FOR DOMESTIC HOT WATER

solar
collectors

COLD
WATER
SUPPLY

HOT
WATER
SERVICE

EXPANSION
TANK

HOT WATER
HEATER

HEAT EXCHANGE
LOOP

SOLAR
STORAGE
TANK

DRAIN VALVE

Blueprint Price Code A

Plan K-166-T

TO ORDER THIS BLUEPRINT,
CALL TOLL-FREE 1-800-820-1283

*PRICES AND DETAILS
ON PAGES 12-15*

101

Perfect Repose

- This perfectly planned home is well suited to serve as the haven your family retreats to for repose and relaxation.
- Out front, a covered porch includes just the right amount of space for your favorite two rockers and a side table.
- Inside, the foyer flows right into the Great Room, which will serve as home base for family gatherings. A fireplace flanked by a media center turns this room into a home theater.
- Nearby, sunlight pours into the versatile dining room. Along one wall, a beautiful built-in cabinet holds linens, china and other fine collectibles.
- Afternoon treats take on a fun twist at the kitchen's snack bar. For easy serving, the snack bar extends to a peninsula counter.
- A 10-ft., 8-in. tray ceiling and a cheery bay window in the master suite turn this space into a stylish oasis. A dressing area with a vanity table for morning preening leads to the master bath, where a skylight and a 15-ft. vaulted ceiling brighten the room.

Plan AX-95347

Bedrooms: 3	Baths: 2½
Living Area:	
Main floor	1,709 sq. ft.
Total Living Area:	**1,709 sq. ft.**
Standard basement	1,709 sq. ft.
Garage and storage	448 sq. ft.
Exterior Wall Framing:	2x4

Foundation Options:

Standard basement

Crawlspace

Slab

(All plans can be built with your choice of foundation and framing. A generic conversion diagram is available. See order form.)

BLUEPRINT PRICE CODE: B

REAR VIEW

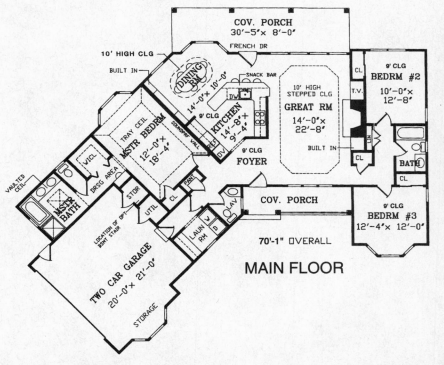

MAIN FLOOR

TO ORDER THIS BLUEPRINT, CALL TOLL-FREE 1-800-820-1283

Plan AX-95347

PRICES AND DETAILS ON PAGES 12-15

This Is It!

- This comfortable design is just the plan you're looking for. The affordable design includes all the features—both inside and out—today's family needs.
- The first days of spring will feel even better when you settle into a rocker on the porch and watch the kids play a game of Kick the Can in the front yard.
- Inside, the dining room awaits formal dinners. Built-in cabinets hold the fine china you pull out to celebrate a job promotion or a good report card.
- In the kitchen, a snack bar is the perfect place to feed the kids a snack. The sunshine that pours into the morning room will rouse the spirits of even the sleepiest family member.
- Friends and family will show up at your home to celebrate the Fourth of July on your fun-packed deck.
- In the busy living room, plenty of room is available to dance to your favorite music or gather the clan together to watch the newest release on video.
- When you need a break, retreat to the master suite, where you can savor the peace and quiet in the sitting area.

Plan DD-1716

Bedrooms: 3	Baths: 2
Living Area:	
Main floor	1,738 sq. ft.
Total Living Area:	**1,738 sq. ft.**
Standard basement	1,466 sq. ft.
Garage	425 sq. ft.
Exterior Wall Framing:	2x4

Foundation Options:

Standard basement

Crawlspace

Slab

(All plans can be built with your choice of foundation and framing. A generic conversion diagram is available. See order form.)

BLUEPRINT PRICE CODE:	B

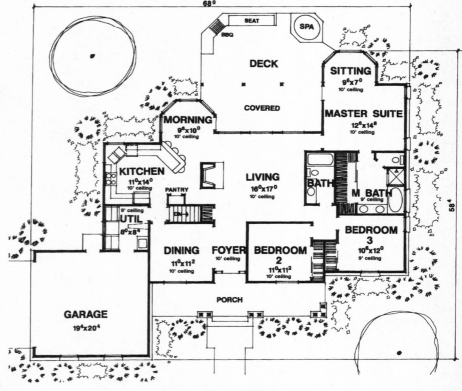

MAIN FLOOR

Scintillating Conversation

- This delightful home is full of inviting spaces that are sure to foster scintillating conversation!
- In the Great Room, a 10-ft. tray ceiling presides over a welcoming fireplace and a refreshing wet bar that will draw you and your loved ones together. French doors lead to a screened porch, where cool breezes waft gently on spring mornings.
- The serene master bedroom lets you relax in a cozy bayed window, while a 10-ft. tray ceiling expands the room. The bath coaxes you to rejuvenate with its whirlpool tub and bracing shower.
- A long porch at the front of the home is defined by a decorative rail and the dining room's bayed window. It's a great spot to chat with neighbors or to enjoy a glass of iced coffee on balmy summer mornings. If it gets too chilly for you, slip through the sliding glass doors and enjoy a meal indoors.

Plan AX-94339

Bedrooms: 3	Baths: 2
Living Area:	
Main floor	1,747 sq. ft.
Total Living Area:	**1,747 sq. ft.**
Screened porch	177 sq. ft.
Standard basement	1,747 sq. ft.
Garage/utility/storage	451 sq. ft.
Exterior Wall Framing:	2x4

Foundation Options:

Standard basement

Crawlspace

Slab

(All plans can be built with your choice of foundation and framing. A generic conversion diagram is available. See order form.)

BLUEPRINT PRICE CODE:	B

VIEW INTO GREAT ROOM

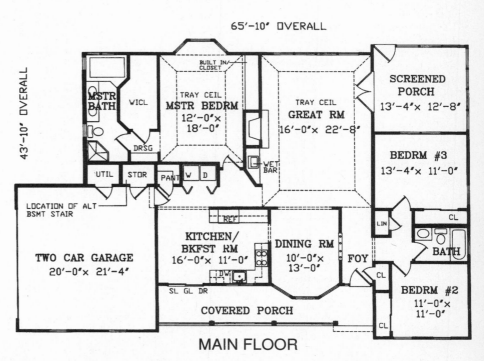

MAIN FLOOR

Dramatic Dining Room

- The highlight of this lovely one-story design is its dramatic dining room, which boasts a 14-ft.-high ceiling and a soaring window wall.
- The airy foyer ushers guests through a 14-ft.-high arched opening and into the 18-ft. vaulted Great Room, which is warmed by an inviting fireplace.
- The kitchen features a large pantry, a serving bar and a handy pass-through to the Great Room. The bright breakfast area offers a convenient laundry closet and outdoor access.
- The two secondary bedrooms share a compartmentalized bath.
- The removed master suite features a 14-ft. tray ceiling, overhead plant shelves and an adjoining 13½-ft. vaulted sitting room. An exciting garden tub is found in the luxurious master bath.

Plan FB-5008-ALLE

Bedrooms: 3	Baths: 2
Living Area:	
Main floor	1,715 sq. ft.
Total Living Area:	**1,715 sq. ft.**
Daylight basement	1,715 sq. ft.
Garage	400 sq. ft.
Exterior Wall Framing:	2x4

Foundation Options:

Daylight basement

Crawlspace

Slab

(All plans can be built with your choice of foundation and framing. A generic conversion diagram is available. See order form.)

BLUEPRINT PRICE CODE: B

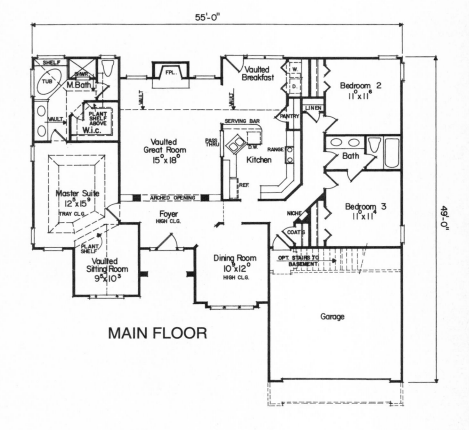

MAIN FLOOR

Porch Offers Three Entries

- Showy window treatments, stately columns and three sets of French doors give this Plantation-style home an inviting exterior.
- High 12-ft. ceilings in the living room, dining room and kitchen add volume to the economically-sized home.
- A corner fireplace and a view to the back porch are found in the living room. The porch is accessed from a door in the dining room.
- The adjoining kitchen features an angled snack bar that easily serves the dining room and the casual eating area.
- The secluded master suite offers a cathedral ceiling, a walk-in closet and a luxurious private bath with a spa tub and a separate shower.
- Across the home, two additional bedrooms share a second full bath.

Plan E-1602

Bedrooms: 3	Baths: 2
Living Area:	
Main floor	1,672 sq. ft.
Total Living Area:	**1,672 sq. ft.**
Standard basement	1,672 sq. ft.
Garage	484 sq. ft.
Exterior Wall Framing:	2x6

Foundation Options:

Standard basement
Crawlspace
Slab

(All plans can be built with your choice of foundation and framing. A generic conversion diagram is available. See order form.)

BLUEPRINT PRICE CODE: **B**

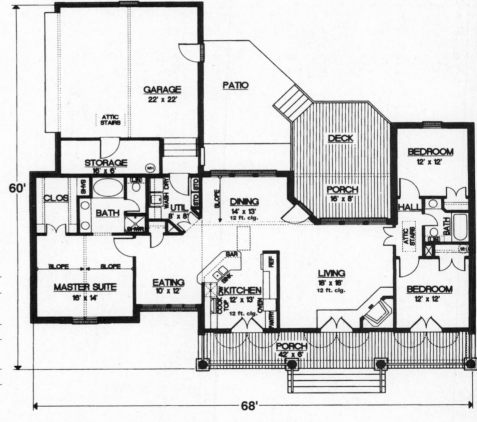

MAIN FLOOR

Plan E-1602

PRICES AND DETAILS ON PAGES 12-15

Fine Dining

- This fine stucco home showcases a huge round-top window arrangement, which augments the central dining room with its 14½-ft. ceiling.
- A cute covered porch opens to the bright foyer, where a 13-ft.-high ceiling extends past a decorative column to the airy Great Room.
- The sunny dining room merges with the Great Room, which features a warm

fireplace, a kitchen pass-through and a French door to the backyard.
- The kitchen boasts a pantry closet, a nice serving bar and an angled sink. The vaulted breakfast nook with an optional bay hosts casual meals.
- The secluded master suite has a tray ceiling and a vaulted bath with a dual-sink vanity, a large garden tub and a separate shower. Across the home, two secondary bedrooms share another full bath.

Plan FB-5351-GENE	
Bedrooms: 3	**Baths: 2**
Living Area:	
Main floor	1,670 sq. ft.
Total Living Area:	**1,670 sq. ft.**
Daylight basement	1,670 sq. ft.
Garage	400 sq. ft.
Exterior Wall Framing:	2x4

Foundation Options:
Daylight basement
Crawlspace
(All plans can be built with your choice of foundation and framing. A generic conversion diagram is available. See order form.)

BLUEPRINT PRICE CODE:	**B**

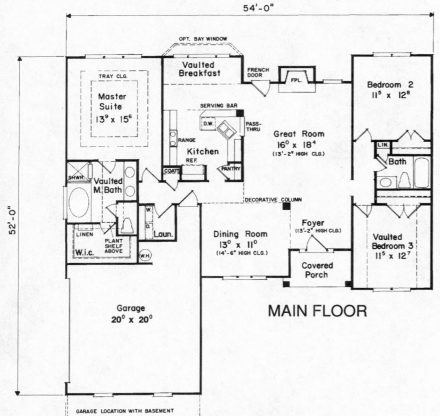

MAIN FLOOR

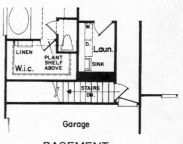

BASEMENT
STAIRWAY
LOCATION

Cozy Covered Porches

- Twin dormers give this raised one-story design the appearance of a two-story. Two covered porches and a deck supplement the main living areas with plenty of outdoor entertaining space.
- The large central living room features a dramatic fireplace, a 12-ft. ceiling with a skylight and access to both porch areas.
- Double doors open to a bayed eating area, which overlooks the adjoining deck and includes a sloped ceiling that rises to 12 ft. in the kitchen. An angled snack bar and a pantry are also featured.
- The elegant master suite is tucked to one side of the home and also overlooks the backyard and deck. Laundry facilities and garage access are nearby.
- Across the home, two additional bedrooms share another full bath.

Plan E-1826

Bedrooms: 3	Baths: 2
Living Area:	
Main floor	1,800 sq. ft.
Total Living Area:	**1,800 sq. ft.**
Garage	550 sq. ft.
Storage	84 sq. ft.
Exterior Wall Framing:	2x6

Foundation Options:

Crawlspace
Slab
(All plans can be built with your choice of foundation and framing. A generic conversion diagram is available. See order form.)

BLUEPRINT PRICE CODE:	**B**

MAIN FLOOR

Plan E-1826

PRICES AND DETAILS ON PAGES 12-15

Winsome Heart

- This stately home's nostalgic facade and welcoming interior recall winsome days of innocence and carefree living.
- The sprawling front porch has plenty of room for a porch swing. Twilight cuddling might make the neighbors whisper, but it will also bring the two of you closer together.
- When the mosquitoes get bad, head indoors for more conversation by the living room's crackling fireplace. Or, share a healthy dessert in the spacious skylighted dining area.
- If privacy is your aim, the cool patio in the backyard is a nice spot to unwind.
- Clustering the bedrooms together creates a reassuring feeling of safety for all family members. At night, the kids can listen for Dad's footsteps if he tries to sneak a midnight snack in the kitchen!
- On the upper floor, expansion ideas are limited only by your imagination. How about an exciting game room, complete with a ping-pong table or billiard table? Or savor a movie with buttery popcorn.

Plan J-9509

Bedrooms: 3+	Baths: 2
Living Area:	
Main floor	1,625 sq. ft.
Total Living Area:	**1,625 sq. ft.**
Future upper floor	710 sq. ft.
Standard basement	1,625 sq. ft.
Garage	533 sq. ft.
Storage	54 sq. ft.
Exterior Wall Framing:	2x6
Foundation Options:	
Standard basement	
Crawlspace	
Slab	

(All plans can be built with your choice of foundation and framing. A generic conversion diagram is available. See order form.)

BLUEPRINT PRICE CODE:	B

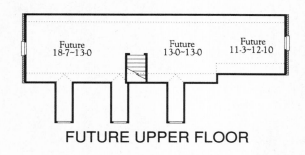

FUTURE UPPER FLOOR

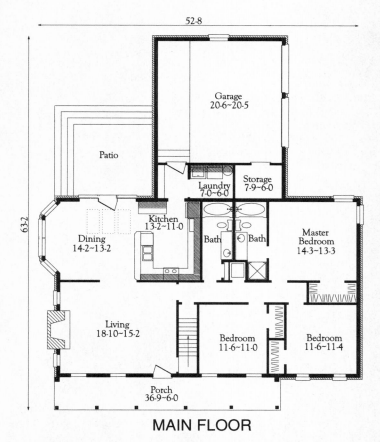

MAIN FLOOR

Free-Flowing Floor Plan

- This exciting luxury home is characterized by a fluid floor plan with open indoor/outdoor living spaces.
- The stylish columned porch opens to a spacious living room and dining room expanse that overlooks the outdoor spaces. The breathtaking view also includes a dramatic corner fireplace.
- The dining room opens to a bright kitchen with an angled eating bar. The overall spaciousness of the living areas is increased with high 12-ft. ceilings.
- A sunny, informal eating area adjoins the kitchen, and an angled set of doors opens to a convenient main-floor laundry room near the garage entrance.
- The master suite features a 13-ft. vaulted ceiling, a walk-in closet and a sumptuous bath with an oval tub.
- A separate wing houses two additional bedrooms and another full bath.
- Attic space is accessible from stairs in the garage and in the bedroom wing.

Plan E-1710

Bedrooms: 3	Baths: 2
Living Area:	
Main floor	1,792 sq. ft.
Total Living Area:	**1,792 sq. ft.**
Standard basement	1,792 sq. ft.
Garage	484 sq. ft.
Storage	96 sq. ft.
Exterior Wall Framing:	2x6

Foundation Options:

Standard basement

Crawlspace

Slab

(All plans can be built with your choice of foundation and framing. A generic conversion diagram is available. See order form.)

BLUEPRINT PRICE CODE: **B**

REAR VIEW

MAIN FLOOR

Emotional Connection

- With radiant windows adorning much of the rear facade, this home promises an emotional connection with the rolling landscape surrounding it.
- Imagine the view from the bayed hearth room, which basks in the warmth from a cheery peninsula fireplace. An eating bar introduces the island kitchen, which boasts a tidy step-in pantry and plenty

of counter space. You can serve breakfast with ease in the corner nook.
- Dazzle your neighbors by displaying the Christmas tree in the windowed corner of the family room. There's plenty of space to gather around for a little family bonding.
- The master suite pampers you with an opulent bath that includes two walk-in closets, twin sinks, a corner whirlpool tub and a sit-down shower.
- For the family on the go, the single garage bay makes a great home for a boat, a snowmobile or a golf cart!

Plan KLF-955	
Bedrooms: 3+	**Baths:** 2
Living Area:	
Main floor	2,394 sq. ft.
Total Living Area:	**2,394 sq. ft.**
Split 3-car garage/storage	818 sq. ft.
Exterior Wall Framing:	2x4
Foundation Options:	
Slab	

(All plans can be built with your choice of foundation and framing. A generic conversion diagram is available. See order form.)

BLUEPRINT PRICE CODE:	C

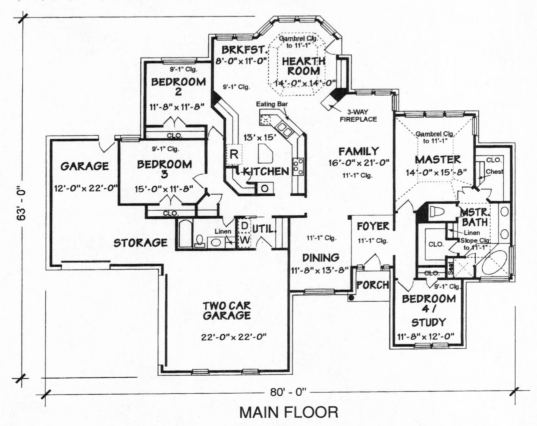

MAIN FLOOR

Simply Beautiful

- This four-bedroom design offers simplistic beauty, economical construction and ample space for both family life and formal entertaining—all on one floor.
- The charming cottage-style exterior gives way to a spacious interior. A 13-ft. vaulted, beamed ceiling soars above the huge living room, which features a massive fireplace, built-in bookshelves and access to a backyard patio.
- The efficient galley-style kitchen flows between a sunny bayed eating area and the formal dining room.
- The deluxe master suite includes a dressing room, a large walk-in closet and a private bath.
- The three remaining bedrooms are larger than average and offer ample closet space.
- A nice-sized storage area and a deluxe utility room are accessible from the two-car garage.

Plan E-1702	
Bedrooms: 4	**Baths:** 2
Living Area:	
Main floor	1,751 sq. ft.
Total Living Area:	**1,751 sq. ft.**
Garage	484 sq. ft.
Storage	105 sq. ft.
Exterior Wall Framing:	2x4

Foundation Options:
Crawlspace
Slab
(All plans can be built with your choice of foundation and framing. A generic conversion diagram is available. See order form.)

BLUEPRINT PRICE CODE:	**B**

MAIN FLOOR

77 '

32 '

PATIO

EATING 11 ' x 9 '

STORAGE 13 ' x 8 '

UTILITY 9 ' x 8 '

WASH. DRYER

BRM'S. STOR.

PANTRY
DISHWASHER

KIT

SINK

SURF. UNIT

REF

OVEN

SLOPE

SLOPE

LIVING 19 ' x 16 '

BEAMS

BOOKS

SHV'S.

CLO.

LINEN

LINEN

BOOKS

BATH

BATH

SHELVES

POST ON 1/2 WALL

DRESS

MASTER SUITE 16 ' x 13 '

CLO.

CLO.

GARAGE 22 ' x 22 '

DINING 11 ' x 10 '

ENTRY 10 ' x 5 '

DISAPPEARING STAIRS

HALL

CLO.

BED RM. 12 ' x 10 '

CLO.

BED RM. 12 ' x 11 '

BED RM. 12 ' x 12 '

PORCH

Plan E-1702

Morning Glory

- This melodious country-style home opens itself to the sights and sounds of nature with front and rear porches, and dazzling window treatments.
- From the sidelighted entry, a long hall leads to the right, introducing three secondary bedrooms. Along the way, you'll find plenty of closet space for coats and board games.
- There's plenty of gathering room in the family room, where a solid fireplace warms the spirit. The bird-watcher in your family can set up camp at the large boxed-out window to the rear.

- The cheery breakfast nook flaunts its own boxed-out window and a glassy door to the backyard porch.
- A raised bar joins the nook to the kitchen, which incorporates cabinets into its center island. Just a few steps brings you to the formal dining room for an exquisite meal.
- On the other side of the home, the master suite is enhanced by a charming window seat. The private bath is packed with essentials, including twin walk-in closets, a whirlpool tub beneath a radiant window, and a dual-sink vanity. The sit-down shower is sure to be a morning eye-opener!

Plan RD-1944	
Bedrooms: 4	**Baths:** 2
Living Area:	
Main floor	1,944 sq. ft.
Total Living Area:	**1,944 sq. ft.**
Standard basement	1,750 sq. ft.
Garage and storage	538 sq. ft.
Exterior Wall Framing:	2x4
Foundation Options:	
Standard basement	
Crawlspace	
Slab	

(All plans can be built with your choice of foundation and framing. A generic conversion diagram is available. See order form.)

BLUEPRINT PRICE CODE:	B

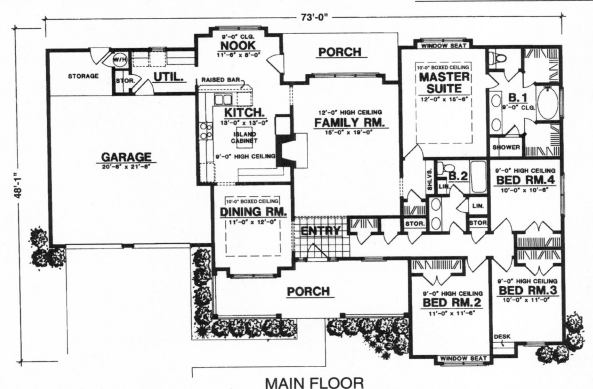

MAIN FLOOR

Sought-After Elegance

- Decorative corner quoins, copper accents and gorgeous windows take the brick and stucco facade of this home to the height of elegance.
- Luxurious appointments continue inside, with a sidelighted 11-ft.-high foyer leading to the formal living and dining rooms. The living room boasts a 14-ft. vaulted ceiling, while the dining room has an 11-ft. ceiling.
- Smoothly accessed from the dining room, the flow-through kitchen offers a serving counter to the breakfast nook. Bright windows light the two areas, which share an 11-ft. vaulted ceiling.

- Adjacent to the nook, the luxurious family room sports a handsome fireplace and access to a sprawling backyard deck. A fancy fan hangs from the soaring 14-ft. vaulted ceiling.
- Just off the family room, two roomy secondary bedrooms share a nice compartmentalized bath.
- The sumptuous master bedroom flaunts its own deck access, a quaint morning porch for quiet cups of coffee and a large walk-in closet.
- The master bath is highlighted by a plant shelf, a garden tub and a separate shower. An 11-ft. ceiling crowns the master bedroom and bath.
- Unless otherwise noted, all rooms have 9-ft. ceilings.
- A bonus room above the garage offers expansion possibilities.

Plan APS-2018	
Bedrooms: 3+	**Baths:** 2½
Living Area:	
Main floor	2,088 sq. ft.
Total Living Area:	**2,088 sq. ft.**
Bonus room (unfinished)	282 sq. ft.
Daylight basement	2,088 sq. ft.
Garage	460 sq. ft.
Storage	35 sq. ft.
Exterior Wall Framing:	2x4
Foundation Options:	

Daylight basement
(All plans can be built with your choice of foundation and framing. A generic conversion diagram is available. See order form.)

BLUEPRINT PRICE CODE:	C

◀ 68 ▶

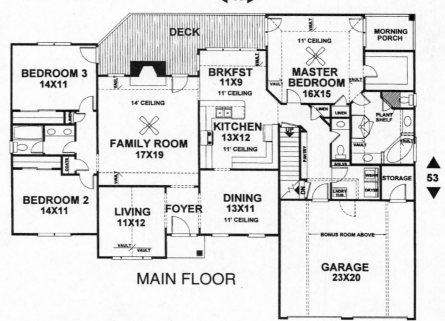

MAIN FLOOR

Tudor-Style Exterior, Modern Interior

Specify crawlspace or slab foundation.

AREAS

Living	2311 sq. ft.
Garage & Storage	576 sq. ft.
Porches	163 sq. ft.
Total	3050 sq. ft.

**TO ORDER THIS BLUEPRINT,
CALL TOLL-FREE 1-800-820-1283**

Blueprint Price Code C
Plan E-2300

**PRICES AND DETAILS
ON PAGES 12-15**

115

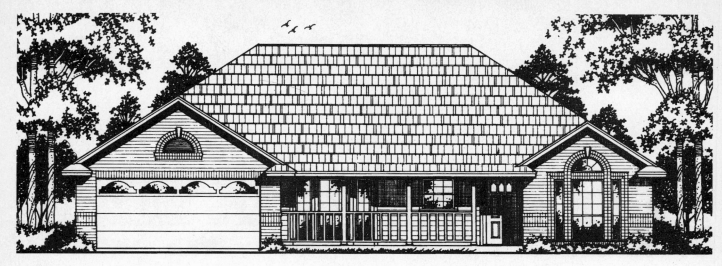

All the Best

- This stylish country home offers the best in amenities and comfortable touches.
- An inviting railed front porch flatters the entry, which opens immediately to the living areas.
- The massive living room will glow warmly with light from its central fireplace. A cozy backyard patio is easily accessed.
- A nifty breakfast bar separates the living room from the walk-through kitchen, which flows into the bay-windowed dining room.
- Secluded from the rest of the home, the master bedroom is brightly lit by a tall, arched window arrangement. The sumptuous master bath boasts his-and-hers walk-in closets, a fabulous garden tub and a sit-down shower. The dual-sink vanity is enhanced by an overhead plant shelf and a makeup area.
- Two more bedrooms, one with an attractive window arrangement, share a convenient hall bath.

Plan KD-1606

Bedrooms: 3	Baths: 2
Living Area:	
Main floor	1,606 sq. ft.
Total Living Area:	**1,606 sq. ft.**
Garage and storage	453 sq. ft.
Exterior Wall Framing:	2x4

Foundation Options:

Slab

(All plans can be built with your choice of foundation and framing. A generic conversion diagram is available. See order form.)

BLUEPRINT PRICE CODE: **B**

55'-6"

43'-0"

patio

f.p.

hearth

BED RM. 1
12'8" x 15'8"
10'0" clg.

bath 1
10'0" clg.

clos.

clos.

shwr

w.h.

w.

d.

util.

storage
9'1" x 5'6"

stor.

hall

LIVING
19'4" x 19'4"
10'0" clg.

BED RM. 3
11'0" x 11'0"
10'0" clg.

h/ac

clos.

hall

bath 2

linen

clos.

clos.

brkfst. bar

DINING RM.
10'0" x 13'0"

KITCH.
9'4" x 11'0"

entry

BED RM. 2
11'0" x 11'0"
10'0" clg.

DOUBLE GARAGE
19'10" x 20'11"

porch

MAIN FLOOR

Regal Poise

- With its stately brick facade, gorgeous half-round transoms and striking gables, this regal home will grace the most upscale neighborhood.
- A warmly appointed family room anchors the home, boasting a prominent fireplace flanked by built-in cabinets. French doors lead to a covered porch that is suitable for neighborly barbecue parties. Transom windows add dazzle.
- The exciting wraparound kitchen boasts an angled bar and stacked ovens with cookie sheet storage above. The adjoining bayed breakfast nook nestles between two porches.
- Shielded from kitchen noise by double doors, the formal dining room provides an intimate space for special meals.
- Natural light floods the master suite through a brilliant bayed window arrangement. In the master bath, a lush plant shelf overlooks a whirlpool tub and a neat split vanity with knee space.
- In the opposite wing of the home, two good-sized secondary bedrooms share a compartmentalized bath, allowing the kids an extra measure of privacy.
- To the right of the sidelighted foyer, French doors introduce a peaceful study that may also be used as a bedroom.

Plan KLF-941

Bedrooms: 3+	Baths: 2½
Living Area:	
Main floor	2,437 sq. ft.
Total Living Area:	**2,437 sq. ft.**
Garage and storage	589 sq. ft.
Exterior Wall Framing:	2x4

Foundation Options:

Slab

(All plans can be built with your choice of foundation and framing. A generic conversion diagram is available. See order form.)

BLUEPRINT PRICE CODE: C

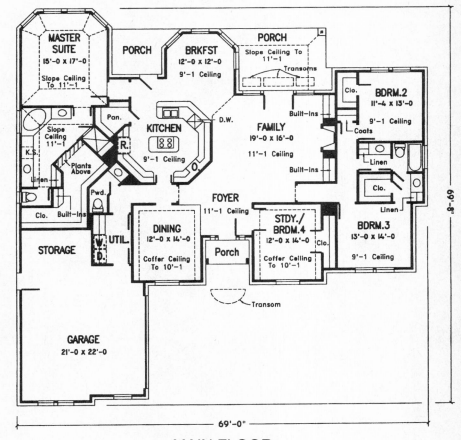

MAIN FLOOR

Distinguished Living

- Beautiful arches, sweeping rooflines and a dramatic entry court distinguish this one-story from all the rest.
- Elegant columns outline the main foyer. To the right, the dining room has a 13-ft. coffered ceiling and an ale bar with a wine rack.
- The centrally located Grand Room can be viewed from the foyer and gallery. French doors and flanking windows allow a view of the veranda as well.
- A large island kitchen and sunny morning room merge with the casual Gathering Room. The combination offers a big fireplace, a TV niche, bookshelves and a handy snack bar.
- The extraordinary master suite flaunts a 12-ft. ceiling, an exciting three-sided fireplace and a TV niche shared with the private bayed lounge. A luxurious bath, a private library and access to the veranda are also featured.
- The two smaller bedroom suites have private baths and generous closets.

Plan EOF-62

Bedrooms: 3	Baths: 3½
Living Area:	
Main floor	3,090 sq. ft.
Total Living Area:	**3,090 sq. ft.**
Garage	660 sq. ft.
Exterior Wall Framing:	2x6

Foundation Options:

Slab

(All plans can be built with your choice of foundation and framing. A generic conversion diagram is available. See order form.)

BLUEPRINT PRICE CODE: E

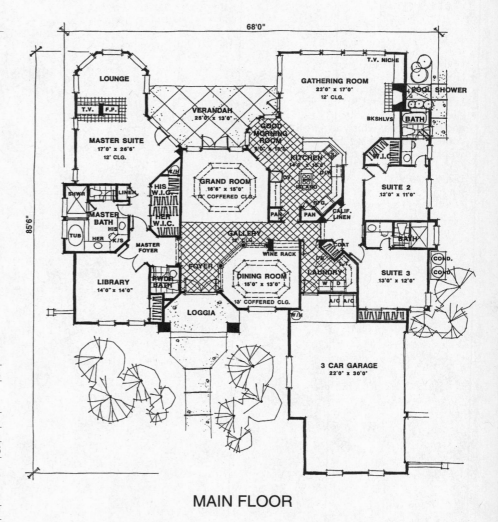

MAIN FLOOR

Plan EOF-62

PRICES AND DETAILS ON PAGES 12-15

French Garden Design

- A creative, angular design gives this traditional French garden home an exciting, open and airy floor plan.
- Guests enter through a covered, columned porch that opens into the large, angled living and dining rooms.
- High 12-ft. ceilings highlight the living and dining area, which also features corner windows, a wet bar, a cozy fireplace and access to a huge covered backyard porch.
- The angled walk-through kitchen, also with a 12-ft.-high ceiling, offers plenty of work space and an adjoining informal eating nook that faces a delightful private courtyard. The nearby utility area has extra freezer space, a walk-in pantry and garage access.
- The home's bedrooms are housed in two separate wings. One wing boasts a luxurious master suite, which features a large walk-in closet, an angled tub and a separate shower.
- Two large bedrooms in the other wing share a hall bath. Each bedroom has a walk-in closet.

Plan E-2004

Bedrooms: 3	Baths: 2
Living Area:	
Main floor	2,023 sq. ft.
Total Living Area:	**2,023 sq. ft.**
Garage	484 sq. ft.
Storage	87 sq. ft.
Exterior Wall Framing:	2x6

Foundation Options:

Crawlspace
Slab
(All plans can be built with your choice of foundation and framing. A generic conversion diagram is available. See order form.)

BLUEPRINT PRICE CODE:	C

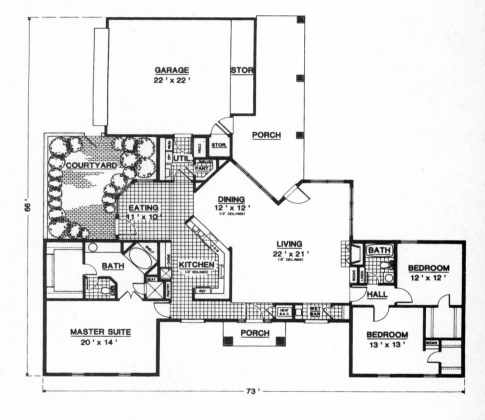

MAIN FLOOR

TO ORDER THIS BLUEPRINT,
CALL TOLL-FREE 1-800-820-1283

Plan E-2004

PRICES AND DETAILS
ON PAGES 12-15

119

Bright Design

- Sweeping rooflines, arched transom windows and a stucco exterior give this exciting design a special flair.
- Inside the high, dramatic entry, guests are greeted with a stunning view of the living room, which is expanded by a 12-ft. volume ceiling. This formal expanse is augmented by an oversized bay that looks out onto a covered patio and possible pool area.
- To the left of the foyer is the formal dining room, accented by columns and a 14-ft. receding tray ceiling.
- The island kitchen overlooks a sunny breakfast nook and a large family room, each with 12-ft.-high ceilings. A handy pass-through transports food to the patio, which offers a summer kitchen.
- The master wing includes a large bedroom with a 10-ft.-high coffered ceiling, a sitting area with patio access, a massive walk-in closet and a sun-drenched garden bath.
- The private den/study could also serve as an extra bedroom.
- Two to three more bedrooms share two full baths. The front bedrooms boast 12-ft. ceilings and the rear bedroom is accented by a 10-ft. ceiling.

Plan HDS-90-814

Bedrooms: 3+	Baths: 3½
Living Area:	
Main floor	3,743 sq. ft.
Total Living Area:	**3,743 sq. ft.**
Garage	725 sq. ft.

Exterior Wall Framing:
2x4 and 8-in. concrete block

Foundation Options:
Slab
(All plans can be built with your choice of foundation and framing. A generic conversion diagram is available. See order form.)

BLUEPRINT PRICE CODE: **F**

MAIN FLOOR

Plan HDS-90-814

Country Charm, Cottage Look

- An interesting combination of stone and stucco gives a charming cottage look to this attactive country home.
- Off the inviting sidelighted entry, the formal dining room is defined by striking columns.
- The dining room expands into the living room, which boasts a fireplace and built-in shelves. A French door provides access to a cute backyard patio.
- The galley-style kitchen unfolds to a sunny morning room.
- All of the living areas are expanded by 10-ft. ceilings.
- The master bedroom features a 10-ft. ceiling and a nice bayed sitting area. The luxurious master bath boasts an exciting garden tub and a glass-block shower, as well as a big walk-in closet and a dressing area with two sinks.
- Across the home, two additional bedrooms with walk-in closets and private dressing areas share a tidy compartmentalized bath.

Plan DD-1790

Bedrooms: 3	Baths: 2½
Living Area:	
Main floor	1,790 sq. ft.
Total Living Area:	**1,790 sq. ft.**
Standard basement	1,790 sq. ft.
Garage	438 sq. ft.
Exterior Wall Framing:	2x4
Foundation Options:	
Standard basement	
Crawlspace	
Slab	

(All plans can be built with your choice of foundation and framing. A generic conversion diagram is available. See order form.)

BLUEPRINT PRICE CODE:	B

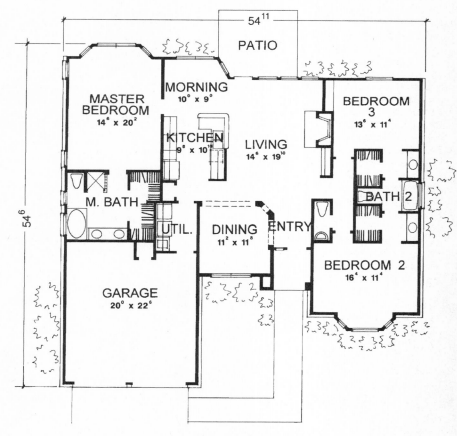

MAIN FLOOR

Interior Angles Add Excitement

- Interior angles add a touch of excitement to this one-story home.
- A pleasantly charming exterior combines wood and stone to give the plan a solid, comfortable look for any neighborhood.
- Formal living and dining rooms flank the entry, which leads into the large family room, featuring a fireplace, a 19-ft. high vaulted ceiling and built-in bookshelves. A covered porch and a sunny patio are just steps away.
- The adjoining eating area with a built-in china cabinet angles off the roomy kitchen. Note the pantry and the convenient utility room.
- The master bedroom suite is both spacious and private, and includes a dressing room, a large walk-in closet and a secluded bath.
- The three secondary bedrooms are also zoned for privacy, and share a compartmentalized bath.

Plan E-1904	
Bedrooms: 4	**Baths:** 2½
Living Area:	
Main floor	1,997 sq. ft.
Total Living Area:	**1,997 sq. ft.**
Garage	484 sq. ft.
Storage	104 sq. ft.
Exterior Wall Framing:	2x4

Foundation Options:

Crawlspace
Slab
(All plans can be built with your choice of foundation and framing. A generic conversion diagram is available. See order form.)

BLUEPRINT PRICE CODE: **B**

MAIN FLOOR

70'—0"

48'—0"

BEDROOM
12'-6" x 12'

PATIO
12'-6" x 12'

MASTER BEDROOM
14' x 14'

CLOSET

DRESSING

BEDROOM
12' x 11'

PORCH
12'-6" x 12'

EATING
11' x 10'

CHINA

CLOSET

STORAGE
13' x 8'

W/H

SHLVS
SHELVES
SLOPE CEILING

FAMILY
18'-6" x 15'

SLOPE CEILING

DRESSING

KITCHEN
14' x 12'

DW

REF

PTRY

DISAPPEARING STAIRS

GARAGE
22' x 22'

BEAMS

SHLVS

OVEN

BRM

BEDROOM
12' x 11'

LIVING
12'-6" x 12'

ENTRY

DINING
12'-6" x 12'

UTIL
8'x6'
W
D

PORCH

Smashing Master Suite!

- Corniced gables accented with arched louvers and a covered front porch with striking columns take this one-story design beyond the ordinary.
- The vaulted ceiling in the foyer rises to join the 19-ft. vaulted ceiling in the family room. A central fireplace heats the casual areas and is framed by a window and a French door.
- An angled serving bar/snack counter connects the family room to the sunny dining room and kitchen. The adjoining breakfast room has easy access to the garage, the optional basement and the laundry room with a plant shelf.
- The master suite is simply smashing, with a 10-ft. tray ceiling and private access to the backyard. The master bath has an 11½-ft. vaulted ceiling and all the amenities, while the 13-ft.-high vaulted sitting area offers an optional fireplace.

Plan FB-1671

Bedrooms: 3	Baths: 2

Living Area:

Main floor	1,671 sq. ft.
Total Living Area:	**1,671 sq. ft.**
Daylight basement	1,671 sq. ft.
Garage	240 sq. ft.
Exterior Wall Framing:	2x4

Foundation Options:

Daylight basement
Crawlspace

(All plans can be built with your choice of foundation and framing. A generic conversion diagram is available. See order form.)

BLUEPRINT PRICE CODE:	B

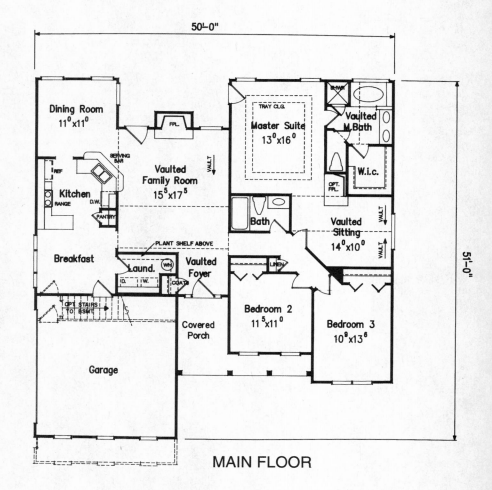

MAIN FLOOR

TO ORDER THIS BLUEPRINT,
CALL TOLL-FREE 1-800-820-1283

Plan FB-1671

PRICES AND DETAILS
ON PAGES 12-15

123

Impressive Master Suite

- This attractive one-story home features an impressive master suite located apart from the secondary bedrooms.
- A lovely front porch opens to the entry, which flows to the formal dining room, the rear-oriented living room and the secondary bedroom wing.
- The living room boasts a large corner fireplace, a ceiling that slopes to 11 ft. and access to a backyard patio.
- A U-shaped kitchen services the dining room and its own eating area. It also boasts a built-in desk, a handy pantry closet and access to the nearby laundry room and carport.
- The wide master bedroom hosts a lavish master bath with a spa tub, a separate shower and his-and-hers dressing areas.
- Across the home, the two secondary bedrooms share another full bath.

Plan E-1818

Bedrooms: 3	Baths: 2
Living Area:	
Main floor	1,868 sq. ft.
Total Living Area:	**1,868 sq. ft.**
Carport	484 sq. ft.
Storage	132 sq. ft.
Exterior Wall Framing:	2x6

Foundation Options:

Crawlspace

Slab

(All plans can be built with your choice of foundation and framing. A generic conversion diagram is available. See order form.)

BLUEPRINT PRICE CODE: B

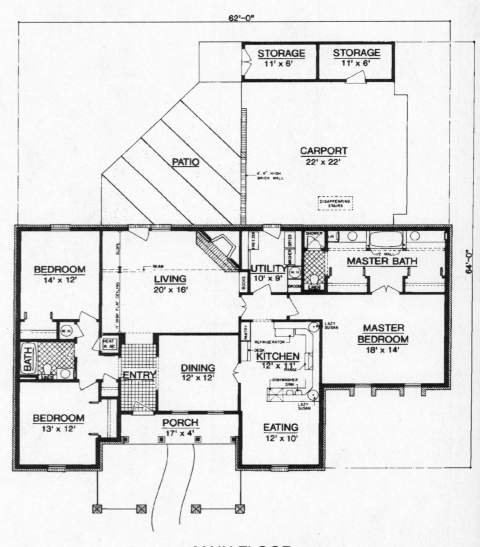

MAIN FLOOR

 Plan E-1818   *PRICES AND DETAILS ON PAGES 12-15*

Upscale Charm

- Country charm and the very latest in conveniences mark this upscale home. To add extra appeal, all of the living areas are housed on one floor, yet may be expanded to the upper floor later.
- Set off from the foyer, the dining room is embraced by elegant columns. Arched windows in the dining room and in the bedroom across the hall echo the delicate detailing of the covered front porch.
- Straight ahead, the family room flaunts a wall of French doors overlooking a covered back porch and a large deck.
- A curved island snack bar smoothly connects the gourmet kitchen to the sunny breakfast area, which features a dramatic 13-ft. vaulted ceiling brightened by skylights. All other rooms have 9-ft. ceilings. A nearby computer room and a laundry/utility room with a recycling center are other amenities.
- The master bedroom's private bath includes a dual-sink vanity and a floor-to-ceiling storage unit with a built-in chest of drawers. Other extras include a step-up spa tub and a separate shower.

Plan J-92100

Bedrooms: 3+	Baths: 2
Living Area:	
Main floor	1,877 sq. ft.
Total Living Area:	**1,877 sq. ft.**
Upper floor (future areas)	1,500 sq. ft.
Standard basement	1,877 sq. ft.
Garage and storage	551 sq. ft.
Exterior Wall Framing:	2x4

Foundation Options:

Standard basement
Crawlspace
Slab
(All plans can be built with your choice of foundation and framing. A generic conversion diagram is available. See order form.)

BLUEPRINT PRICE CODE:	B

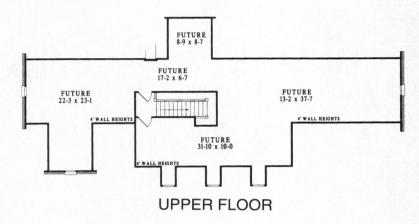

UPPER FLOOR

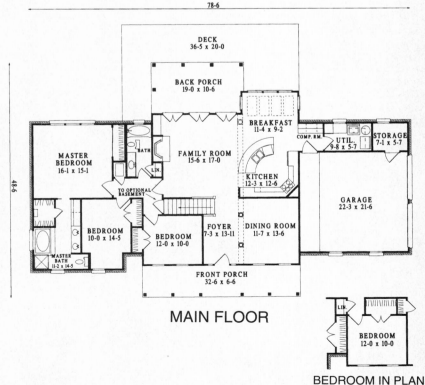

MAIN FLOOR

BEDROOM IN PLAN WITHOUT BASEMENT

Quiet Relaxation

- This elegant brick one-story home features a stunning master bedroom with a sunny morning porch for quiet relaxation. The bedroom's 11-ft. vaulted ceiling extends into the master bath, which boasts a corner garden tub and an attractive plant shelf.
- A few steps away, the open kitchen shares its 11-ft. ceiling and handy snack bar with the bright breakfast nook.
- A handsome fireplace warms the spacious family room, which is enhanced by a soaring 14-ft. ceiling. A striking French door provides access to a roomy deck that may also be reached from the master bedroom.
- The formal living areas flank the sidelighted foyer. The living room shows off a 14-ft. cathedral ceiling.
- Three secondary bedrooms with 9-ft. ceilings have easy access to a split bath. The center bedroom features a built-in desk with shelves above. Two of the bedrooms have walk-in closets.
- A convenient half-bath and a good-sized laundry room are located near the two-car garage, which offers additional storage space and excellent lighting from three bright windows.

Plan APS-2117

Bedrooms: 4	Baths: 2½
Living Area:	
Main floor	2,187 sq. ft.
Total Living Area:	**2,187 sq. ft.**
Garage	460 sq. ft.
Exterior Wall Framing:	2x4

Foundation Options:

Crawlspace
(All plans can be built with your choice of foundation and framing. A generic conversion diagram is available. See order form.)

BLUEPRINT PRICE CODE: C

MAIN FLOOR

- BEDRM 4 11X12
- BEDRM 3 11X12
- BEDRM 2 12X11
- DECK
- FAMILY ROOM 17X19
- LIVING 11X12
- FOYER
- BRKFST 11X9
- KITCHEN 13X12
- DINING 13X11
- MASTER BEDROOM 16X15
- MORNING PORCH
- GARAGE 23X20
- STORAGE / MECH.

70

47

TO ORDER THIS BLUEPRINT, CALL TOLL-FREE 1-800-820-1283

Plan APS-2117

PRICES AND DETAILS ON PAGES 12-15

Classic Ranch

- With decorative brick quoins, a columned porch and stylish dormers, the exterior of this classic one-story provides an interesting blend of Early American and European design.
- Flowing from the foyer, the bay-windowed dining room is enhanced by an 11½-ft.-high stepped ceiling.
- The spacious Great Room, separated from the dining room by a columned arch, features a stepped ceiling, a built-in media center and a striking fireplace. Lovely French doors lead to a big backyard patio.
- The breakfast room, which shares an eating bar with the kitchen, boasts a ceiling that slopes to 12 feet. French doors access a covered rear porch.
- The master bedroom has a 10-ft. tray ceiling, a sunny bay window and a roomy walk-in closet. The master bath features a whirlpool tub in a bayed nook and a separate shower.
- The front-facing bedroom is enhanced by a 10-ft.-high vaulted area over an arched transom window.

Plan AX-93304

Bedrooms: 3	Baths: 2
Living Area:	
Main floor	1,860 sq. ft.
Total Living Area:	**1,860 sq. ft.**
Standard basement	1,860 sq. ft.
Garage/utility/storage	434 sq. ft.
Exterior Wall Framing:	2x4

Foundation Options:

Standard basement
Crawlspace
Slab

(All plans can be built with your choice of foundation and framing. A generic conversion diagram is available. See order form.)

BLUEPRINT PRICE CODE: B

VIEW INTO GREAT ROOM

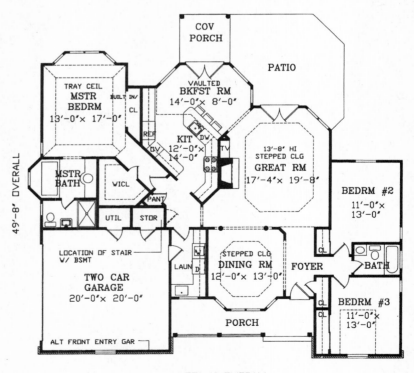

MAIN FLOOR

All-Inclusive

- The stylish facade of this one-story home welcomes all, with its assortment of windows and columned front porch.
- Inside, another column graces the entry, which flows into the dining room on the left and straight ahead to the central living room.
- The crossroads of the home are in the living room, where a window wall expands the area to a backyard deck. The soothing fireplace may be enjoyed throughout the living spaces.
- The kitchen offers an L-shaped serving counter to both the living room and the sunny breakfast bay.
- Secluded behind the kitchen, the master bedroom has a nice sitting bay and an elaborate private bath. Found here are a dual-sink vanity, a dual walk-in closet, a garden bath and a separate shower.
- Across the home, two good-sized secondary bedrooms each have private access to a roomy full bath.

Plan DD-1596

Bedrooms: 3	Baths: 2
Living Area:	
Main floor	1,680 sq. ft.
Total Living Area:	**1,680 sq. ft.**
Standard basement	1,680 sq. ft.
Garage	413 sq. ft.
Exterior Wall Framing:	2x4

Foundation Options:

Standard basement
Crawlspace
Slab

(All plans can be built with your choice of foundation and framing. A generic conversion diagram is available. See order form.)

BLUEPRINT PRICE CODE: B

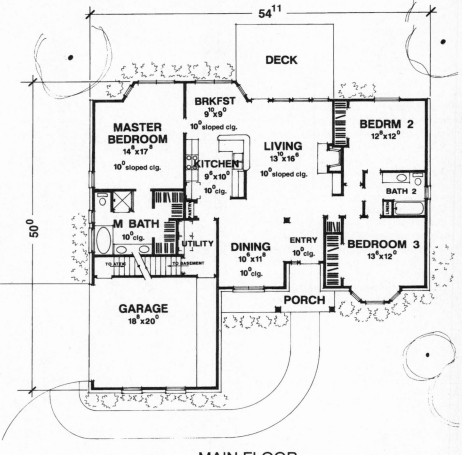

MAIN FLOOR

Plan DD-1596

PRICES AND DETAILS ON PAGES 12-15

Sweet Home

- The sweet facade of this charming home looks as if it were plucked straight out of a European hamlet. The stone exterior, decorated dormers and cute porch combine to present a charming invitation to guests.
- Inside, the floor plan takes advantage of the compact square footage. A tiled foyer leads into a unique curved gallery that wraps around the central Great Room. On the left, a half-wall allows a view into the dining room.
- A wall of windows adds brightness and cheer to the Great Room, where a shuttered pass-through to the kitchen lets the chef visit with guests. French doors open to a railed deck that is the perfect site for drinks with friends.
- Between the kitchen and the breakfast nook, a serving counter provides a spot to set snacks. The kitchen's island cooktop makes meal preparation easier.
- The Great Room, the breakfast nook and the kitchen boast 12-ft. ceilings. All other rooms feature 9-ft. ceilings.
- The master suite's sunny bay serves as a cozy sitting area to retreat to each day.

Plan DW-1892

Bedrooms: 3	Baths: 2
Living Area:	
Main floor	1,892 sq. ft.
Total Living Area:	**1,892 sq. ft.**
Standard basement	1,892 sq. ft.
Exterior Wall Framing:	2x4

Foundation Options:

Standard basement

Crawlspace

Slab

(All plans can be built with your choice of foundation and framing. A generic conversion diagram is available. See order form.)

BLUEPRINT PRICE CODE:	B

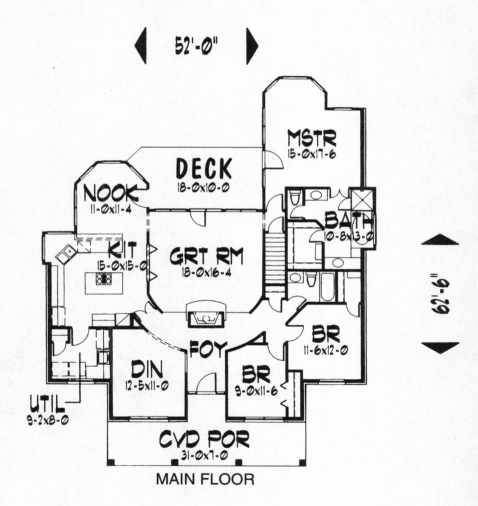

MAIN FLOOR

52'

Classic Design Features Luxurious Master Bath

PLAN E-1907
WITHOUT BASEMENT

Exterior walls are 2x6 construction.
Specify crawlspace or slab foundation.

76'

BATH

STEP

LIN MC

LIN MC

CLO.

CLO.

MASTER SUITE
18' x 6'

PORCH
14' x 6'

PORCH
14' x 10'
SKYLIGHT

CLO.

CLO.

BED RM.
14' x 12'

KITCHEN
SLOPE CEILING
14' x 12'
SKYLIGHT
REF
SINK
OVEN DW
COOK TOP
BAR
PANT.

DINING
14' x 14'
SLOPE CEILING

BATH
VANITY

HALL
LIN
STOR

STORAGE
10' x 6'
WH

UTIL
8' x 6'
DRY WASH

STORAGE

CLO.
HEAT B/A/C

LIVING
20' x 18'

GARAGE
22' x 22'
ATTIC STAIRS

PORCH
18' x 8'

BED RM.
14' x 12'

AREAS

Living	1951 sq. ft.
Porches	376 sq. ft.
Garage & Storage	555 sq. ft.
Total	2882 sq. ft.

Blueprint Price Code B

Plan E-1907

Open Invitation

- The wide front porch of this friendly country farmhouse presents an open invitation to all who visit.
- Highlighted by a round-topped transom, the home's entrance opens directly into the spacious living room, which features a warm fireplace flanked by windows.
- The adjoining dining area is enhanced by a lovely bay window and is easily serviced by the updated kitchen's angled snack bar.
- A bright sun room off the kitchen provides a great space for informal meals or relaxation. Access to a covered backyard porch is nearby.
- The good-sized master bedroom is secluded from the other sleeping areas. The lavish master bath includes a garden tub, a separate shower, a dual-sink vanity and a walk-in closet.
- Two more bedrooms share a second full bath. A laundry/utility room is nearby.
- An additional 1,007 sq. ft. of living space can be made available by finishing the upper floor.
- All ceilings are 9 ft. high for added spaciousness.

Plan J-91078

Bedrooms: 3	Baths: 2
Living Area:	
Main floor	1,846 sq. ft.
Total Living Area:	**1,846 sq. ft.**
Future upper floor	1,007 sq. ft.
Standard basement	1,846 sq. ft.
Garage	484 sq. ft.
Exterior Wall Framing:	2x6

Foundation Options:

Standard basement
Crawlspace
Slab
(All plans can be built with your choice of foundation and framing. A generic conversion diagram is available. See order form.)

BLUEPRINT PRICE CODE: B

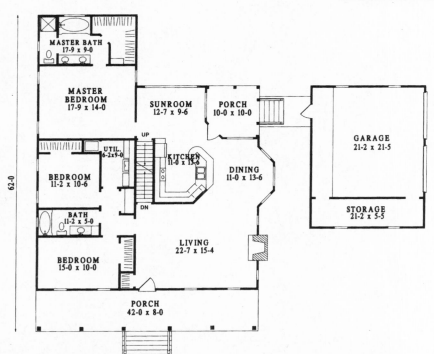

MAIN FLOOR

Welcome Home

- An inviting covered porch welcomes you home to this country-kissed ranch.
- Inside, a 16-ft. cathedral ceiling soars over the expansive living room, which boasts a fireplace flanked by windows.
- Bathed in sunlight from more windows, the dining room flaunts an elegant French door that opens to a delightful backyard porch.
- The gourmet kitchen features a planning desk, a pantry and a unique, angled bar—a great place to settle for an afternoon snack. Garage access is conveniently nearby.

- Smartly secluded in one corner of the home is the lovely and spacious master bedroom, crowned by a 10-ft. tray ceiling. Other amenities include huge his-and-hers walk-in closets and a private bath with a garden tub and a dual-sink vanity.
- A neat laundry closet near the master bedroom is handy for last-minute loads.
- Two secondary bedrooms round out this wonderful design. The front-facing bedroom is complemented by a 10-ft. vaulted ceiling, while the rear bedroom offers a sunny window seat. A full bath accented by a stylish round window is shared by both rooms.

Plan J-91085

Bedrooms: 3	**Baths:** 2

Living Area:

Main floor	1,643 sq. ft.
Total Living Area:	**1,643 sq. ft.**
Standard basement	1,643 sq. ft.
Garage and storage	480 sq. ft.
Exterior Wall Framing:	2x4

Foundation Options:

Standard basement
Crawlspace
Slab

(All plans can be built with your choice of foundation and framing. A generic conversion diagram is available. See order form.)

BLUEPRINT PRICE CODE:	**B**

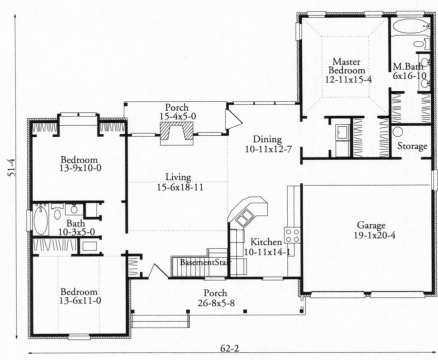

MAIN FLOOR

Master Bedroom 12-11x15-4

M. Bath 6x16-10

Storage

Porch 15-4x5-0

Dining 10-11x12-7

Bedroom 13-9x10-0

Living 15-6x18-11

Garage 19-1x20-4

Bath 10-3x5-0

Kitchen 10-11x14-1

BasementStair

Bedroom 13-6x11-0

Porch 26-8x5-8

51-4

62-2

Plan J-91085

PRICES AND DETAILS ON PAGES 12-15

Just Perfect

- This well-planned design is the perfect solution for a family in search of an affordable yet comfortable home.
- A quiet porch out front gives you a peaceful spot to retreat to with a book or just your thoughts. A charming rail lends warmth to the home.
- Inside, the formal dining room sits to the right of the entry. This is the ideal spot to entertain friends or celebrate a promotion with a good meal.
- At the core of the home, the living room awaits years of visiting, good

conversation, homework, TV watching and other regular activities. A handy bar between the living room and the kitchen holds chips, sodas and other refreshments during get-togethers.
- You will enjoy everyday dinners and leisurely breakfasts with coffee and the Sunday paper in the casual breakfast nook. A nearby door offers escape to a nice-sized covered patio.
- The cozy master suite makes getting out of bed even harder. In the skylighted bath, a dual-sink vanity and an oversized tub give the heads of the household extra-special treatment.

Plan KD-1648

Bedrooms: 3	**Baths:** 2

Living Area:	
Main floor	1,648 sq. ft.
Total Living Area:	**1,648 sq. ft.**
Garage	446 sq. ft.
Storage	61 sq. ft.
Exterior Wall Framing:	2x4

Foundation Options:

Slab
(All plans can be built with your choice of foundation and framing. A generic conversion diagram is available. See order form.)

BLUEPRINT PRICE CODE: **B**

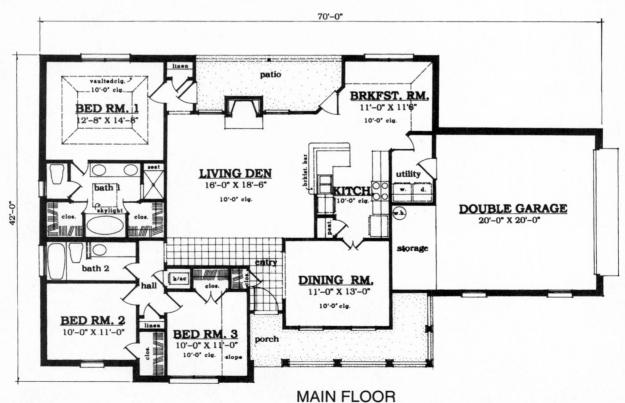

MAIN FLOOR

A Home Run

- The designer hit a home run with this plan. The compact square footage makes the home affordable, while the floor plan includes plenty of open spaces and amenities to please even the most demanding homeowners.
- A sunny transom above the front entry, gorgeous arched window arrangements and decorative keystones add flair to the otherwise modest exterior.
- Inside, the Great Room serves as the home's heart and soul. In this good-sized room, your family will celebrate birthdays, watch favorite movies and enjoy raucous games of Pictionary. Built-in cabinets by the fireplace hold your home entertainment system.
- The cheerful bayed dining room merges with the island kitchen. This convenient layout simplifies the chore of serving even the grandest meals, while a pantry closet nearby maximizes storage space.
- The master bedroom is secluded from the other bedrooms to ensure peace and quiet for the heads of the household. A raised tub under a beautiful window lends a touch of magnificence to the master bath.

Plan KD-1701

Bedrooms: 4	Baths: 2
Living Area:	
Main floor	1,701 sq. ft.
Total Living Area:	**1,701 sq. ft.**
Garage and storage	472 sq. ft.
Exterior Wall Framing:	2x4

Foundation Options:

Slab

(All plans can be built with your choice of foundation and framing. A generic conversion diagram is available. See order form.)

BLUEPRINT PRICE CODE: **B**

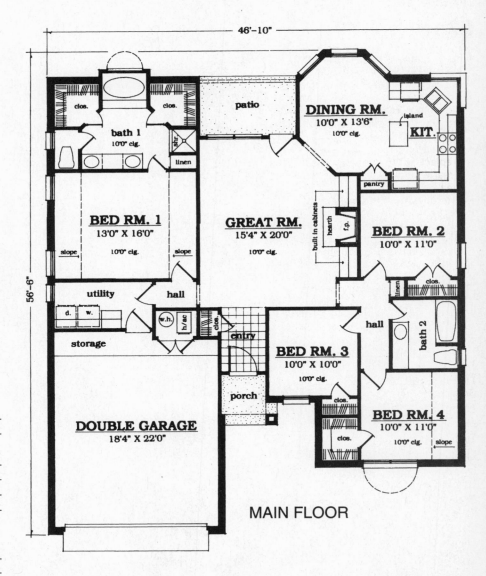

MAIN FLOOR

Plan KD-1701

PRICES AND DETAILS ON PAGES 12-15

Sophisticated One-Story

- Beautiful windows accentuated by elegant keystones highlight the exterior of this sophisticated one-story design.
- An open floor plan is the hallmark of the interior, beginning with the foyer that provides instant views of the study as well as the dining and living rooms.
- The spacious living room boasts a fireplace with built-in bookshelves and a rear window wall that stretches into the morning room.
- The sunny morning room has a snack bar to the kitchen. The island kitchen includes a walk-in pantry, a built-in desk and easy access to the utility room and the convenient half-bath.
- The master suite features private access to a nice covered patio, plus an enormous walk-in closet and a posh bath with a spa tub and glass-block shower.
- A hall bath serves the two secondary bedrooms. These three rooms, plus the utility area, have standard 8-ft. ceilings. Other ceilings are 10 ft. high.

Plan DD-2455

Bedrooms: 3+	Baths: 2½
Living Area:	
Main floor	2,457 sq. ft.
Total Living Area:	**2,457 sq. ft.**
Standard basement	2,457 sq. ft.
Garage	585 sq. ft.
Exterior Wall Framing:	2x4

Foundation Options:

Standard basement
Crawlspace
Slab

(All plans can be built with your choice of foundation and framing. A generic conversion diagram is available. See order form.)

BLUEPRINT PRICE CODE: C

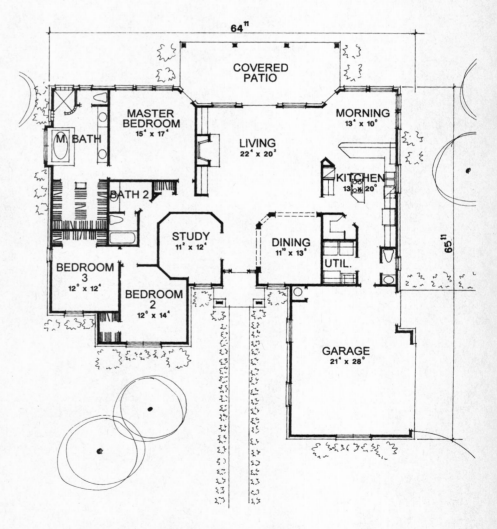

MAIN FLOOR

Wonderful Windows

- This one-story's striking stucco and stone facade is enhanced by great gables and wonderful windows.
- A beautiful bay augments the living room/den, which can be closed off.
- A wall of windows lets sunbeams brighten the exquisite formal dining room, which is defined by decorative columns and a high 14-ft. ceiling.
- The spacious family room offers a handsome fireplace flanked by glass.
- The kitchen boasts a large pantry, a corner sink and two convenient serving bars. A 13-ft. vaulted ceiling presides over the adjoining breakfast room.
- A lovely window seat highlights one of the two secondary bedrooms, which are serviced by a full bath with a 13-ft., 10-in. vaulted ceiling.
- The magnificent master suite features a symmetrical tray ceiling that sets off an attractive round-top window. The elegant master bath offers a 15-ft.-high vaulted ceiling, a garden tub and dual vanities, one with knee space.
- Ceilings not specified are 9 ft. high.

Plan FB-5009-CHAD

Bedrooms: 3	Baths: 2
Living Area:	
Main floor	2,115 sq. ft.
Total Living Area:	**2,115 sq. ft.**
Daylight basement	2,115 sq. ft.
Garage and storage	535 sq. ft.
Exterior Wall Framing:	2x4

Foundation Options:

Daylight basement

Slab

(All plans can be built with your choice of foundation and framing. A generic conversion diagram is available. See order form.)

BLUEPRINT PRICE CODE:	C

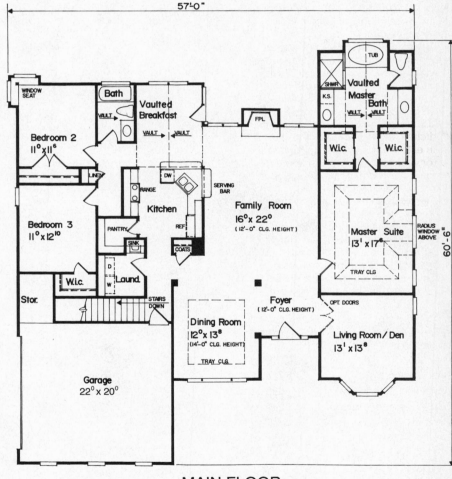

MAIN FLOOR

Breathtaking Open Space

- Soaring ceilings and an open floor plan add breathtaking volume to this charming country-style home.
- The inviting covered-porch entrance opens into the spacious living room, which boasts a spectacular 21-ft.-high cathedral ceiling. Two overhead dormers fill the area with natural light, while a fireplace adds warmth.
- Also under the cathedral ceiling, the kitchen and bayed breakfast room share an eating bar. Skylights brighten the convenient laundry room and the computer room, which provides access to a covered rear porch.
- The secluded master bedroom offers private access to another covered porch. The skylighted master bath has a walk-in closet and a 10-ft. sloped ceiling above a whirlpool tub.
- Optional upper-floor areas provide future expansion space for the needs of a growing family.

Plan J-9302

Bedrooms: 3	Baths: 2
Living Area:	
Main floor	1,745 sq. ft.
Total Living Area:	**1,745 sq. ft.**
Upper floor (future area)	500 sq. ft.
Future area above garage	241 sq. ft.
Standard basement	1,745 sq. ft.
Garage and storage	559 sq. ft.
Exterior Wall Framing:	2x4

Foundation Options:

Standard basement
Crawlspace
Slab

(All plans can be built with your choice of foundation and framing. A generic conversion diagram is available. See order form.)

BLUEPRINT PRICE CODE: B

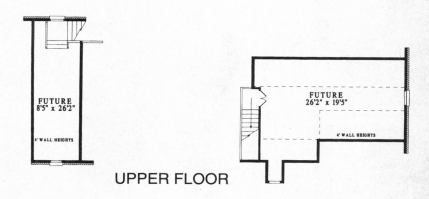

UPPER FLOOR

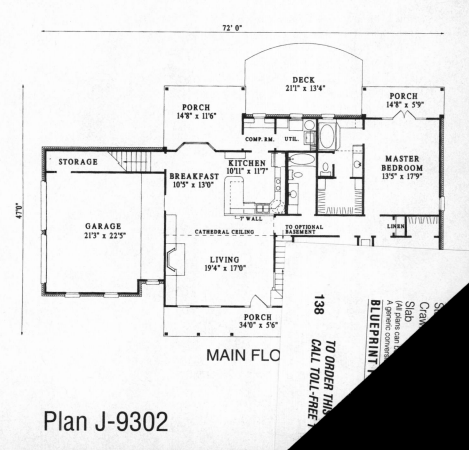

MAIN FLOOR

Plan J-9302

Morning Room with a View

- This modern-looking ranch is stylishly decorated with a pair of arched-window dormers, handsome brick trim and a covered front porch.
- Inside, the dining room is set off by columns, as it merges with the entry.
- The main living areas are oriented to the rear, where a huge central family room offers a patio view and a fireplace that may also be enjoyed from the bayed morning room and adjoining kitchen.
- The walk-through kitchen features a pantry, a snack bar to the family room and easy service to the formal dining room across the hall.
- The secluded master suite boasts a wide window seat and a private bath with a walk-in closet, a corner garden tub and a separate shower.
- Across the home, the three secondary bedrooms share another full bath. The fourth bedroom may double as a study.
- High 10-ft. ceilings are found throughout the home, except in the secondary bedrooms.

Plan DD-1962-1

Bedrooms: 3+	Baths: 2
Living Area:	
Main floor	1,962 sq. ft.
Total Living Area:	**1,962 sq. ft.**
Standard basement	1,962 sq. ft.
Garage	386 sq. ft.
Exterior Wall Framing:	2x4

Foundation Options:
Standard basement
~~~dspace

...e built with your choice of foundation and framing.
...on diagram is available. See order form.)

PRICE CODE: B

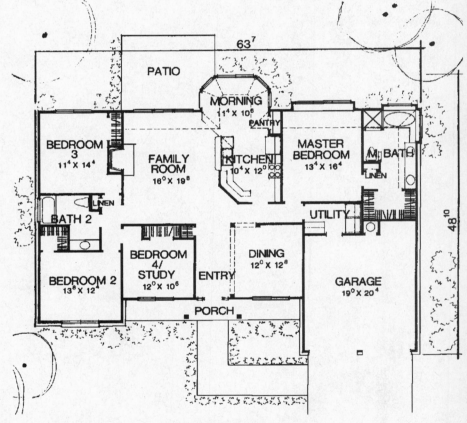

MAIN FLOOR

Stunning Style

- The stunning detailing of this three-bedroom stucco home includes a stately roofline, round louvers and a sidelighted entry door topped with a half-round transom.
- The open floor plan begins at the foyer, where a decorative column is all that separates the dining room from the living room. Lovely French doors and windows overlook the backyard, while a 13½-ft. ceiling creates a dramatic effect for this spacious area.

- A sunny breakfast room and a great kitchen with a huge serving bar adjoin a 14½-ft.-high vaulted family room.
- A laundry/mudroom lies near the garage, which is supplemented by a handy storage or shop area.
- The opulent master suite has an 11-ft. tray ceiling, a rear window wall and a French door to the outdoors. The master bath includes a spa tub, a separate shower, a spacious walk-in closet and a dual-sink vanity with a sit-down makeup area. Another full bath serves the two remaining bedrooms.

Plan FB-1802	
Bedrooms: 3	**Baths:** 2
Living Area:	
Main floor	1,802 sq. ft.
Total Living Area:	**1,802 sq. ft.**
Garage and storage	492 sq. ft.
Exterior Wall Framing:	2x4

Foundation Options:
Crawlspace
Slab
(All plans can be built with your choice of foundation and framing. A generic conversion diagram is available. See order form.)

BLUEPRINT PRICE CODE: **B**

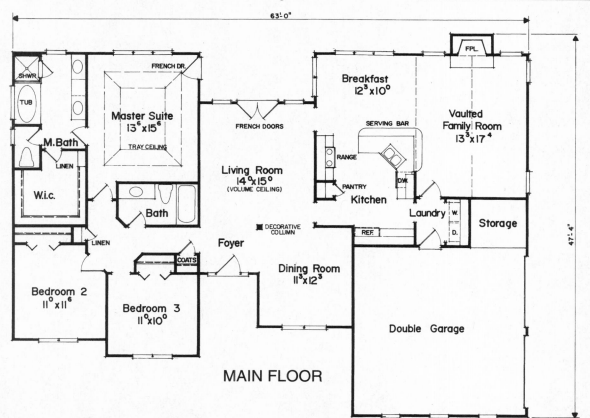

MAIN FLOOR

TO ORDER THIS BLUEPRINT,
CALL TOLL-FREE 1-800-820-1283

Plan FB-1802

PRICES AND DETAILS
ON PAGES 12-15

139

Appealing, Angled Ranch

- This unique, angled ranch boasts a striking interior, which is highlighted by a dramatic domed ceiling at its center.
- The gabled entryway opens to a spacious pentagonal living area. A handsome fireplace, lots of glass and an adjoining backyard terrace are showcased, in addition to the 14-ft.-high domed ceiling.
- The dining room can be extended into the nearby den by opening the folding doors. The den features a 14-ft. sloped ceiling, an exciting solar bay and terrace access.
- A casual eating area and a nice-sized kitchen expand to the front of the home, ending at a windowed sink.
- The nearby mudroom area includes laundry facilities and an optional powder room.
- The sleeping wing offers four bedrooms, including an oversized master suite with a private terrace and a skylighted bath with dual sinks and a whirlpool tub. The secondary bedrooms share another full bath.

Plan K-669-N

Bedrooms: 4	Baths: 2-2½
Living Area:	
Main floor	1,728 sq. ft.
Total Living Area:	**1,728 sq. ft.**
Standard basement	1,545 sq. ft.
Garage and storage	468 sq. ft.
Exterior Wall Framing:	2x4 or 2x6

Foundation Options:

Standard basement

Slab

(All plans can be built with your choice of foundation and framing. A generic conversion diagram is available. See order form.)

BLUEPRINT PRICE CODE:	**B**

VIEW INTO DINING ROOM AND LIVING ROOM

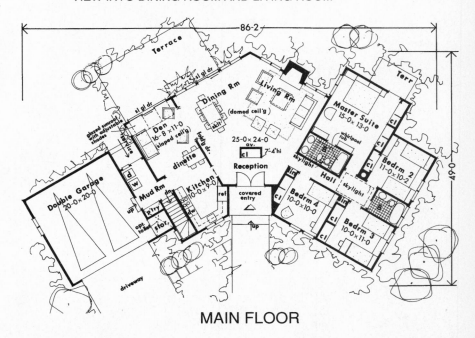

MAIN FLOOR

TO ORDER THIS BLUEPRINT, CALL TOLL-FREE 1-800-820-1283 Plan K-669-N *PRICES AND DETAILS ON PAGES 12-15*

Indoor/Outdoor Delights

- A curved porch in the front and a garden sun room in the back make this home an indoor/outdoor delight.
- Inside, a roomy kitchen is open to a five-sided, glassed-in dining room that views out to the porch.
- The living room features a fireplace along a glass wall that adjoins the gloriously sunny garden room.

- Wrapped in windows, the garden room accesses the backyard as well as a large storage area in the unobtrusive, side-entry garage.
- The master suite is no less luxurious, featuring a a sumptuous master bath with a garden spa tub, a corner shower and a walk-in closet.
- Each of the two remaining bedrooms has a boxed-out window and a walk-in closet. A full bath with a corner shower and a dual-sink vanity is close by.
- A stairway leads to the attic, which provides more potential living space.

Plan DD-1852	
Bedrooms: 3	**Baths: 2**
Living Area:	
Main floor	1,852 sq. ft.
Total Living Area:	**1,852 sq. ft.**
Standard basement	1,852 sq. ft.
Garage	528 sq. ft.
Exterior Wall Framing:	2x4

Foundation Options:

Standard basement
Crawlspace
Slab
(All plans can be built with your choice of foundation and framing. A generic conversion diagram is available. See order form.)

BLUEPRINT PRICE CODE:	**B**

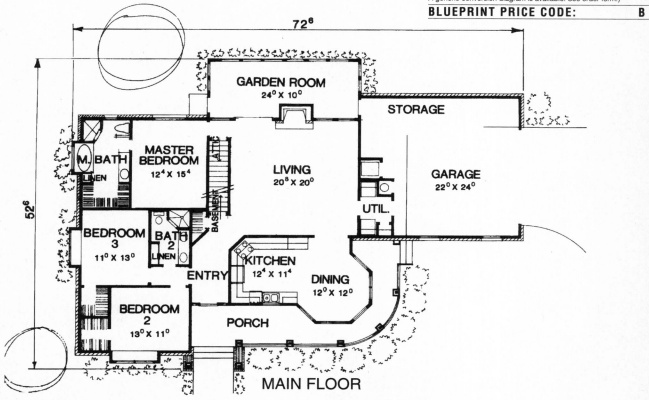

MAIN FLOOR

Shady Porches, Sunny Patio

- Designed with stylish country looks, this attractive one-story also has shady porches and a sunny patio for relaxed indoor/outdoor living.
- The inviting foyer flows into the spacious living room, which is warmed by a handsome fireplace.
- The adjoining dining room has a door to a screened-in porch, which opens to the backyard and serves as a breezeway to the nearby garage
- The U-shaped kitchen has a pantry closet and plenty of counter space. Around the corner, a space-efficient laundry/utility room exits to a big backyard patio.
- The master bedroom is brightened by windows on two sides and includes a wardrobe closet. The compartmentalized master bath offers a separate dressing area and a walk-in closet.
- Another full bath serves two additional good-sized bedrooms.

Plan C-7557	
Bedrooms: 3	**Baths:** 2
Living Area:	
Main floor	1,688 sq. ft.
Total Living Area:	**1,688 sq. ft.**
Daylight basement	1,688 sq. ft.
Garage	400 sq. ft.
Exterior Wall Framing:	2x4

Foundation Options:
Daylight basement
Crawlspace
Slab
(All plans can be built with your choice of foundation and framing. A generic conversion diagram is available. See order form.)

BLUEPRINT PRICE CODE:	**B**

PATIO
18-0 x 10-0

GARAGE
20-0 x 20-0

SCREENED PORCH
12-0 x 20-6

DINING ROOM
12-0 x 13-4

KITCHEN
10 x 13

UTILITY

BEDROOM
11-0 x 13-4

CLOSET

DRESS

BATH

PAN

CLOSET

CLOSET

BEDROOM
12-0 x 18-0

LIVING ROOM
15-6 x 17-8

DOWN

CLOSET

LINEN

32-0

COAT

BEDROOM
12-0 x 11-4

DRESSING

BATH

FOYER

PORCH
26 x 6

88-8

MAIN FLOOR

Plan C-7557

Stunning and Sophisticated

- A well-balanced blend of brick, stucco, and glass gives this stunning one-story home a sophisticated look.
- Past the recessed entry, the 16-ft.-high foyer is highlighted by a round-topped transom window. An arched opening introduces the formal dining room.
- The spectacular living room boasts an elegant 16-ft. coffered ceiling and is brightened by a trio of tall windows topped by a radius transom.
- The spacious island kitchen includes a roomy corner pantry and a built-in desk. A serving bar is convenient to the family room and the sunny breakfast area.
- A window-flanked fireplace is the focal point of the family room, which features a 16-ft. vaulted ceiling.
- A tray ceiling adorns the luxurious master suite. The vaulted master bath has a 16-ft. ceiling and includes a garden tub, a separate shower and his-and-hers vanities and walk-in closets.

Plan FB-5074-ARLI

Bedrooms: 3+	Baths: 2½
Living Area:	
Main floor	2,492 sq. ft.
Total Living Area:	**2,492 sq. ft.**
Daylight basement	2,492 sq. ft.
Garage	400 sq. ft.
Exterior Wall Framing:	2x4

Foundation Options:

Daylight basement
Crawlspace
(All plans can be built with your choice of foundation and framing. A generic conversion diagram is available. See order form.)

BLUEPRINT PRICE CODE:	C

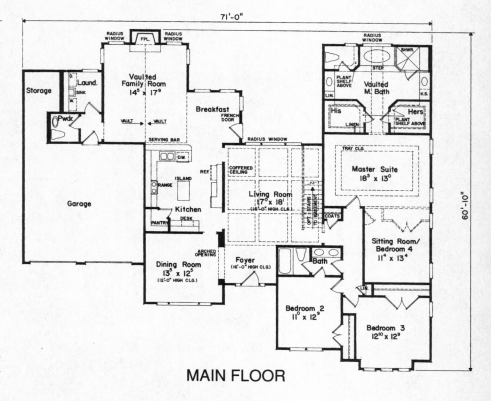

MAIN FLOOR

Showy
One-Story

- Dramatic windows embellish the exterior of this showy one-story home.
- Inside, the entry provides a sweeping view of the living room, where sliding glass doors open to the backyard patio and flank a dramatic fireplace.
- Skylights accent the living room's 12-ft. sloped ceiling, while arched openings define the formal dining room.
- Double doors lead from the dining room to the kitchen and informal eating area. The kitchen features a built-in work desk and a pantry. An oversized utility room adjoins the kitchen and accesses the two-car garage.
- A 10-ft. tray ceiling adorns the master suite. The private bath is accented with a skylight above the fabulous fan-shaped marble tub. His-and-hers vanities, a separate shower and a huge walk-in closet are also featured.
- Two more bedrooms and a full bath are located at the other end of the home.
- The front-facing bedroom boasts a 12-ft. sloped ceiling.

Plan E-1830

Bedrooms: 3	**Baths:** 2

Living Area:	
Main floor	1,868 sq. ft.
Total Living Area:	**1,868 sq. ft.**
Garage and storage	616 sq. ft.
Exterior Wall Framing:	2x6

Foundation Options:

Crawlspace
Slab
(All plans can be built with your choice of foundation and framing. A generic conversion diagram is available. See order form.)

BLUEPRINT PRICE CODE: B

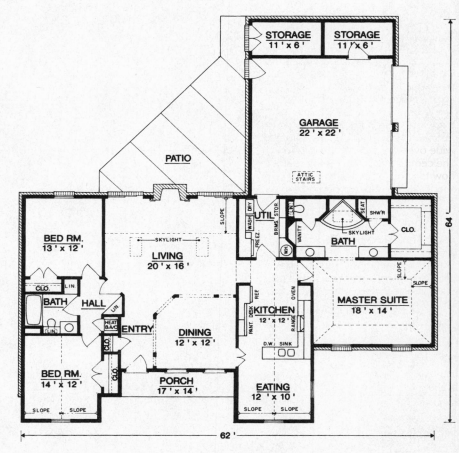

MAIN FLOOR

Plan E-1830

PRICES AND DETAILS ON PAGES 12-15

REAR VIEW

FRONT VIEW

Year-Round Comfort

- Designed for the energy-conscious, this passive-solar home provides year-round comfort with much lower fuel costs.
- The open, airy interior is a delight. In the winter, sunshine penetrates deep into the living spaces. In the summer, wide overhangs shade the interior.
- The central living and dining rooms flow together, creating a bright, open space. Sliding glass doors open to a terrace and an enclosed sun spot.
- In the airy casual space, the kitchen has an eating bar and a sunny breakfast nook. The adjoining family room boasts a woodstove that warms the entire area.
- The master bedroom suite includes a private terrace, a personal bath and a walk-in closet. Two other bedrooms share another full bath.

Plan K-392-T

Bedrooms: 3	Baths: 2½
Living Area:	
Main floor	1,592 sq. ft.
Sun spot	125 sq. ft.
Total Living Area:	**1,717 sq. ft.**
Partial basement	634 sq. ft.
Garage	407 sq. ft.
Exterior Wall Framing:	2x4 or 2x6

Foundation Options:

Partial basement

Slab

(All plans can be built with your choice of foundation and framing. A generic conversion diagram is available. See order form.)

BLUEPRINT PRICE CODE:	B

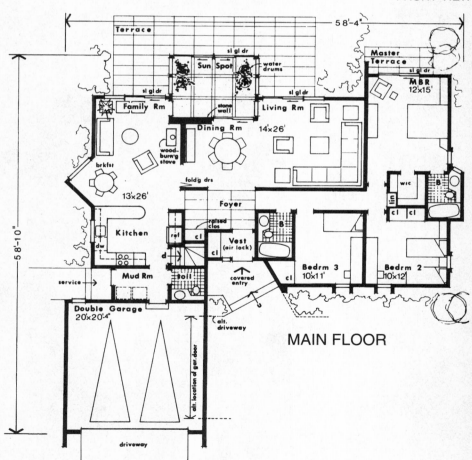

MAIN FLOOR

Spacious Contemporary

- Perfect for a sloping or scenic site, this home features a large deck, a patio, lots of windows and a walk-out basement.
- Guests are welcomed by a roomy front porch with a decorative planter.
- The 14-ft. vaulted entry leads to a spectacular Great Room with a 13-ft. vaulted ceiling, a fireplace and a rear window wall. The dining area's vaulted ceiling rises to 14 feet. French doors provide deck access.
- The kitchen boasts a unique angled serving counter and a bright sink.
- The main-floor master suite offers a window seat, a walk-in closet and a private bath with a skylighted dressing area that has his-and-hers sinks. A 14-ft. vaulted ceiling adds a dramatic effect.
- Two bedrooms and a full bath share the daylight basement with a roomy family room, which boasts a second fireplace and sliding glass doors to a sunny patio.

Plan P-6606-2D

Bedrooms: 3	Baths: 2½
Living Area:	
Main floor	1,140 sq. ft.
Daylight basement	935 sq. ft.
Total Living Area:	**2,075 sq. ft.**
Garage	451 sq. ft.
Exterior Wall Framing:	2x6

Foundation Options:

Daylight basement

(All plans can be built with your choice of foundation and framing. A generic conversion diagram is available. See order form.)

BLUEPRINT PRICE CODE:	C

MAIN FLOOR

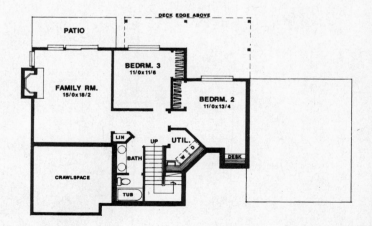

DAYLIGHT BASEMENT

Plan P-6606-2D

PRICES AND DETAILS ON PAGES 12-15

Playful Floor Plan

- High, hip roofs and a recessed entry give this home a smart-looking exterior. A dynamic floor plan—punctuated with angled walls, high ceilings and playful window treatments—gives the home an exciting interior.
- The sunken Great Room, the circular dining room and the angled island kitchen are the heartbeat of the home. The Great Room offers a 14-ft. vaulted ceiling, a fireplace, a built-in corner entertainment center and tall arched windows overlooking the backyard.

- An angled railing separates the Great Room from the open kitchen and dining room. An atrium door next to the glassed-in dining area leads to the backyard. The kitchen includes an island snack bar and a garden window.
- The master bedroom is nestled into one corner for quiet and privacy. This deluxe suite features two walk-in closets and a luxurious whirlpool bath.
- An extra-large laundry area, complete with a clothes-folding counter and a coat closet, is accessible from the three-car garage.
- The home is expanded by 9-ft. ceilings throughout, with the exception of the vaulted Great Room.

Plan PI-90-435	
Bedrooms: 3	**Baths:** 2
Living Area:	
Main floor	1,896 sq. ft.
Total Living Area:	**1,896 sq. ft.**
Daylight basement	1,889 sq. ft.
Garage	667 sq. ft.
Exterior Wall Framing:	2x6
Foundation Options:	

Daylight basement
(All plans can be built with your choice of foundation and framing. A generic conversion diagram is available. See order form.)

BLUEPRINT PRICE CODE:	**B**

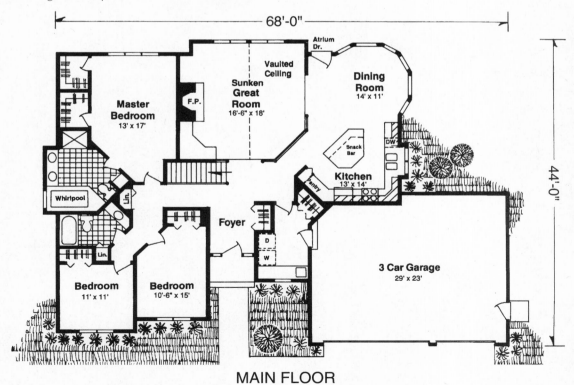

MAIN FLOOR

Ever-Popular Floor Plan

- Open living spaces that are well integrated with outdoor areas give this plan its popularity.
- The covered porch ushers guests into a roomy entry that separates the formal entertaining areas.
- Double doors open to the huge family room, which boasts a 13-ft. vaulted ceiling accented by rustic beams, a raised-hearth fireplace and built-in book-shelves. Glass doors lead to a covered porch and an adjoining patio, creating a perfect poolside setting.
- A bayed eating area is open to the family room, separated only by a decorative half-wall, and features a large china hutch and great views. The adjacent kitchen has an angled sink for easy service to the family room and the eating area. The utility room and the garage are close by.
- The master suite is secluded to the rear of the home, with a private bath and access to the patio. The two remaining bedrooms share a dual-access bath.

Plan E-2000	
Bedrooms: 3	**Baths:** 2
Living Area:	
Main floor	2,009 sq. ft.
Total Living Area:	**2,009 sq. ft.**
Garage and storage	550 sq. ft.
Exterior Wall Framing:	2x4
Foundation Options:	
Crawlspace	
Slab	

(All plans can be built with your choice of foundation and framing. A generic conversion diagram is available. See order form.)

BLUEPRINT PRICE CODE:	**C**

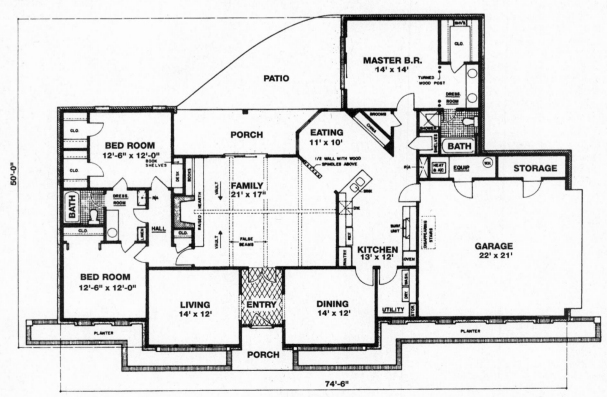

MAIN FLOOR

Plan E-2000

PRICES AND DETAILS ON PAGES 12-15

Super Features!

- Super indoor/outdoor living features are the main ingredients of this sprawling one-story home.
- Beyond the columned entry, the foyer features a 16-ft.-high ceiling and is brightened by a fantail transom. The dining room and the living room enjoy ceilings that vault to nearly 11 feet.
- The family room, with a 15-ft. vaulted ceiling, sits at the center of the floor plan and extends to the outdoor living spaces. A handsome fireplace flanked by built-in shelves adds excitement.
- The adjoining kitchen shares the family room's vaulted ceiling and offers a cooktop island, a large pantry and a breakfast nook that opens to the patio.
- The master suite is intended to offer the ultimate in comfort. A double-door entry, a 10-ft. tray ceiling and private patio access are featured in the bedroom. The master bath shares a see-through fireplace with the bedroom.
- Three secondary bedrooms share two full baths at the other end of the home.

Plan HDS-99-164

Bedrooms: 4	Baths: 3
Living Area:	
Main floor	2,962 sq. ft.
Total Living Area:	**2,962 sq. ft.**
Garage	567 sq. ft.

Exterior Wall Framing:
2x4 and 8-in. concrete block

Foundation Options:
Slab
(All plans can be built with your choice of foundation and framing. A generic conversion diagram is available. See order form.)

BLUEPRINT PRICE CODE:	D

MAIN FLOOR

Spacious Single-Story

- Vaulted ceilings distinguish this bright, open single-story home.
- Designed for both formal entertaining and casual family living, this airy home features an inviting stone-hearth fireplace in the living room and a dramatic woodstove in the corner of the family room.
- The living room flows into the formal dining room, which boasts a coffered ceiling and a built-in china hutch.
- The efficiently designed kitchen is positioned to serve both the formal and the informal areas. A functional island range, a pantry, a work desk and a serving bar to the large deck are featured in the kitchen.
- A skylight brightens the hallway to the sleeping wing, which includes three bedrooms, an oversized laundry room and two bathrooms. The sumptuous master suite offers a whirlpool garden tub, a double-basin vanity and a huge walk-in closet.

Plan LMB-9576-T

Bedrooms: 3+	Baths: 2
Living Area:	
Main floor	2,185 sq. ft.
Total Living Area:	**2,185 sq. ft.**
Garage	600 sq. ft.
Exterior Wall Framing:	2x6

Foundation Options:

Crawlspace

(All plans can be built with your choice of foundation and framing. A generic conversion diagram is available. See order form.)

BLUEPRINT PRICE CODE: C

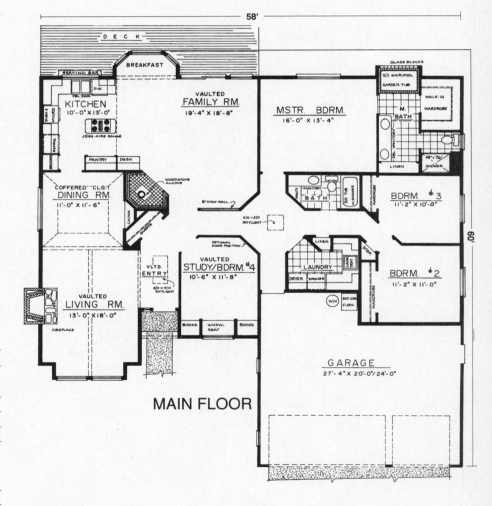

MAIN FLOOR

TO ORDER THIS BLUEPRINT, CALL TOLL-FREE 1-800-820-1283 Plan LMB-9576-T *PRICES AND DETAILS ON PAGES 12-15*

Ultimate French Comfort

- Delightful interior touches coupled with a striking French facade make this home the ultimate in one-story comfort.
- In the sidelighted entry, an attractive overhead plant ledge captures the eye.
- The entry opens to the formal dining and living rooms—both of which boast 10-ft. ceilings.
- In the living room, a handy wet bar and a media center flank a handsome fireplace. Large windows frame wide backyard views. Around the corner, French doors open to a back porch.
- Adjacent to the dining room, the kitchen offers a speedy serving bar. A bayed nook lights up with morning sun.
- Double doors open to the master bedroom, with its cute window seat and TV shelf. A 10-ft. ceiling tops it off.
- Two walk-in closets with glamorous mirror doors flank the walkway to the master bath, which offers an exotic garden tub and a separate shower.
- One of the two roomy secondary bedrooms offers a walk-in closet, a built-in desk and a gorgeous window.

Plan RD-1895

Bedrooms: 3	Baths: 2
Living Area:	
Main floor	1,895 sq. ft.
Total Living Area:	**1,895 sq. ft.**
Garage and storage	485 sq. ft.
Exterior Wall Framing:	2x4

Foundation Options:

Crawlspace
Slab
(All plans can be built with your choice of foundation and framing. A generic conversion diagram is available. See order form.)

BLUEPRINT PRICE CODE:	B

MAIN FLOOR

Charming One-Story

- The charming facade of this home conceals an exciting angled interior with many accesses to the outdoors.
- At the center of the floor plan is a spacious family activity area that combines the Great Room, the breakfast room and the kitchen.
- The sunny sunken Great Room features a 12½-ft. cathedral ceiling and an exciting two-sided fireplace. The adjacent breakfast room offers French doors to a covered backyard patio.

- The unique angled kitchen has a bright sink, a serving bar and plenty of counter space. Across the hall are the dining room, the laundry room and access to the three-car garage.
- The secluded master bedroom boasts a 12½-ft. cathedral ceiling, a roomy walk-in closet and French doors to a private covered patio. The lavish master bath has a bright garden tub, a separate shower and a dual-sink vanity.
- The secondary bedrooms both have walk-in closets. The rear-facing bedroom has patio access through its own full bath. The parlor off the entry could serve as a fourth bedroom, a guest room or a home office.

Plan Q-2033-1A	
Bedrooms: 3+	**Baths: 3**
Living Area:	
Main floor	2,033 sq. ft.
Total Living Area:	**2,033 sq. ft.**
Garage	592 sq. ft.
Exterior Wall Framing:	2x4

Foundation Options:
Slab
(All plans can be built with your choice of foundation and framing. A generic conversion diagram is available. See order form.)

BLUEPRINT PRICE CODE: **C**

MAIN FLOOR

Plan Q-2033-1A
PRICES AND DETAILS ON PAGES 12-15

European Charm

- This distinguished European home offers today's most luxurious features.
- In the formal living and dining rooms, 15-ft. vaulted ceilings add elegance.
- The informal areas are oriented to the rear of the home, entered through French doors in the foyer. The family room features a 12-ft. tray ceiling, a fireplace with an adjoining media center and a view of a backyard deck.

- The open kitchen and breakfast area is bright and cheerful, with a window wall and French-door deck access.
- Double doors lead into the luxurious master suite, which showcases a 14-ft. vaulted ceiling and a see-through fireplace that is shared with the spa bath. The splashy bath includes a dual-sink vanity, a separate shower and a wardrobe closet and dressing area.
- Two more bedrooms, one with private deck access, and a full bath are located on the opposite side of the home.
- Unless otherwise mentioned, 9-ft. ceilings enhance every room.

Plan APS-2006	
Bedrooms: 3	**Baths:** 2
Living Area:	
Main floor	2,006 sq. ft.
Total Living Area:	**2,006 sq. ft.**
Daylight basement	2,006 sq. ft.
Garage	448 sq. ft.
Exterior Wall Framing:	2x4
Foundation Options:	
Daylight basement	
Slab	

(All plans can be built with your choice of foundation and framing. A generic conversion diagram is available. See order form.)

BLUEPRINT PRICE CODE: C

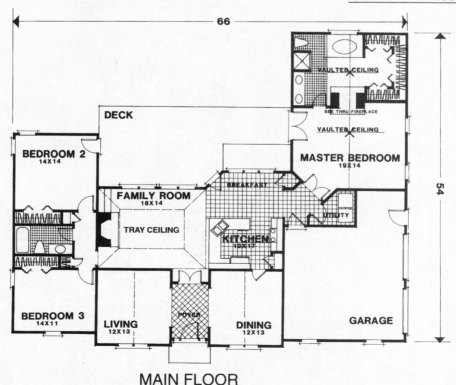

MAIN FLOOR

Angles Add Spark to Floor Plan

- Here's a one-story plan that provides plenty of space for active family living as well as business or personal entertaining.
- A majestic entry leads into a splendid sunken living room with fireplace, vaulted ceiling and built-in planter.
- A uniquely angled dining area is bathed in light from multiple windows and overlooks the living room.

- A stunning multi-sided kitchen includes a convenient island and adjoins a large pantry, breakfast nook and utility area.
- An incredible master suite boasts a magnificent bath, two huge walk-in closets and a striking bow window.
- A second bedroom also includes a large closet, and shares a walk-through bath with the parlor which could easily be a third bedroom, guest room or office.

Plan Q-3009-1A

Bedrooms: 2-3	Baths: 2½

Space:

Total living area:	3,009 sq. ft.
Garage:	632 sq. ft.

Exterior Wall Framing:	2x4

Foundation options:
Slab only.
(Foundation & framing conversion diagram available — see order form.)

Blueprint Price Code:	E

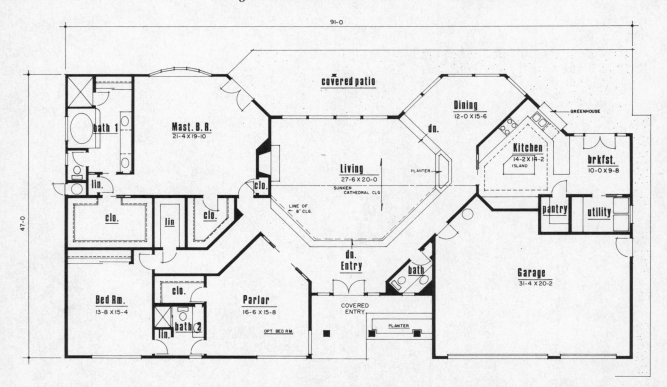

Plan Q-3009-1A

Angled Solar Design

- This passive-solar design with a six-sided core is angled to capture as much sunlight as possible.
- Finished in natural vertical cedar planks and stone veneer, this contemporary three-bedroom requires a minimum of maintenance.
- Double doors at the entry open into the spacious living and dining areas.

- The formal area features a 14-ft. domed ceiling with skylights, a freestanding fireplace and three sets of sliding glass doors. The central sliding doors lead to a glass-enclosed sun room.
- The bright eat-in kitchen merges with the den, where sliding glass doors lead to one of three backyard terraces.
- The master bedroom, in the quiet sleeping wing, boasts ample closets, a private terrace and a luxurious bath, complete with a whirlpool tub.
- The two secondary bedrooms share a convenient hall bath.

Plan K-534-L	
Bedrooms: 3	**Baths:** 2
Living Area:	
Main floor	1,647 sq. ft.
Total Living Area:	**1,647 sq. ft.**
Standard basement	1,505 sq. ft.
Garage	400 sq. ft.
Exterior Wall Framing:	2x4 or 2x6
Foundation Options:	

Standard basement
Slab
(All plans can be built with your choice of foundation and framing. A generic conversion diagram is available. See order form.)

BLUEPRINT PRICE CODE:	**B**

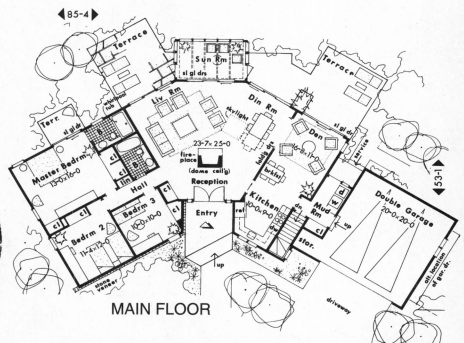

MAIN FLOOR

VIEW INTO LIVING ROOM AND DINING ROOM

TO ORDER THIS BLUEPRINT,
CALL TOLL-FREE 1-800-820-1283

Plan K-534-L

PRICES AND DETAILS
ON PAGES 12-15

155

Sun-Splashed One-Story

- This unique angled design offers spectacular backyard views, a delightful sun room and two enticing terraces.
- The high-ceilinged reception hall is open to the huge combination living and dining area. Here, more high ceilings, a stone fireplace and walls of glass add to the expansive look and the inviting atmosphere.

- The adjoining family room, kitchen and nook are just as appealing. The family room features a built-in entertainment center and sliding glass doors that access the energy-saving sun room. The comfortable kitchen has a handy snack counter facing the sunny dinette.
- The sleeping wing offers three bedrooms and two baths. The master suite boasts a sloped ceiling, a private terrace, a large walk-in closet and a personal bath with a whirlpool tub. The two remaining bedrooms are just steps away from another full bath.

Plan AHP-9330	
Bedrooms: 3	**Baths:** 2
Living Area:	
Main floor	1,626 sq. ft.
Sun room	146 sq. ft.
Total Living Area:	**1,772 sq. ft.**
Standard basement	1,542 sq. ft.
Garage	427 sq. ft.
Exterior Wall Framing:	2x4 or 2x6

Foundation Options:

Standard basement
Crawlspace
Slab

(All plans can be built with your choice of foundation and framing. A generic conversion diagram is available. See order form.)

BLUEPRINT PRICE CODE:	B

MAIN FLOOR

Plan AHP-9330
PRICES AND DETAILS
ON PAGES 12-15

Updated Creole

- This Louisiana-style raised cottage features a tin roof, shuttered windows and three pairs of French doors, all of which add to the comfort and nostalgic appeal of this Creole classic.
- The French doors enter from the cool and relaxing front porch to the formal living areas and a front bedroom.
- The central living room, which features a 12-ft. ceiling, merges with the dining room and the kitchen's eating area. A fireplace warms the whole space while more French doors access a porch.
- The efficient kitchen offers a 12-ft. flat ceiling, an angled snack bar and a bayed nook with a 12-ft. sloped ceiling.
- A secluded master suite showcases a private bath, fit for the most demanding tastes. Across the home, the secondary bedrooms include abundant closet space and share a full bath.
- This full-featured, energy-efficient design also includes a large utility room and extra storage space in the garage.

Plan E-1823

Bedrooms: 3	Baths: 2
Living Area:	
Main floor	1,800 sq. ft.
Total Living Area:	**1,800 sq. ft.**
Garage	550 sq. ft.
Exterior Wall Framing:	2x6

Foundation Options:

Crawlspace

Slab

(All plans can be built with your choice of foundation and framing. A generic conversion diagram is available. See order form.)

BLUEPRINT PRICE CODE:	B

MAIN FLOOR

TO ORDER THIS BLUEPRINT,
CALL TOLL-FREE 1-800-820-1283

Plan E-1823

PRICES AND DETAILS
ON PAGES 12-15

157

A Palette of Pleasures

- This stylish traditional brick home has a palette of popular features that serves to enhance family living.
- The formal living spaces are located at the front of the home, flanking the foyer. The dining room is enhanced by a 9-ft. tray ceiling, while the living room boasts a 12-ft. cathedral ceiling.
- A combination kitchen, breakfast nook and family room is oriented to the rear of the home. A pass-through and a snack bar open to the family room, which features a fireplace, a 14-ft.-high vaulted ceiling and deck access.
- The secluded master bedroom offers a 9-ft. tray ceiling and private deck access. The posh master bath boasts a 13-ft. cathedral ceiling and his-and-hers walk-in closets. Dual vanities sit opposite a garden tub and a separate shower.
- Across the home, two secondary bedrooms have walk-in closets and share another full bath. A laundry/utility room and garage access are nearby.

Plan APS-2309

Bedrooms: 3	Baths: 2
Living Area:	
Main floor	2,275 sq. ft.
Total Living Area:	**2,275 sq. ft.**
Standard basement	2,275 sq. ft.
Garage	418 sq. ft.
Exterior Wall Framing:	2x4
Foundation Options:	

Standard basement
(All plans can be built with your choice of foundation and framing. A generic conversion diagram is available. See order form.)

BLUEPRINT PRICE CODE:	**C**

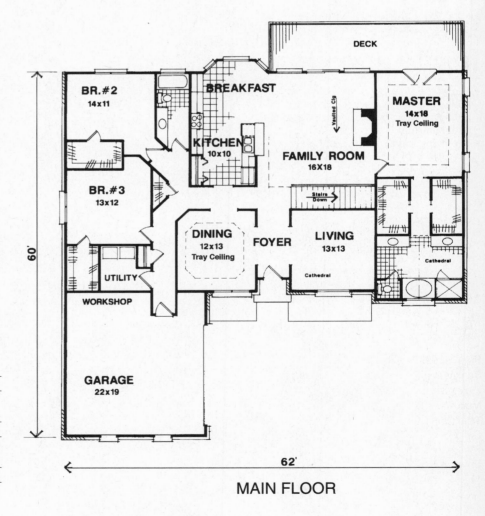

MAIN FLOOR

Plan APS-2309

Elegance
Inside and Out

- The raised front porch of this home is finely detailed with wood columns, railings, moldings, and French doors with half-round transoms.
- The living room, dining room and entry have 12-ft.-high ceilings. Skylights illuminate the living room, which offers a fireplace and access to a roomy deck.
- The efficient kitchen permits easy service to both the dining room and the casual eating area.
- The master suite features a raised tray ceiling and an enormous skylighted bath with a walk-in closet, dual vanities and a large quarter-circle spa tub surrounded by a mirror wall.
- On the left, two secondary bedrooms are insulated from the more active areas of the home by an efficient hallway, and also share another full bath.

Plan E-1909

Bedrooms: 3	Baths: 2
Living Area:	
Main floor	1,936 sq. ft.
Total Living Area:	**1,936 sq. ft.**
Garage	484 sq. ft.
Storage	132 sq. ft.
Exterior Wall Framing:	2x6

Foundation Options:

Crawlspace

Slab

(All plans can be built with your choice of foundation and framing. A generic conversion diagram is available. See order form.)

BLUEPRINT PRICE CODE:	B

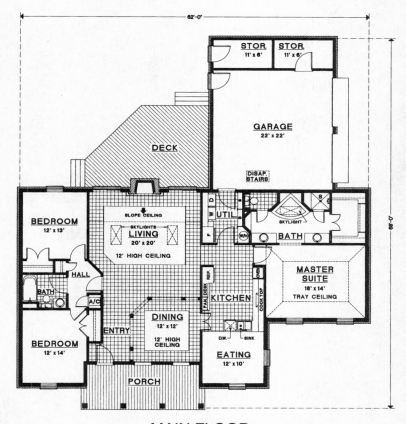

MAIN FLOOR

Comfortable, Open Plan

- This comfortable home defines function and style, with a sharp window wall to brighten the central living areas.
- In from the broad front deck, the living/family room boasts a fireplace, a cathedral ceiling and soaring views. The fireplace visually sets off the dining

room, which extends to the backyard patio through sliding doors.
- The galley-style kitchen offers a bright sink and an abundance of counter space, with a laundry closet and carport access nearby.
- The secluded and spacious master bedroom features private deck access, a walk-in closet and a private bath.
- On the other side of the home, two good-sized secondary bedrooms share another full bath.

Plan C-8160	
Bedrooms: 3	**Baths:** 2
Living Area:	
Main floor	1,669 sq. ft.
Total Living Area:	**1,669 sq. ft.**
Daylight basement	1,660 sq. ft.
Carport	413 sq. ft.
Storage	85 sq. ft.
Exterior Wall Framing:	2x4
Foundation Options:	
Daylight basement	
Crawlspace	
Slab	

(All plans can be built with your choice of foundation and framing. A generic conversion diagram is available. See order form.)

BLUEPRINT PRICE CODE:	B

MAIN FLOOR

PATIO

BEDROOM
17'-3"x10'-10"

DINING
15'-10"x13'-0"

KITCHEN
18'-0"x9'-0"

W. D.

CLOS.

BATH

STORAGE

CLOS.

LIN.

BATH

CARPORT
20'-0"x20'-8"

37'-0"

CATHEDRAL CEILING

CLOS.

COAT

BEDROOM
14'-10"x11'-0"

LIVING-FAMILY
15'-10"x20'-0"

BEDROOM
18'-0"x13'-4"

STORAGE

STORAGE

WOOD DECK

73'-0"

Plan C-8160

Stunning Windows

- This one-story design is enhanced by stunning window arrangements that brighten the formal areas and beyond.
- A step down from the skylighted foyer, the living room sparkles, with a tray ceiling, a striking fireplace and a turret-like bay with high arched windows.
- The island kitchen easily services the sunny bayed dining room and includes a built-in desk, a garden sink and an eating bar to the bright, vaulted nook.
- The adjoining vaulted family room is warmed by a corner woodstove and overlooks the rear patio.
- A decorative plant shelf introduces the bedroom wing. Double doors reveal the master bedroom, which boasts a tray ceiling, a rear window wall and access to the patio. The skylighted master bath includes a raised ceiling, a step-up garden spa tub and a separate shower.
- Across the hall, a den and a second bedroom share another full bath, while the utility room offers garage access.

Plans P-7754-3A & -3D

Bedrooms: 2+	Baths: 2
Living Area:	
Main floor (crawlspace version)	2,200 sq. ft.
Main floor (basement version)	2,288 sq. ft.
Total Living Area:	**2,200/2,288 sq. ft.**
Daylight basement	2,244 sq. ft.
Garage	722 sq. ft.
Exterior Wall Framing:	2x4
Foundation Options:	**Plan #**
Daylight basement	P-7754-3D
Crawlspace	P-7754-3A

(All plans can be built with your choice of foundation and framing. A generic conversion diagram is available. See order form.)

BLUEPRINT PRICE CODE:	C

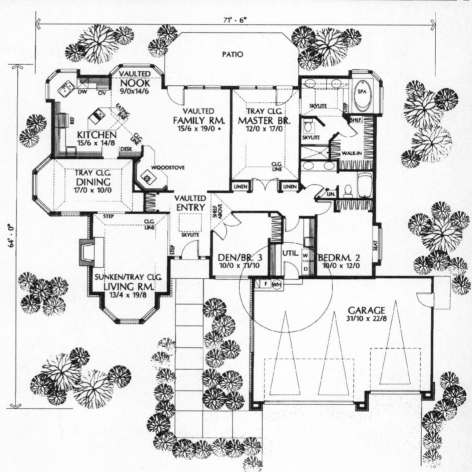

MAIN FLOOR

**NOTE: The above photographed home may have been modified by the homeowner. Please refer to floor plan and/or drawn elevation shown for actual blueprint details.

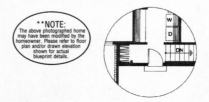

BASEMENT STAIRWAY LOCATION

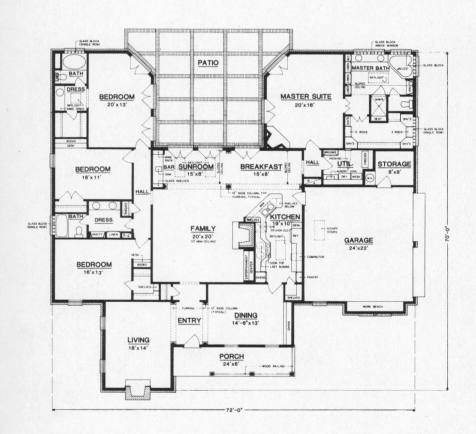

PLAN E-3102
WITHOUT BASEMENT

Exterior walls are 2x6 construction.
Specify crawlspace or slab foundation.

Ranch-Style Designed for Entertaining

- This all-brick home offers both formal living and dining rooms.
- The family room is large scale with 13' ceilings, formal fireplace and an entertainment center. An adjoining sun room reveals a tucked away wet bar.
- The master suite has private patio access and its own fireplace. An adjoining bath offers abundant closet and linen storage, a separate shower and garden tub with glass block walls.
- The home contains three additional bedrooms and two baths. Each bath has glass block above the tubs and separate dressing rooms.
- The master bedroom ceiling is sloped to 14' high. Both the sun room and the breakfast room have sloped ceilings with skylights. Typical ceiling heights are 9'.
- The home is energy efficient.

Heated area:	3,158 sq. ft.
Unheated area:	767 sq. ft.
Total area:	3,925 sq. ft.

Blueprint Price Code E
Plan E-3102

PRICES AND DETAILS
ON PAGES 12-15

Photo by Mark Englund/HomeStyles

Angled Interior

- This plan gives new dimension to one-story living. The exterior has graceful arched windows and a sweeping roofline. The interior is marked by unusual angles and stately columns.
- The living areas are clustered around a large lanai, or covered porch. French doors provide lanai access from the family room, the living room and the master bedroom.
- The central living room also offers arched windows and shares a two-sided fireplace with the family room.
- The island kitchen and the bayed morning room are open to the family room, which features a wet bar next to the striking fireplace.
- The master bedroom features an irresistible bath with a spa tub, a separate shower, dual vanities and two walk-in closets. Two more good-sized bedrooms share another full bath.
- A 12-ft. cathedral ceiling enhances the third bedroom. Standard 8-ft. ceilings are found in the second bedroom and the hall bath. All other rooms boast terrific 10-ft. ceilings.

Plan DD-2802

Bedrooms: 3+	Baths: 2½
Living Area:	
Main floor	2,899 sq. ft.
Total Living Area:	**2,899 sq. ft.**
Standard basement	2,899 sq. ft.
Garage	568 sq. ft.
Exterior Wall Framing:	2x4

Foundation Options:

Standard basement

Crawlspace

Slab

(All plans can be built with your choice of foundation and framing. A generic conversion diagram is available. See order form.)

BLUEPRINT PRICE CODE: D

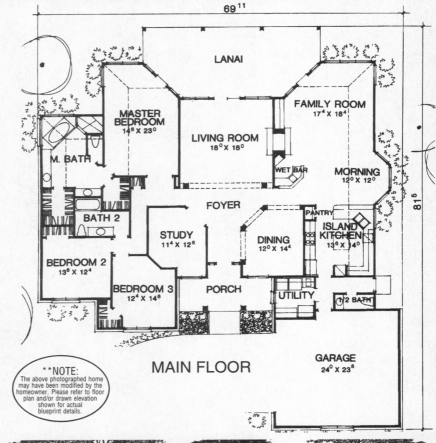

MAIN FLOOR

**NOTE: The above photographed home may have been modified by the homeowner. Please refer to floor plan and/or drawn elevation shown for actual blueprint details.

REAR VIEW

Elegant Approach

- This smart-looking design features an impressive approach, with a beautiful courtyard leading to the front door.
- The Y-shaped tiled entry efficiently directs traffic to all areas of the home.
- To the right, the combined living room and dining area offer a bow window, a fireplace and corner windows that overlook a covered sideyard patio.
- The adjacent sun room showcases a 14-ft. vaulted, skylighted ceiling and access to the patio.
- The corner kitchen has a snack bar that faces the family room, which features a 16-ft. vaulted ceiling, a woodstove and access to a second patio.
- The roomy master suite boasts a compartmentalized bath with a skylighted dressing area, a walk-in wardrobe and a shower.
- Another bath and bedroom, plus a den or possible third bedroom, complete this exciting design.

Plans P-7661-3A & -3D

Bedrooms: 2+	Baths: 2
Living Area:	
Main floor	1,693 sq. ft.
Total Living Area:	**1,693 sq. ft.**
Daylight basement	1,275 sq. ft.
Garage	462 sq. ft.
Exterior Wall Framing:	**2x4**
Foundation Options:	**Plan #**
Daylight basement	P-7661-3D
Crawlspace	P-7661-3A

(All plans can be built with your choice of foundation and framing. A generic conversion diagram is available. See order form.)

BLUEPRINT PRICE CODE:	**B**

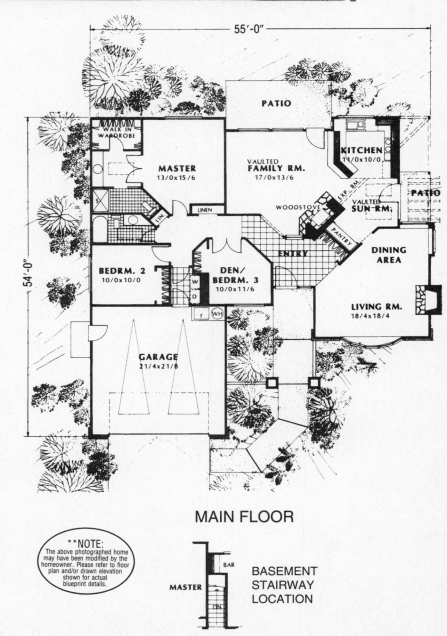

MAIN FLOOR

**NOTE: The above photographed home may have been modified by the homeowner. Please refer to floor plan and/or drawn elevation shown for actual blueprint details.

BASEMENT STAIRWAY LOCATION

TO ORDER THIS BLUEPRINT, CALL TOLL-FREE 1-800-820-1283

Plans P-7661-3A & -3D

PRICES AND DETAILS ON PAGES 12-15

Rustic Comfort

- Rustic charm highlights the exterior of this design, while the interior is filled with all the latest comforts.
- The wide, covered porch opens to a roomy entry, where two 7-ft.-high openings with decorative railings view into the dining room.
- Straight ahead lies the sunken living room, which features a 16-ft.-high vaulted ceiling with exposed beams. The fireplace is faced with floor-to-ceiling fieldstone, adding to the rustic look. A rear door opens to a large patio with luscious plant areas.

- The large and functional U-shaped kitchen features a china niche with glass shelves. Other bonuses include the adjacent sewing/hobby room, the oversized utility room and the storage area and built-in workbench in the side-entry garage.
- The secluded master suite hosts a sunken sleeping area with built-in bookshelves. One step up is a cozy sitting area that is defined by brick columns and a railed room divider. Double doors open to the deluxe bath, which offers a niche with glass shelves.
- Across the home, two more bedrooms share a second full bath.

Plan E-1607	
Bedrooms: 3	**Baths:** 2
Living Area:	
Main floor	1,600 sq. ft.
Total Living Area:	**1,600 sq. ft.**
Standard basement	1,600 sq. ft.
Garage	484 sq. ft.
Storage	132 sq. ft.
Exterior Wall Framing:	2x6
Foundation Options:	

Standard basement
Crawlspace
Slab
(All plans can be built with your choice of foundation and framing. A generic conversion diagram is available. See order form.)

BLUEPRINT PRICE CODE:	B

MAIN FLOOR

TO ORDER THIS BLUEPRINT,
CALL TOLL-FREE 1-800-820-1283

Plan E-1607

PRICES AND DETAILS
ON PAGES 12-15

165

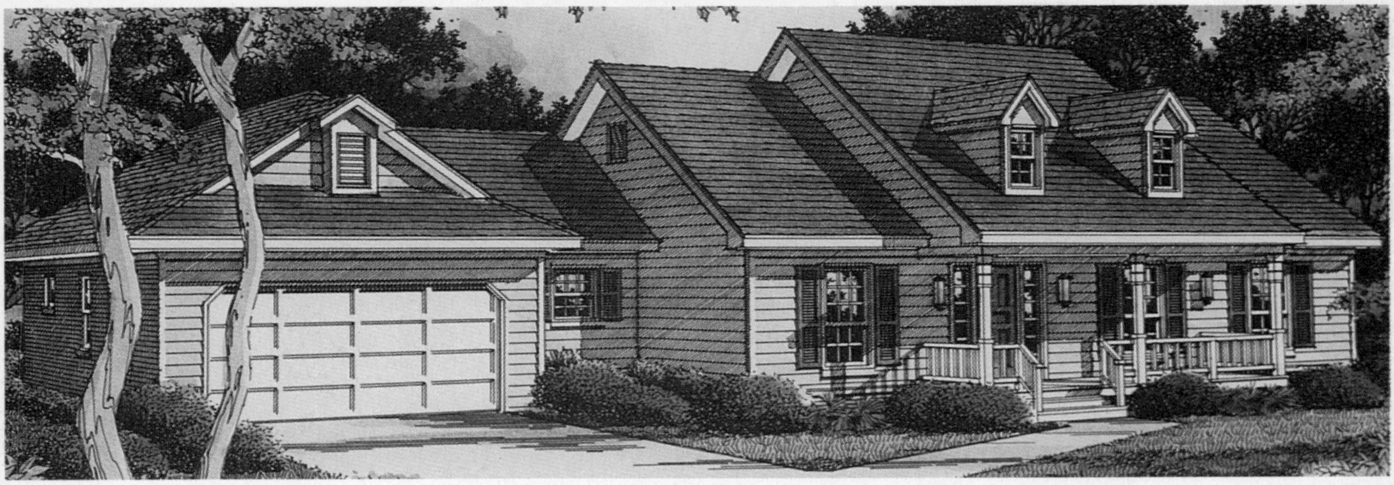

Modern Charmer

- This attractive plan combines country-style charm with a modern floor plan.
- The central foyer ushers guests past a study and on into the huge living room, which is highlighted by an 11-ft. ceiling, a corner fireplace and access to a big, covered backyard porch.
- An angled snack bar joins the living room to the bayed nook and the efficient kitchen. The formal dining room is easily reached from the kitchen and the foyer. A utility room and a half-bath are just off the garage entrance.
- The master suite, isolated for privacy, boasts a magnificent bath with a garden tub, a separate shower, double vanities and two walk-in closets.
- Two more bedrooms are located on the opposite side of the home and are separated by a hall bath.
- Ceilings in all rooms are at least 9 ft. high for added spaciousness.

Plan VL-2069

Bedrooms: 3	**Baths:** 2½
Living Area:	
Main floor	2,069 sq. ft.
Total Living Area:	**2,069 sq. ft.**
Garage	460 sq. ft.
Exterior Wall Framing:	2x4
Foundation Options:	
Crawlspace	
Slab	

(All plans can be built with your choice of foundation and framing. A generic conversion diagram is available. See order form.)

BLUEPRINT PRICE CODE: C

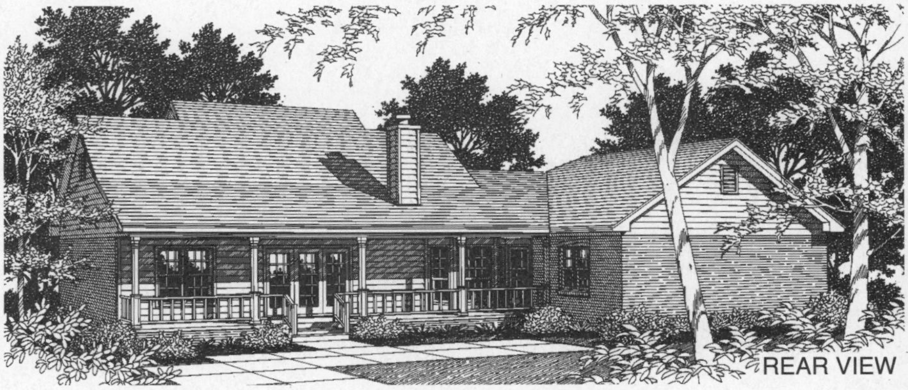

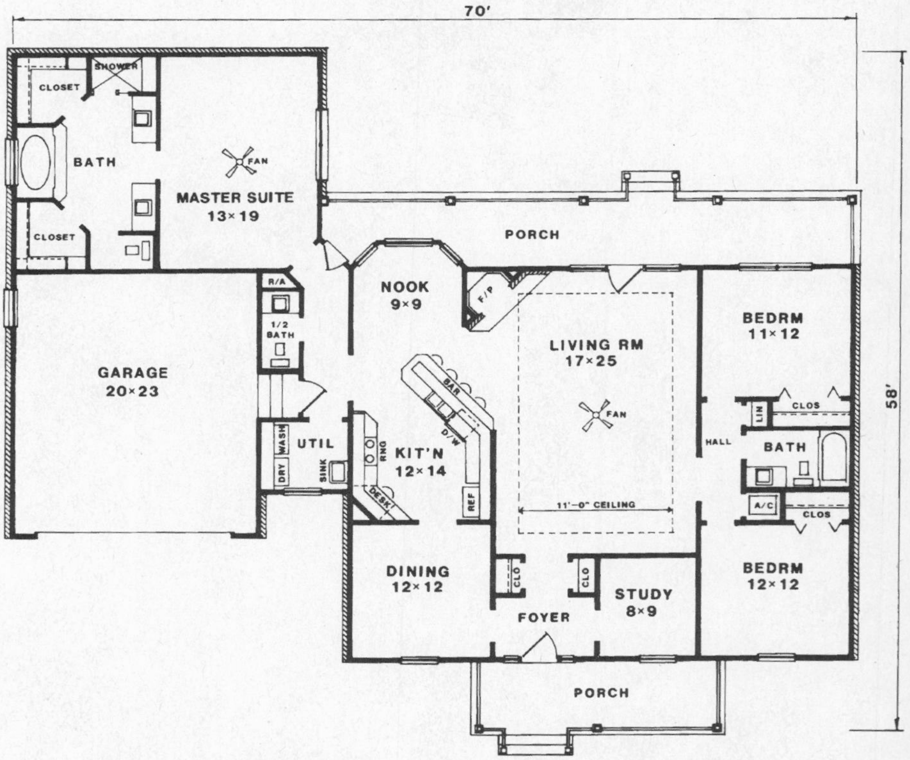

MAIN FLOOR

High Luxury in One Story

- Beautiful arched windows lend a luxurious feeling to the exterior of this one-story home.
- Soaring 12-ft. ceilings add volume to both the wide entry area and the central living room, which boasts a large fireplace and access to a covered porch and the patio beyond.
- Double doors separate the formal dining room from the corridor-style kitchen. Features of the kitchen include a pantry and an angled eating bar. The sunny, bayed eating area is perfect for casual family meals.
- The plush master suite has amazing amenities: a walk-in closet, a skylighted, angled whirlpool tub, a separate shower and private access to the laundry/utility room and the patio.
- Three good-sized bedrooms and a full bath are situated across the home.

Plan E-2302

Bedrooms: 4	Baths: 2
Living Area:	
Main floor	2,396 sq. ft.
Total Living Area:	**2,396 sq. ft.**
Standard basement	2,396 sq. ft.
Garage	484 sq. ft.
Exterior Wall Framing:	2x6

Foundation Options:

Standard basement
Crawlspace
Slab

(All plans can be built with your choice of foundation and framing. A generic conversion diagram is available. See order form.)

BLUEPRINT PRICE CODE: **C**

MAIN FLOOR

Designed for Livability

- As you enter this excitingly spacious traditional home, you see through the extensive windows to the backyard.
- This four-bedroom home was designed for the livability of the maturing family with the separation of the master suite.
- The formal dining room expands spatially to the living room while being set off by a decorative column and plant shelves.
- The bay that creates the morning room and the sitting area for the master suite also adds excitement to this plan, both inside and out.
- The master bath offers an exciting oval tub under glass and a separate shower, as well as a spacious walk-in closet and a dressing area.

Plan DD-1696

Bedrooms: 4	Baths: 2
Living Area:	
Main floor	1,748 sq. ft.
Total Living Area:	**1,748 sq. ft.**
Standard basement	1,748 sq. ft.
Garage	393 sq. ft.
Exterior Wall Framing:	2x4

Foundation Options:

Standard basement
Crawlspace
Slab

(All plans can be built with your choice of foundation and framing. A generic conversion diagram is available. See order form.)

BLUEPRINT PRICE CODE: B

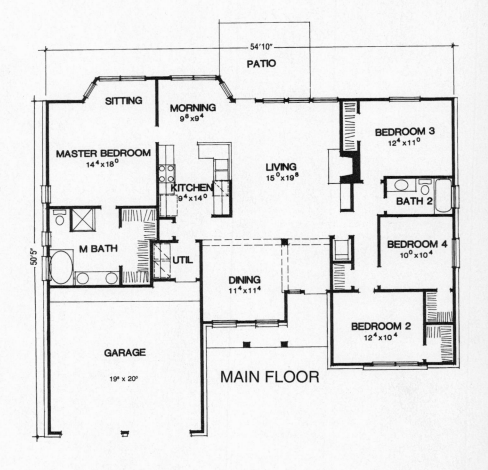

MAIN FLOOR

Photo courtesy of Breland & Farmer Designers, Inc.

Luxurious Master Suite

- The inviting facade of this gorgeous one-story design boasts a sheltered porch, symmetrical architecture and elegant window treatments.
- Inside, beautiful arched openings frame the living room, which features a 12-ft. ceiling, a dramatic fireplace and a wet bar that is open to the deluxe kitchen.
- The roomy kitchen is highlighted by an island cooktop, a built-in desk and a snack bar that faces the bayed eating area and the covered back porch.
- Isolated to the rear of the home, the master suite is a romantic retreat, offering an intimate sitting area and a luxurious bath. Entered through elegant double doors, the private bath showcases a skylighted corner tub, a separate shower, his-and-hers vanities, and a huge walk-in closet.
- The two remaining bedrooms have walk-in closets and share a hall bath.
- Unless otherwise specified, the home has 9-ft. ceilings throughout.

Plan E-2106

Bedrooms: 3	Baths: 2
Living Area:	
Main floor	2,177 sq. ft.
Total Living Area:	**2,177 sq. ft.**
Standard basement	2,177 sq. ft.
Garage and storage	570 sq. ft.
Exterior Wall Framing:	2x4

Foundation Options:

Standard basement
Crawlspace
Slab
(All plans can be built with your choice of foundation and framing. A generic conversion diagram is available. See order form.)

BLUEPRINT PRICE CODE:	C

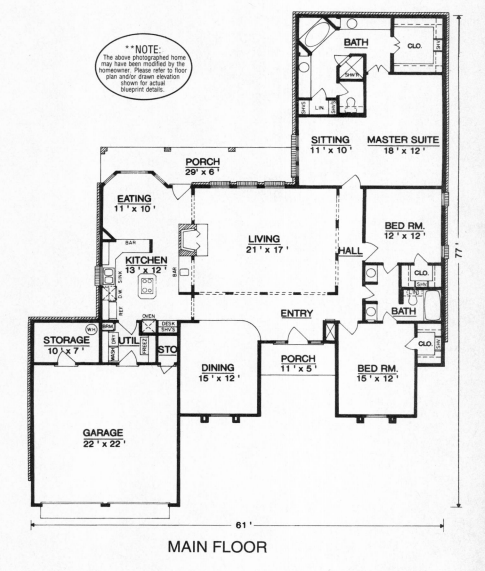

** NOTE:
The above photographed home may have been modified by the homeowner. Please refer to floor plan and/or drawn elevation shown for actual blueprint details.

MAIN FLOOR

TO ORDER THIS BLUEPRINT,
CALL TOLL-FREE 1-800-820-1283

Plan E-2106

PRICES AND DETAILS
ON PAGES 12-15

169

Alluring Arches

- Massive columns, alluring arches and dazzling windows crowned by half-round transoms attract passersby to this gorgeous one-story showcase home.
- Inside, 12-ft. coffered ceilings are found in the foyer, dining room and living room. A bank of windows in the living room provides a sweeping view of the covered backyard patio, creating a bright, open effect that is carried throughout the home.
- The informal, family activity areas are oriented to the back of the home as well. Spectacular window walls in the breakfast room and family room offer tremendous views. The family room's inviting corner fireplace is positioned to be enjoyed from the breakfast area and the spacious island kitchen.
- Separated from the secondary bedrooms, the superb master suite is entered through double doors and features a sitting room and a garden bath. Another full bath is across the hall from the den, which would also make a great guest room or nursery.

Plan HDS-99-179

Bedrooms: 3+	Baths: 3
Living Area:	
Main floor	2,660 sq. ft.
Total Living Area:	**2,660 sq. ft.**
Garage	527 sq. ft.
Exterior Wall Framing:	2x4

Foundation Options:

Slab

(All plans can be built with your choice of foundation and framing. A generic conversion diagram is available. See order form.)

BLUEPRINT PRICE CODE: **D**

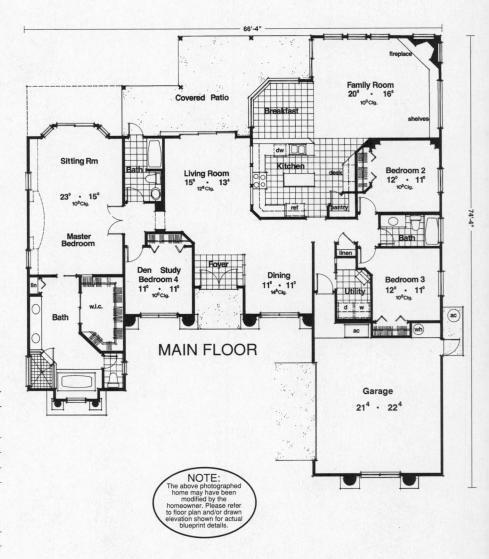

MAIN FLOOR

NOTE:
The above photographed home may have been modified by the homeowner. Please refer to floor plan and/or drawn elevation shown for actual blueprint details.

TO ORDER THIS BLUEPRINT, CALL TOLL-FREE 1-800-820-1283   Plan HDS-99-179   *PRICES AND DETAILS ON PAGES 12-15*

Attainable
Luxury

- This traditional ranch home offers a large, central living room with a 12-ft. ceiling, a corner fireplace and an adjoining patio.
- The U-shaped kitchen easily services both the formal dining room and the bayed eating area.
- The luxurious master suite features a large bath with separate vanities and dressing areas.
- Two secondary bedrooms share a second full bath.
- A covered carport boasts a decorative brick wall and attic space above. Two additional storage areas provide plenty of room for gardening supplies and sports equipment.

Plan E-1812

Bedrooms: 3	Baths: 2
Living Area:	
Main floor	1,860 sq. ft.
Total Living Area:	**1,860 sq. ft.**
Carport	484 sq. ft.
Storage	132 sq. ft.
Exterior Wall Framing:	2x6

Foundation Options:

Crawlspace

Slab

(All plans can be built with your choice of foundation and framing. A generic conversion diagram is available. See order form.)

BLUEPRINT PRICE CODE: B

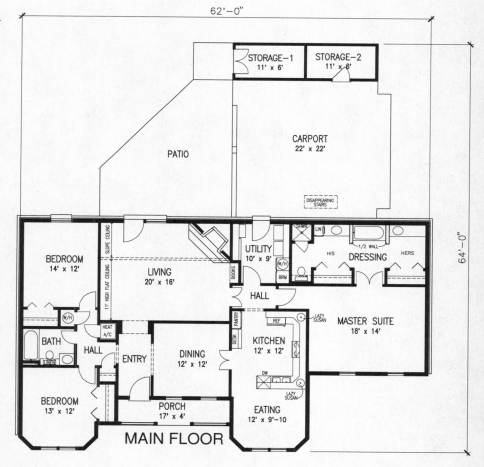

MAIN FLOOR

TO ORDER THIS BLUEPRINT,
CALL TOLL-FREE 1-800-820-1283

Plan E-1812

PRICES AND DETAILS
ON PAGES 12-15

171

Spacious Country-Style

- This distinctive country-style home is highlighted by a wide front porch and multi-paned windows with shutters.
- Inside, the dining room is off the foyer and open to the living room, but is defined by elegant columns and beams above.
- The central living room boasts a 12-ft. cathedral ceiling, a fireplace and French doors to the rear patio.
- The delightful kitchen/nook area is spacious and well planned for both work and play.
- A handy utility room and a half-bath are on either side of a short hallway leading to the carport, which includes a large storage area.
- The master suite offers his-and-hers walk-in closets and an incredible bath that incorporates a plant shelf above the raised spa tub.
- The two remaining bedrooms share a hall bath that is compartmentalized to allow more than one user at a time.

Plan J-86140

Bedrooms: 3	Baths: 2½
Living Area:	
Main floor	2,177 sq. ft.
Total Living Area:	**2,177 sq. ft.**
Standard basement	2,177 sq. ft.
Carport	440 sq. ft.
Storage	120 sq. ft.
Exterior Wall Framing:	2x4

Foundation Options:

Standard basement

Crawlspace

Slab

(All plans can be built with your choice of foundation and framing. A generic conversion diagram is available. See order form.)

BLUEPRINT PRICE CODE: C

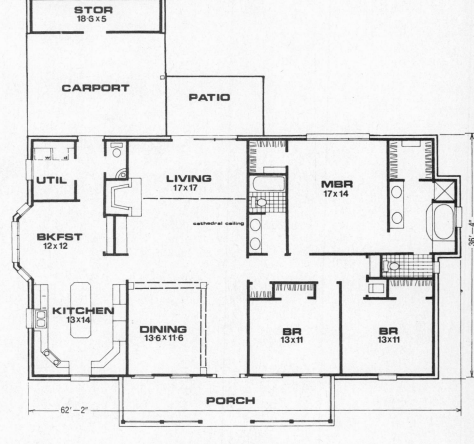

MAIN FLOOR

TO ORDER THIS BLUEPRINT, CALL TOLL-FREE 1-800-820-1283

Plan J-86140

PRICES AND DETAILS ON PAGES 12-15

Planned to Perfection

- This attractive and stylish home offers an interior design that is planned to perfection.
- The covered entry and vaulted foyer create an impressive welcome.
- The vaulted Great Room features a corner fireplace, a wet bar and lots of windows. The adjoining dining room offers a bay window and access to a covered patio.
- The gourmet kitchen includes an island cooktop, a garden window above the sink and a built-in desk. The attached nook is surrounded by windows that overlook a delightful planter.
- The master suite boasts a tray ceiling that rises to 9½ ft. and a peaceful reading area that accesses a private patio. The superb master bath features a garden tub and a separate shower.
- Two secondary bedrooms share a compartmentalized bath.

Plan S-4789

Bedrooms: 3	Baths: 2
Living Area:	
Main floor	1,665 sq. ft.
Total Living Area:	**1,665 sq. ft.**
Standard basement	1,665 sq. ft.
Garage	400 sq. ft.
Exterior Wall Framing:	2x6

Foundation Options:

Standard basement
Crawlspace
Slab
(All plans can be built with your choice of foundation and framing. A generic conversion diagram is available. See order form.)

BLUEPRINT PRICE CODE:	B

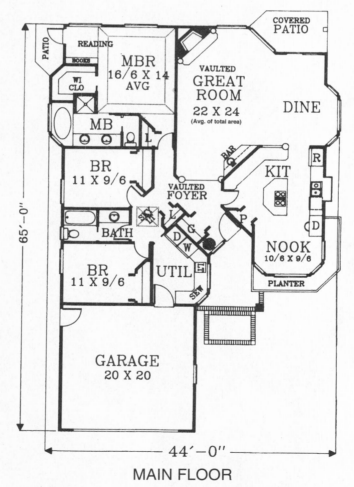

MAIN FLOOR

BASEMENT STAIRWAY LOCATION

Vaulted Ceilings Expand Interior

- A dignified exterior and a gracious, spacious interior combine to make this an outstanding plan for today's families.
- A step down from the vaulted entry, the living room offers a 12-ft.-high vaulted ceiling brightened by an arch-top boxed window and a nice fireplace.
- The vaulted dining room ceiling rises to more than 15 ft., and sliding glass doors open to a unique central atrium.
- The island kitchen shares a snack bar with the bayed nook and provides easy service to the dining room.
- The spacious family room boasts a sloped ceiling that peaks at 18 ft. and a woodstove that warms the entire area.
- The master suite is first-class all the way, with a spacious sleeping room and an opulent bath, which features a walk-in closet, a sunken garden tub, a separate shower and a skylighted dressing area with a dual-sink vanity.
- Two secondary bedrooms have window seats and share another full bath.

Plans P-7697-4A & -4D

Bedrooms: 3	Baths: 2
Living Area:	
Main floor (crawlspace version)	2,003 sq. ft.
Main floor (basement version)	2,030 sq. ft.
Total Living Area:	**2,003/2,030 sq. ft.**
Daylight basement	2,015 sq. ft.
Garage	647 sq. ft.
Exterior Wall Framing:	**2x6**
Foundation Options:	**Plan #**
Daylight basement	P-7697-4D
Crawlspace	P-7697-4A

(All plans can be built with your choice of foundation and framing. A generic conversion diagram is available. See order form.)

BLUEPRINT PRICE CODE:	**C**

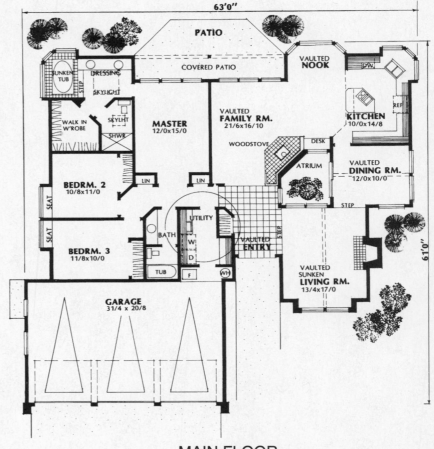

MAIN FLOOR

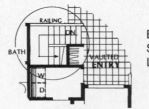

BASEMENT STAIRWAY LOCATION

Plans P-7697-4A & -4D

PRICES AND DETAILS ON PAGES 12-15

Classic Country-Style

- At the center of this rustic country-style home is an enormous living room with a flat beamed ceiling and a massive stone fireplace. A sunny patio and a covered rear porch are just steps away.
- The adjoining eating area and kitchen provide plenty of room for casual dining and meal preparation. The eating area is visually enhanced by a 14-ft. sloped ceiling with false beams. The kitchen includes a snack bar, a pantry closet and a built-in spice cabinet.
- The formal dining room gets plenty of pizzazz from a stone-faced wall and an arched planter facing the living room.
- The secluded master suite has it all, including a private bath, a separate dressing area and a large walk-in closet with built-in shelves.
- The two remaining bedrooms have big closets and easy access to a full bath.

Plan E-1808

Bedrooms: 3	**Baths:** 2

Living Area:	
Main floor	1,800 sq. ft.
Total Living Area:	**1,800 sq. ft.**
Garage	605 sq. ft.
Exterior Wall Framing:	2x4

Foundation Options:

Crawlspace
Slab
(All plans can be built with your choice of foundation and framing. A generic conversion diagram is available. See order form.)

BLUEPRINT PRICE CODE:	B

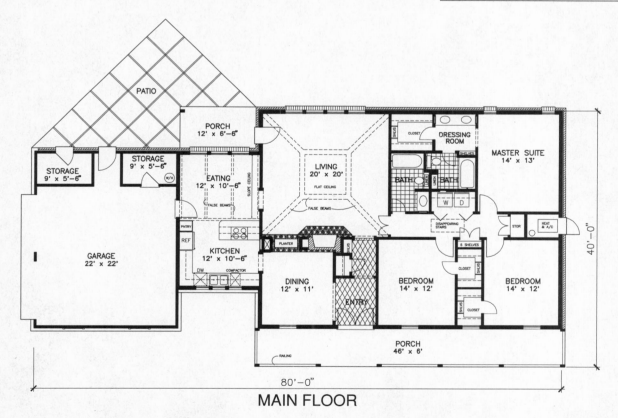

MAIN FLOOR

Spectacular Design

- The spectacular brick facade of this home conceals a stylish floor plan. Endless transoms crown the windows that wrap around the rear of the home, flooding the interior with natural light.
- The foyer opens to a huge Grand Room with a 14-ft. ceiling. French doors access a delightful covered porch.
- A three-sided fireplace warms the three casual rooms, which share a high 12-ft. ceiling. The Gathering Room is surrounded by tall windows; the Good Morning Room features porch access; and the island kitchen offers a double oven, a pantry and a snack bar.
- Guests will dine in style in the formal dining room, with its 13-ft. tray ceiling and trio of tall, arched windows.
- Curl up with a good book in the quiet library, which has an airy 10-ft. ceiling.
- A 12-ft. ceiling enhances the fantastic master suite, which is wrapped in windows. The superb master bath boasts a step-up garden tub, a separate shower, two vanities, a makeup table and a bidet.
- Two sleeping suites on the other side of the home have 10-ft. ceilings and share a unique bath with private vanities.

Plan EOF-8	
Bedrooms: 3+	**Baths:** 3½
Living Area:	
Main floor	3,392 sq. ft.
Total Living Area:	**3,392 sq. ft.**
Garage	871 sq. ft.
Exterior Wall Framing:	2x6
Foundation Options:	
Slab	

(All plans can be built with your choice of foundation and framing. A generic conversion diagram is available. See order form.)

BLUEPRINT PRICE CODE:	E

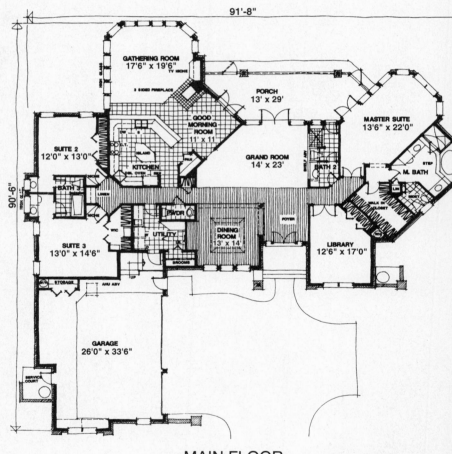

MAIN FLOOR

Plan EOF-8

Symmetry and Style

- This appealing one-story home boasts a striking facade with symmetrical rooflines, stately columns and terrific transoms.
- The formal living spaces have a classic split design, perfect for quiet times and conversation.
- The unique design of the bedroom wing gives each bedroom easy access to a full bath. The rear bedroom also enjoys pool and patio proximity.
- The huge family room, which opens up to the patio with 12-ft. pocket sliding doors, has plenty of space for a fireplace and media equipment.
- The master suite just off the kitchen and nook is private yet easily accessible. One unique feature is its bed wall with high glass above. The master bath offers a walk-in closet, a corner tub, a step down shower and a private toilet room.
- Throughout the home, volume ceilings to a height of at least ten feet increase the spacious, airy feeling.

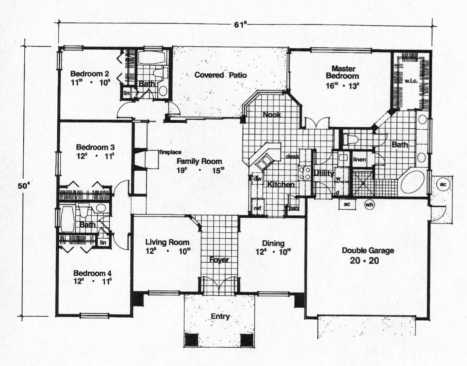

MAIN FLOOR

Plan HDS-99-147	
Bedrooms: 4	**Baths:** 3
Living Area:	
Main floor	2,089 sq. ft.
Total Living Area:	**2,089 sq. ft.**
Garage	415 sq. ft.
Exterior Wall Framing:	2x4

Foundation Options:
Slab
(Typical foundation & framing conversion diagram available—see order form.)

BLUEPRINT PRICE CODE:	C

Fashionable Detailing

- A soaring entry portico and unusual window treatments make a bold, fashionable statement for this home.
- Inside, varied ceiling heights and special features lend a distinctive look and feel to each room.
- A 14-ft. stepped ceiling in the foyer gives way to the columned formal dining room and its 12-ft. stepped ceiling. Soffit planters outline the foyer and the living room.
- Decorative columns and a 12-ft. raised ceiling also highlight the living room, where sliding doors open to an expansive covered patio.
- A huge, angular counter with a floating soffit distinguishes the kitchen from the sunny breakfast nook. The adjoining family room has a 10-ft. ceiling and a fireplace accented with high, fixed glass and built-in shelves.
- The master suite has sliding glass doors to the patio and an arched opening to the lavish bath. The raised spa tub has louvered shutters to the sleeping area.
- Across from the den is a dual-access bath. The two bedrooms at the opposite side of the home enjoy private access to another full bath.

Plan HDS-99-161

Bedrooms: 3+	Baths: 3½
Living Area:	
Main floor	2,691 sq. ft.
Total Living Area:	**2,691 sq. ft.**
Garage	520 sq. ft.
Exterior Wall Framing:	2x4

Foundation Options:

Slab

(All plans can be built with your choice of foundation and framing. A generic conversion diagram is available. See order form.)

BLUEPRINT PRICE CODE: **D**

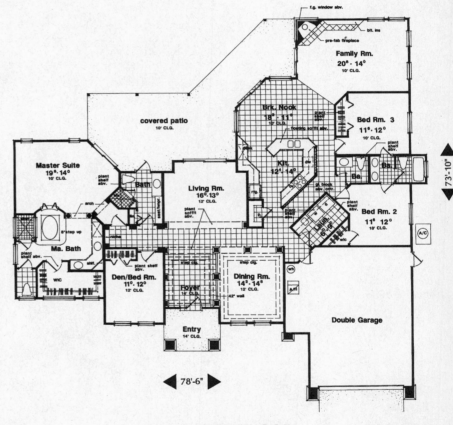

MAIN FLOOR

 TO ORDER THIS BLUEPRINT, CALL TOLL-FREE 1-800-820-1283 Plan HDS-99-161 PRICES AND DETAILS ON PAGES 12-15

Flexible Design

- Dramatic angled glass, natural stone and a flexible floor plan give contemporary appeal to this attractive ranch.
- The welcoming recessed entry offers double doors that open into a wide reception hall, which views the dining room and the backyard beyond.
- The stunning living room boasts a 14-ft. cathedral ceiling and a handsome fireplace framed by a wall of glass.
- Highlighted by skylights in a 14-ft. cathedral ceiling, the kitchen serves the sunny dinette over a stylish breakfast bar. Sliding glass doors lead to a bright backyard terrace. The adjoining family room has a high-efficiency fireplace.
- The charming master bedroom opens to a private backyard terrace. The master bath includes a whirlpool tub.
- This plan is available with either three or four bedrooms. Please specify your choice when ordering blueprints.

Plans K-645-PA & -PB

Bedrooms: 3+	Baths: 2
Living Area:	
Main floor (3 bedrooms)	1,635 sq. ft.
Main floor (4 bedrooms)	1,839 sq. ft.
Total Living Area:	**1,635/1,839 sq. ft.**
Garage and storage	476 sq. ft.
Standard basement	1,592/1,796 sq. ft.
Exterior Wall Framing:	2x4 or 2x6

Foundation Options:

Standard basement

(All plans can be built with your choice of foundation and framing. A generic conversion diagram is available. See order form.)

BLUEPRINT PRICE CODE: B

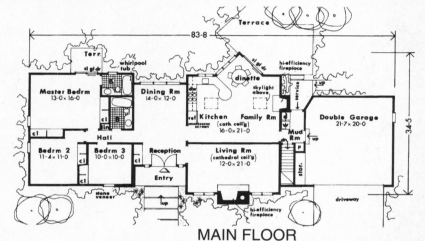

MAIN FLOOR
(K-645-PA)

MAIN FLOOR
(K-645-PB)

VIEW INTO DINETTE AND FAMILY ROOM

Arched Entry

- A beautiful arched entry introduces this grand Mediterranean home.
- Elegant double doors open into a tiled foyer, which is flanked by the home's formal living and dining rooms. Both rooms boast 12-ft. ceilings, and the dining room offers a tray ceiling.
- In the huge family room, sliding glass doors open to a covered patio. A fireplace flanked by built-in cabinets sets the stage for fun evenings at home.
- An 8-ft. wall separates the family room from the kitchen, which shares an

angled serving counter with the sunny bayed breakfast nook. A built-in desk nearby is a great spot to pay the bills.
- The secluded master suite includes a sprawling overhead plant shelf and sliding glass doors to the patio. A dramatic arch introduces the private bath, which includes a huge tub, a separate shower and a dual-sink vanity.
- Across the home, two more bedrooms share a hall bath. A quiet rear bedroom is serviced by another full bath. Each room boasts a neat plant shelf.
- Unless otherwise noted, a 10-ft. ceiling enhances every room in the home.

Plan HDS-99-233	
Bedrooms: 4	**Baths: 3**
Living Area:	
Main floor	2,140 sq. ft.
Total Living Area:	**2,140 sq. ft.**
Garage	430 sq. ft.
Exterior Wall Framing:	8-in. concrete block

Foundation Options:

Slab
(All plans can be built with your choice of foundation and framing. A generic conversion diagram is available. See order form.)

BLUEPRINT PRICE CODE: C

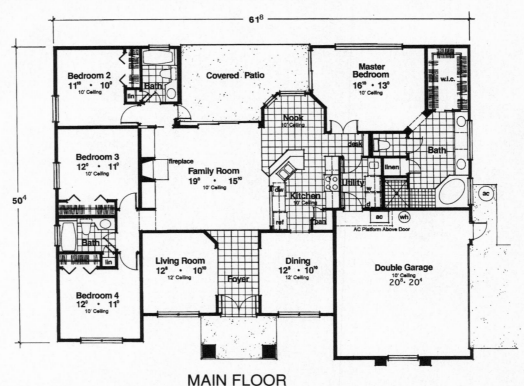

MAIN FLOOR

Plan HDS-99-233

PRICES AND DETAILS ON PAGES 12-15

Enjoyable Porch

- This stylish home offers an exciting four-season porch and a large deck. Transom windows adorn the exterior and allow extra light into the interior.
- The airy 17-ft., 4-in.-high foyer provides views into all of the living areas.
- The sunken Great Room boasts a see-through fireplace, a Palladian window and a 13-ft., 4-in. cathedral ceiling.
- An island cooktop highlights the corner kitchen, which is open to both the formal dining room and the casual dinette. Double doors access the porch, with its 12-ft. vaulted ceiling and French door to the inviting deck.
- The master bedroom is enhanced by a 10-ft., 3-in. tray ceiling and the see-through fireplace. The master bath has a whirlpool tub and a separate shower, each with striking glass-block walls.
- The front bedroom boasts an arched window under an 11-ft., 9-in. ceiling.
- The den off the foyer may be used to accommodate overnight guests.
- Unless otherwise noted, all rooms have 9-ft. ceilings.

Plan PI-92-535

Bedrooms: 2+	Baths: 2½
Living Area:	
Main floor	2,302 sq. ft.
Four-season porch	208 sq. ft.
Total Living Area:	**2,510 sq. ft.**
Daylight basement	2,302 sq. ft.
Garage	912 sq. ft.
Exterior Wall Framing:	2x6

Foundation Options:

Daylight basement

(All plans can be built with your choice of foundation and framing. A generic conversion diagram is available. See order form.)

BLUEPRINT PRICE CODE: D

MAIN FLOOR

Garden Home with a View

- This clever design proves that privacy doesn't have to be compromised even in high-density urban neighborhoods. From within, views are oriented to a beautiful, lush entry courtyard and a covered rear porch.
- The exterior appearance is sheltered, but warm and welcoming.
- The innovative interior design centers on a unique kitchen, which directs traffic away from the working areas while still serving the entire home.
- The sunken family room features a 14-ft. vaulted ceiling and a warm fireplace.
- The master suite is highlighted by a sumptuous master bath with an oversized shower and a whirlpool tub, plus a large walk-in closet.
- The formal living room is designed and placed in such a way that it can become a third bedroom, a den, or an office or study room, depending on family needs and lifestyles.

Plan E-1824

Bedrooms: 2+	Baths: 2
Living Area:	
Main floor	1,891 sq. ft.
Total Living Area:	**1,891 sq. ft.**
Garage	506 sq. ft.
Storage	60 sq. ft.
Exterior Wall Framing:	2x4

Foundation Options:

Crawlspace
Slab
(All plans can be built with your choice of foundation and framing. A generic conversion diagram is available. See order form.)

BLUEPRINT PRICE CODE: B

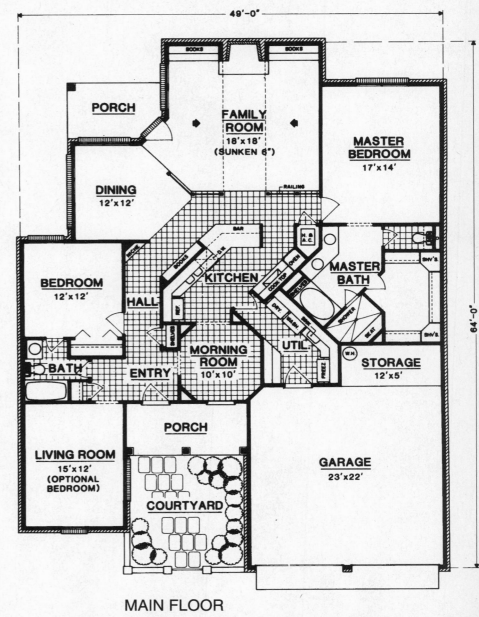

MAIN FLOOR

Plan E-1824

PRICES AND DETAILS ON PAGES 12-15

Captivating Facade

- This home attracts the eye with stately columns, half-round transoms and a sidelighted entry.
- A tall, barrel-vaulted foyer flows between the radiant formal areas at the front of the home.
- The barrel vault opens from the foyer to an overwhelming 14½-ft. vaulted family room, where a striking fireplace and a media center are captivating features.
- The central kitchen offers a dramatic 14½-ft. vaulted ceiling and a snack bar to the breakfast nook and family room. The nook's bay window overlooks a covered backyard patio.
- Formal occasions are hosted in the dining room, which boasts its own bay window and a 10½-ft. vaulted ceiling.
- The secluded master bedroom opens to the patio and flaunts an 11-ft. vaulted ceiling. A large walk-in closet and a posh bath with a step-up garden tub and a separate shower are also featured. On the other side of the home are three additional vaulted bedrooms and two more full baths.

Plan HDS-90-807

Bedrooms: 4	Baths: 3

Living Area:

Main floor	2,171 sq. ft.
Total Living Area:	**2,171 sq. ft.**
Garage	405 sq. ft.

Exterior Wall Framing:
2x4 and 8-in. concrete block

Foundation Options:

Slab
(All plans can be built with your choice of foundation and framing. A generic conversion diagram is available. See order form.)

BLUEPRINT PRICE CODE:	C

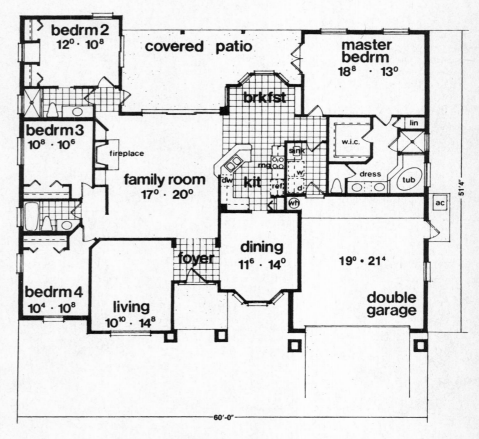

MAIN FLOOR

TO ORDER THIS BLUEPRINT,
CALL TOLL-FREE 1-800-820-1283

Plan HDS-90-807

PRICES AND DETAILS
ON PAGES 12-15

183

Arranged for Family Living

- This distinguished ranch home has a neatly arranged floor plan with a large activity area at the center and a strategically placed master bedroom.
- The formal living room and dining room flank the entry. The dining room provides views out to the covered front porch and a decorative planter with brick veneer. The living room boasts corner windows and a display niche with shelves.
- The double-doored entry also opens to a large sunken family room with a 13-ft. cathedral ceiling, a handsome fireplace, a patio view and a 10-ft-high decorative bridge.
- The huge modern kitchen offers a handy snack counter to the adjacent family room. The bayed breakfast room has French-door access to an expansive covered patio.
- Secluded to one end of the home is the deluxe master bedroom, which offers an 11-ft. cathedral ceiling, a spacious walk-in closet and French-door patio access. The master bath has a dual-sink vanity and outdoor access.
- Three additional bedrooms and two more baths are located at the opposite end of the home.

Plan Q-2266-1A

Bedrooms: 4	Baths: 3
Living Area:	
Main floor	2,266 sq. ft.
Total Living Area:	**2,266 sq. ft.**
Garage	592 sq. ft.
Exterior Wall Framing:	2x4

Foundation Options:

Slab

(All plans can be built with your choice of foundation and framing. A generic conversion diagram is available. See order form.)

BLUEPRINT PRICE CODE:	C

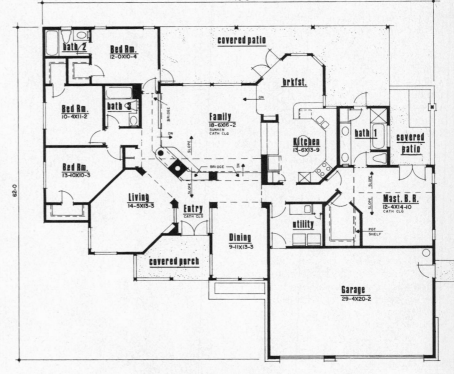

MAIN FLOOR

Plan Q-2266-1A

Well-Planned Walk-Out

- A handsome exterior, combined with an excellent interior design, makes this plan a popular and smart choice.
- The tiled entry opens to the formal dining room and the Great Room, which are separated by stylish columns and heightened by vaulted ceilings.
- A see-through fireplace with an adjacent wet bar highlights the Great Room. A window wall offers wonderful views of the expansive backyard deck.
- The fantastic kitchen, which is also warmed by the fireplace, offers a built-in desk, a walk-in pantry and an angled snack bar that faces an octagonal breakfast bay.
- The spacious main-floor master suite includes a raised ceiling, a huge walk-in closet and a lavish bath.
- An elegant den, a handy half-bath and a roomy laundry complete the main floor.
- A dramatic, open stairway overlooking an eye-catching planter leads to the walk-out basement. Included are two bedrooms and a full bath, plus an optional bonus room or family room.

Plan AG-9105

Bedrooms: 3+	Baths: 2½
Living Area:	
Main floor	1,838 sq. ft.
Daylight basement (finished)	800 sq. ft.
Total Living Area:	**2,638 sq. ft.**
Daylight basement (unfinished)	1,038 sq. ft.
Garage	462 sq. ft.
Exterior Wall Framing:	2x6

Foundation Options:
Daylight basement
(All plans can be built with your choice of foundation and framing. A generic conversion diagram is available. See order form.)

BLUEPRINT PRICE CODE:	**D**

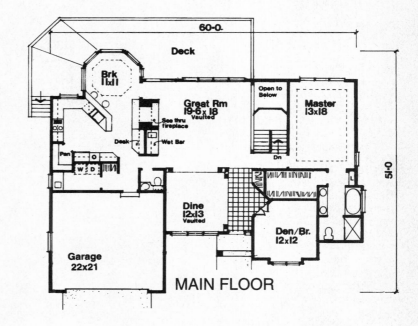

MAIN FLOOR

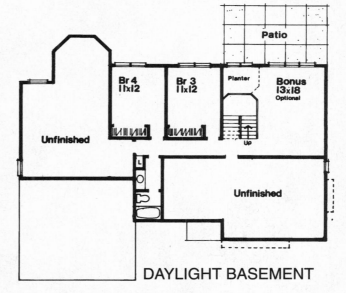

DAYLIGHT BASEMENT

Master Suite
Fit for a King

- This sprawling one-story features an extraordinary master suite that stretches from the front of the home to the back.
- Eye-catching windows and columns introduce the foyer, which flows back to the Grand Room. French doors open to the covered veranda, which offers a fabulous summer kitchen.
- The kitchen and bayed morning room are nestled between the Grand Room and a warm Gathering Room. A striking fireplace, an entertainment center and an ale bar are found here. This exciting core of living spaces also offers dramatic views of the outdoors.
- The isolated master suite features a stunning two-sided fireplace and an octagonal lounge area with veranda access. His-and-hers closets, separate dressing areas and a garden tub are other amenities. Across the home, three additional bedroom suites have private access to one of two more full baths.
- The private dining room at the front of the home has a 13-ft. coffered ceiling and a niche for a china cabinet.
- An oversized laundry room is located across from the kitchen and near the entrance to the three-car garage.

Plan EOF-60

Bedrooms: 4	Baths: 3

Living Area:	
Main floor	3,002 sq. ft.
Total Living Area:	**3,002 sq. ft.**
Garage	660 sq. ft.
Exterior Wall Framing:	2x6

Foundation Options:

Slab
(All plans can be built with your choice of foundation and framing. A generic conversion diagram is available. See order form.)

BLUEPRINT PRICE CODE:	E

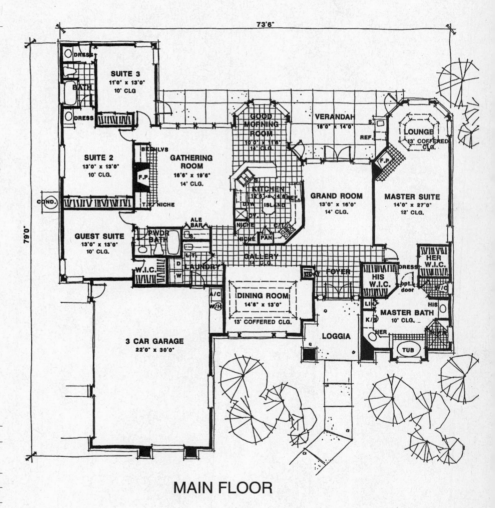

MAIN FLOOR

Plan EOF-60

PRICES AND DETAILS
ON PAGES 12-15

Enticing Interior

- Filled with elegant features, this modern country home's exciting floor plan is as impressive as it is innovative.
- Past the inviting columned porch, the entrance gallery flows into the spacious living room/dining room area.
- Boasting a 14-ft.-high sloped ceiling, the living room is enhanced by a semi-circular window bay and includes a handsome fireplace. The adjoining dining room offers sliding glass doors to a backyard terrace.
- The skylighted kitchen features an eating bar that serves the sunny bayed dinette. A convenient half-bath and a laundry/mudroom are nearby.
- Brightened by a bay window, the luxurious master bedroom shows off his-and-hers walk-in closets. The master bath showcases a whirlpool garden tub under a glass sunroof.
- Two additional bedrooms share a skylighted hallway bath.

Plan K-685-DA

Bedrooms: 3	Baths: 2½
Living Area:	
Main floor	1,760 sq. ft.
Total Living Area:	**1,760 sq. ft.**
Standard basement	1,700 sq. ft.
Garage	482 sq. ft.
Exterior Wall Framing:	2x4 or 2x6

Foundation Options:

Standard basement
Slab
(All plans can be built with your choice of foundation and framing. A generic conversion diagram is available. See order form.)

BLUEPRINT PRICE CODE:	B

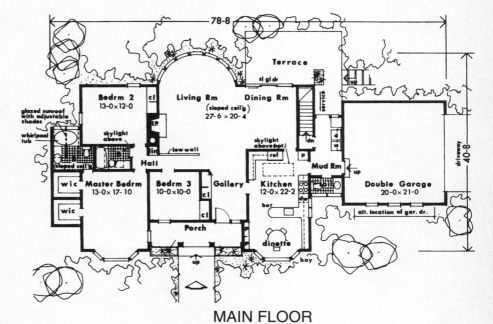

MAIN FLOOR

VIEW INTO LIVING AND DINING ROOMS

Exquisite Farmhouse

- This exquisite home is characterized by a nostalgic facade that disguises a uniquely modern floor plan.
- The covered front porch leads guests to the bright, sidelighted foyer. The foyer is flanked by the formal dining room and a quiet study as it flows to the living room.
- The spacious living room boasts an 11-ft. stepped ceiling and a handsome corner fireplace. French doors open to a covered back porch.
- The walk-through kitchen features a sunny bayed breakfast nook, a nifty work desk and an angled sink and snack counter.
- A half-bath, a laundry room and access to the two-car garage are all close by.
- The isolated master suite boasts two walk-in closets and a lavish private bath with a bayed garden tub, a separate shower and a dual-sink vanity.
- At the opposite end of the home, three additional bedrooms are serviced by two full baths.

Plan VL-2483	
Bedrooms: 4	**Baths:** 3½
Living Area:	
Main floor	2,483 sq. ft.
Total Living Area:	**2,483 sq. ft.**
Garage	504 sq. ft.
Exterior Wall Framing:	2x4

Foundation Options:
Crawlspace
Slab
(All plans can be built with your choice of foundation and framing. A generic conversion diagram is available. See order form.)

BLUEPRINT PRICE CODE:	C

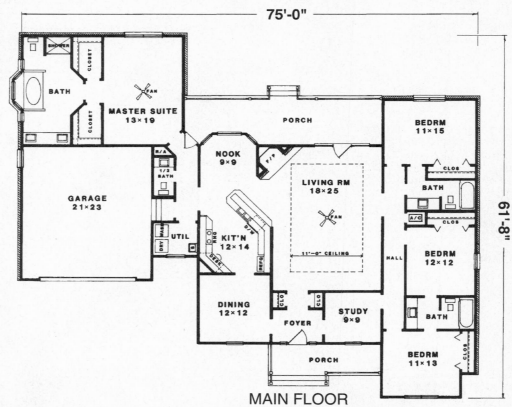

MAIN FLOOR

TO ORDER THIS BLUEPRINT, CALL TOLL-FREE 1-800-820-1283

Plan VL-2483

PRICES AND DETAILS ON PAGES 12-15

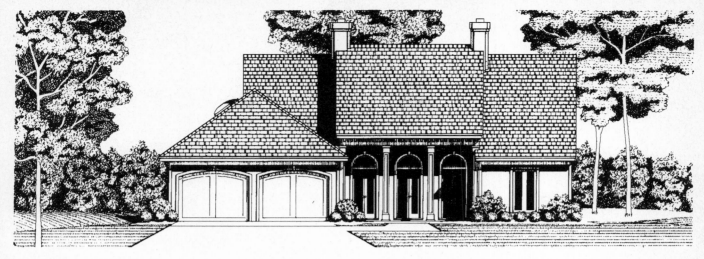

Distinctive and Elegant

- A distinctive look is captured in the exterior of this elegant one-story. Half-round transoms grace the three glass doors that open to the columned, covered front porch.
- The spacious living room at the center of the homer commands attention, with its 15-ft. ceiling and inviting fireplace. A glass door flanked by windows opens to a skylighted porch, which is also accessible from the secondary bedroom at the back of the home.
- The unique dining room overlooks the two backyard porches and boasts an elegant octagonal design, shaped by columns and cased openings.
- A 14-ft. sloped, skylighted ceiling adds drama to the gourmet kitchen, which also showcases an angled cooktop bar and a windowed sink. Laundry facilities and storage space are nearby.
- The luxurious master suite is secluded at the rear of the home, with private access to the porch. The sumptuous master bath features an oval spa tub, a separate shower, dual vanities and a huge walk-in closet.

Plan E-1628

Bedrooms: 3	Baths: 2
Living Area:	
Main floor	1,655 sq. ft.
Total Living Area:	**1,655 sq. ft.**
Garage and storage	549 sq. ft.
Exterior Wall Framing:	2x6

Foundation Options:

Crawlspace

Slab

(All plans can be built with your choice of foundation and framing. A generic conversion diagram is available. See order form.)

BLUEPRINT PRICE CODE:	**B**

MAIN FLOOR

TO ORDER THIS BLUEPRINT,
CALL TOLL-FREE 1-800-820-1283

Plan E-1628

PRICES AND DETAILS
ON PAGES 12-15

189

Circular Dining Room Featured

- An attractive stone facade, innovative architectural features and a functional, light-filled floor plan are the hallmarks of this attractive design.
- Guests are welcomed in the skylighted gallery, which boasts an 11-ft.-high sloped ceiling. The living room features a stone fireplace and opens to the circular dining room.
- The dining room is highlighted by a curved wall of windows and an 11-ft. domed ceiling, making an expansive space for entertaining.
- The open kitchen is set up for efficient operation and adjoins the sunny dinette and the cozy family room.
- The bedrooms are zoned to the left, with the master suite including a private bath, a large walk-in closet and access to an outdoor terrace. The additional bedrooms share another full bath.

Plan K-663-N

Bedrooms: 3	Baths: 2
Living Area:	
Main floor	1,682 sq. ft.
Total Living Area:	**1,682 sq. ft.**
Standard basement	1,645 sq. ft.
Garage	453 sq. ft.
Exterior Wall Framing:	2x4 or 2x6

Foundation Options:

Standard basement
Slab

(All plans can be built with your choice of foundation and framing. A generic conversion diagram is available. See order form.)

BLUEPRINT PRICE CODE:	**B**

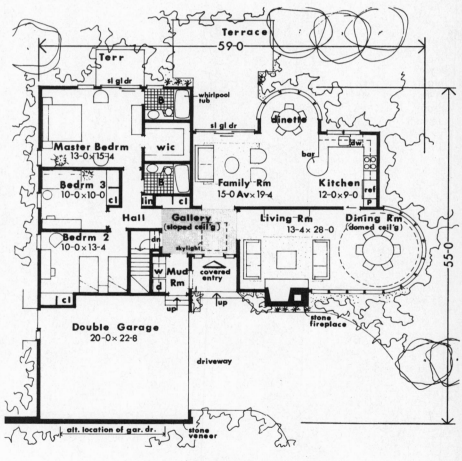

MAIN FLOOR

Plan K-663-N
PRICES AND DETAILS ON PAGES 12-15

Large, Stylish Spaces

- This stylish brick home greets guests with a beautiful entry court that leads to the recessed front porch.
- Beyond the porch, the bright entry flows into the Great Room, which features an 11-ft. sloped ceiling. This airy space also offers a fireplace, a sunny dining area and sliding glass doors to a backyard patio.
- The kitchen has a walk-in pantry, an open serving counter above the sink and convenient access to the laundry facilities and the garage.
- Isolated from the secondary bedrooms, the master suite boasts a 9-ft. tray ceiling, an oversized walk-in closet and an exquisite bath with two distinct sink areas, a corner garden tub and a separate shower.
- The third bedroom, which features lovely double doors and a front-facing bay window, would also make a perfect home office.

Plan SDG-91188

Bedrooms: 2+	Baths: 2
Living Area:	
Main floor	1,704 sq. ft.
Total Living Area:	**1,704 sq. ft.**
Garage	484 sq. ft.
Exterior Wall Framing:	2x4

Foundation Options:

Slab

(All plans can be built with your choice of foundation and framing. A generic conversion diagram is available. See order form.)

BLUEPRINT PRICE CODE: **B**

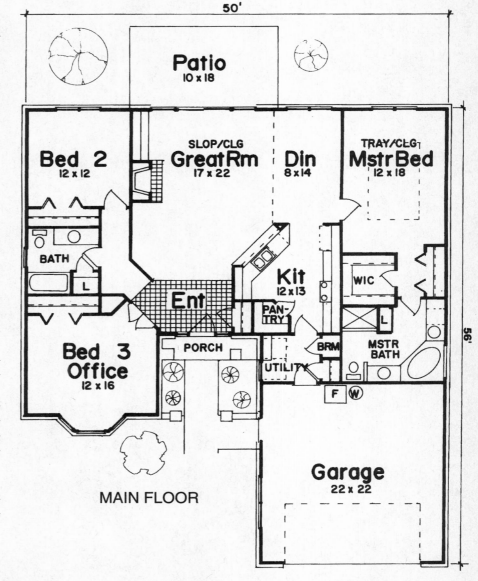

MAIN FLOOR

TO ORDER THIS BLUEPRINT,
CALL TOLL-FREE 1-800-820-1283

Plan SDG-91188

PRICES AND DETAILS
ON PAGES 12-15

191

Bold, Sweeping Architecture

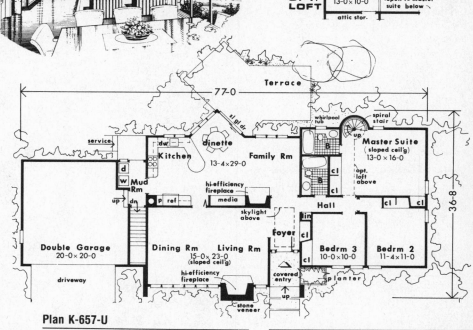

- The immediate architectural appeal of this contemporary three-bedroom design is characterized by the interplay of sloping rooflines and a dominating stone chimney.
- Inside, the open airy plan is cleverly organized in three natural zones: active, private and service.
- A sloped ceiling and wood-burning fireplace grace the formal living and dining rooms.
- The kitchen, dinette and family room area, ideal for casual living and informal meals, faces the rear and opens onto a back-yard terrace.
- A second fireplace in the family room generates much warmth.
- Three bedrooms and two full baths are sequestered in a private zone.
- Master suite features many amenities, including a personal bath and an optional loft, situated over the bathrooms and served by a spiral stairway.
- The loft, which is an added bonus, can double as a hobby corner, study spot or just a cozy private den. Basement is optional.

Plan K-657-U

Bedrooms: 3		Baths: 2
Space:		
Total living area:		1,506 sq. ft.
Basement:		1,552 sq. ft.
Garage:		400 sq. ft.
Mud room, etc.:		90 sq. ft.

Exterior Wall Framing:	2x4 or 2x6

Foundation options:
Standard basement.
Slab.
(Foundation & framing conversion diagram available — see order form)

Blueprint Price Code:	B

Plan K-657-U

Distinctly Different

- This traditional, ranch-style home offers three distinct living areas—a formal area for entertaining, a casual one to enjoy everyday life in and a sleeping wing when you want privacy.
- An inviting porch greets visitors and ushers them into a welcoming foyer. On the right, the living room extends to the formal dining room, providing a large yet intimate place to entertain.
- A versatile family room at the rear of the home serves as the focal point of casual

gatherings. This good-sized room is a comfortable spot to watch a movie, enjoy a book or catch up on family matters. You will spend plenty of easy, bug-free, summer afternoons on the screened porch nearby.
- The efficient kitchen includes lots of counter space to prepare meals, and a roomy pantry that maximizes storage space. The sunny breakfast bay is great for casual meals and morning pastries.
- Across the home, the spacious master bedroom is a peaceful retreat. A neat dressing area with a dual-sink vanity and a large walk-in closet leads to the master bath, where a raised tub ends the day with a splash!

Plan C-8625	
Bedrooms: 3	**Baths:** 2½
Living Area:	
Main floor	2,306 sq. ft.
Total Living Area:	**2,306 sq. ft.**
Screened porch	276 sq. ft.
Daylight basement	2,306 sq. ft.
Garage and storage	583 sq. ft.
Exterior Wall Framing:	2x4
Foundation Options:	

Daylight basement
Crawlspace
Slab
(All plans can be built with your choice of foundation and framing. A generic conversion diagram is available. See order form.)

BLUEPRINT PRICE CODE:	C

Floor Plan

SCR. PORCH
23'-0" x 12'-0"

M. BEDROOM
17'-0" x 13'-6"

BATH

CLOSET

LINEN

DRESSING

CLOSET

LINEN

CLOSET

BEDROOM
14'-0" x 12'-0"

BATH

BEDROOM
12'-0" x 12'-0"

COATS

CLOSET

FOYER

STEP

DOWN

FAMILY ROOM
22'-6" x 13'-6"

KITCHEN
10'-0" x 13'-6"

BREAKFAST
10'-0" x 13'-0"

BATH

D W

UTILITY

PANTRY

LIVING ROOM
16'-0" x 15'-0"

DINING ROOM
10'-0" x 12'-6"

GARAGE
22'-0" x 20'-0"

32'-8"

PORCH

STORAGE

93'-10"

MAIN FLOOR

A Taste of Europe

- This tasteful one-story home is characterized by a European exterior and an ultra-modern interior.
- High 10-ft. ceilings grace the central living areas, from the foyer to the Great Room, and from the nook through the kitchen to the dining room.
- The inviting Great Room showcases a fireplace framed by glass that overlooks the covered back porch.
- A snack bar unites the Great Room with the bayed nook and the galley-style

kitchen. A spacious utility room is just off the kitchen and accessible from the two-car garage as well.
- The secluded master suite boasts a luxurious private bath and French doors that open to the covered backyard porch.
- The master bath features a raised garden spa tub set into an intimate corner, with a separate shower nearby. A large walk-in closet and two sinks separated by a built-in makeup table are also included.
- Two additional bedrooms, a second full bath and a front study or home office make up the remainder of this up-to-date design.

Plan VL-2162

Bedrooms: 3	Baths: 2
Living Area:	
Main floor	2,162 sq. ft.
Total Living Area:	**2,162 sq. ft.**
Garage	498 sq. ft.
Exterior Wall Framing:	2x4

Foundation Options:

Crawlspace
Slab
(All plans can be built with your choice of foundation and framing. A generic conversion diagram is available. See order form.)

BLUEPRINT PRICE CODE: C

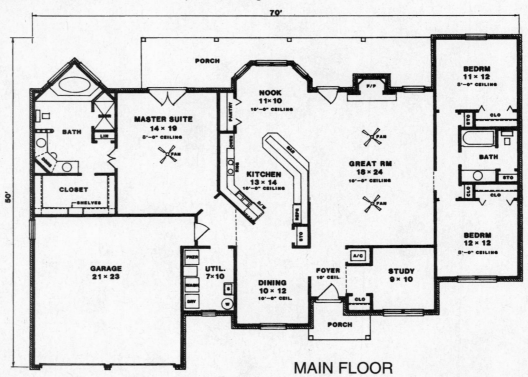

MAIN FLOOR

Plan VL-2162

PRICES AND DETAILS ON PAGES 12-15

Low-profile Country Classic

Total living area:	1,790 sq. ft.
Porches:	352 sq. ft.
Carport:	474 sq. ft.
Storage:	146 sq. ft.
Total:	2,762 sq. ft.

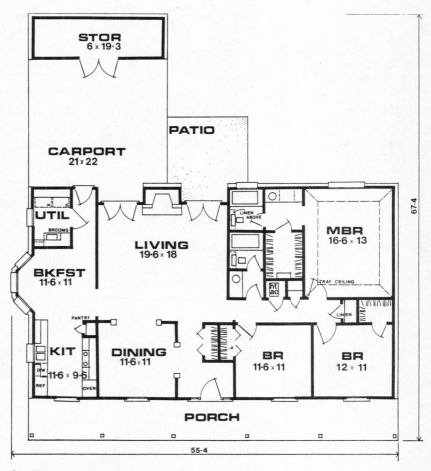

STOR
6 x 19·3

PATIO

CARPORT
21 x 22

UTIL

BROOMS

BKFST
11·6 x 11

LIVING
19·6 x 18

LINEN
ABOVE

MBR
16·6 x 13

TRAY CEILING

LINEN

PANTRY

KIT
11·6 x 9·6

DW

REF

OVEN

DINING
11·6 x 11

BR
11·6 x 11

BR
12 x 11

PORCH

67·4

55·4

Specify basement, crawlspace or slab foundation.

Blueprint Price Code B

Plan J-8606

Family Home, Formal Accents

- Captivating roof angles and European detailing highlight the exterior of this graceful home.
- The generous foyer is flanked by the spacious living and dining rooms, both with tall, ornate windows.
- Beyond the foyer lies an expansive family room, highlighted by a dramatic fireplace and sliding glass doors that open to a sunny patio.
- The kitchen makes use of an L-shaped counter and a central island to maximaze efficiency. The adjacent breakfast room offers casual dining. A nearby utility room features a washer and dryer and a door to the backyard.
- The large master suite boasts two closets and a private bath with a dual-sink vanity and a step-up tub.
- Across the hall, two additional bedrooms share a second full bath.

Plan C-8103	
Bedrooms: 3	**Baths:** 2
Living Area:	
Main floor	1,940 sq. ft.
Total Living Area:	**1,940 sq. ft.**
Daylight basement	1,870 sq. ft.
Garage	400 sq. ft.
Exterior Wall Framing:	2x4
Foundation Options:	
Daylight basement	
Crawlspace	
Slab	

(All plans can be built with your choice of foundation and framing. A generic conversion diagram is available. See order form.)

BLUEPRINT PRICE CODE:	**B**

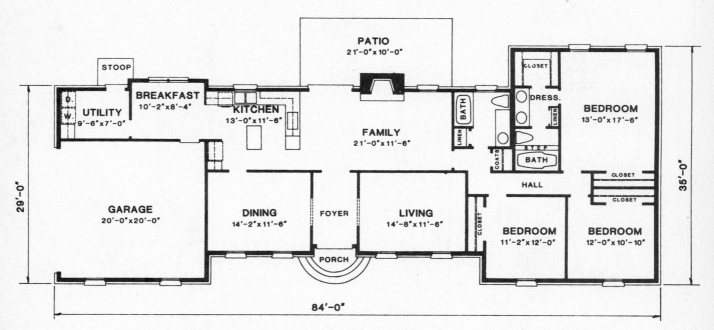

MAIN FLOOR

Plan C-8103
PRICES AND DETAILS ON PAGES 12-15

Distinctive Design

- This well-designed home is neatly laid out to provide distinctive formal and informal living areas.
- The entry guides guests into the combination living and dining room. Straight ahead, double doors open to a large family room that overlooks an inviting patio. An 11-ft. vaulted ceiling with exposed beams and a dramatic fireplace with a raised hearth give the room added appeal.
- The galley-style kitchen offers easy service to the dining room and the bayed eating area. Nearby, a deluxe utility room features laundry facilities and access to the garage.
- Three bedrooms, each with a walk-in closet, make up the sleeping wing. The master suite offers a private bath with a separate dressing area set off by a decorative half-wall.

Plan E-1601	
Bedrooms: 3	**Baths:** 2
Living Area:	
Main floor	1,630 sq. ft.
Total Living Area:	**1,630 sq. ft.**
Garage and storage	610 sq. ft.
Exterior Wall Framing:	2x4

Foundation Options:
Crawlspace
Slab
(All plans can be built with your choice of foundation and framing. A generic conversion diagram is available. See order form.)

BLUEPRINT PRICE CODE:	**B**

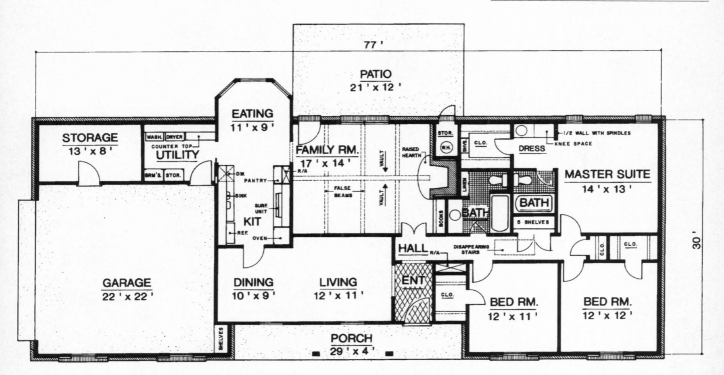

MAIN FLOOR

Triple Treat!

- With three exciting and distinctive front elevation options included, this ranch design is sure to please.
- The interior has something for everyone as well. The formal dining room, to the right of the foyer, is graced with an elegant transom window-wall.
- The formal living room has a vaulted ceiling and handsome columns to define its perimeter.
- The heart of the plan is the family room, which has a fireplace flanked by sliders which lead to the rear covered patio.
- The galley kitchen overlooks the family room and the sunny breakfast eating area.
- Two bedrooms lie on the left side of the plan, while the master suite lies on the right side with a den/fourth bedroom which can be privately used as a master sitting room.

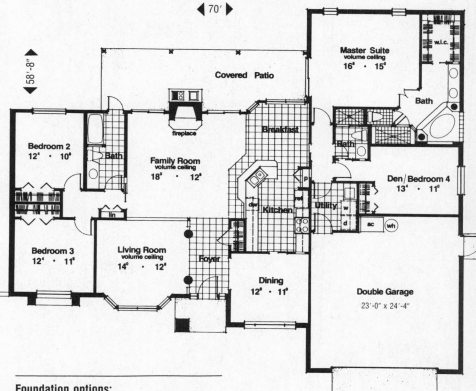

Plan HDS-90-804

Bedrooms: 3-4	Baths: 2½
Space:	
Total living area:	2,321 sq. ft.
Garage:	498 sq. ft.
Exterior Wall Framing:	2x4 and concrete

Foundation options:
Slab.
(Foundation & framing conversion diagram available — see order form.)

Blueprint Price Code: C

Luxurious Living on One Level

- The elegant exterior of this spacious one-story presents a classic air of quality and distinction.
- Three French doors brighten the inviting entry, which flows into the spacious living room. Boasting a 13-ft. ceiling, the living room enjoys a fireplace with a wide hearth and adjoining built-in bookshelves. A wall of glass, including a French door, provides views of the sheltered backyard porch.
- A stylish angled counter joins the spacious kitchen to the sunny bay-windowed eating nook.
- Secluded for privacy, the master suite features a nice dressing area, a large walk-in closet and private backyard access. A convenient laundry/utility room is adjacent to the master bath.
- At the opposite end of the home, double doors lead to three more bedrooms, a compartmentalized bath and lots of closet space.

Plan E-2208	
Bedrooms: 4	**Baths:** 2
Living Area:	
Main floor	2,252 sq. ft.
Total Living Area:	**2,252 sq. ft.**
Standard basement	2,252 sq. ft.
Garage and storage	592 sq. ft.
Exterior Wall Framing:	2x6

Foundation Options:

Standard basement
Crawlspace
Slab

(All plans can be built with your choice of foundation and framing. A generic conversion diagram is available. See order form.)

BLUEPRINT PRICE CODE: **C**

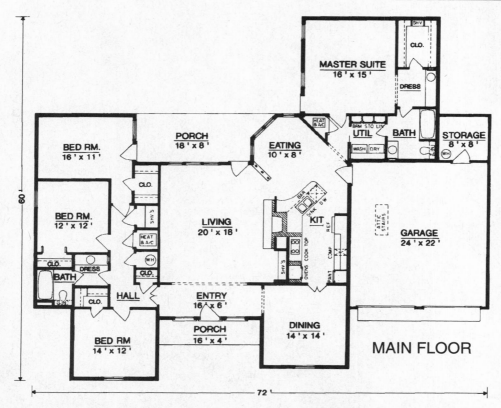

MAIN FLOOR

TO ORDER THIS BLUEPRINT,
CALL TOLL-FREE 1-800-820-1283

Plan E-2208

PRICES AND DETAILS
ON PAGES 12-15

199

One-Floor Gracious Living

- An impressive roofscape, stately brick with soldier coursing and an impressive columned entry grace the exterior of this exciting single-story home.
- The entry opens to the the free-flowing interior, where the formal areas merge near the den, or guest room.
- The living room offers a window wall to a wide backyard deck, and the dining room is convenient to the kitchen.
- The octagonal island kitchen area offers a sunny breakfast nook with a large corner pantry.
- The spacious family room adjoins the kitchen and features a handsome fireplace and deck access. Laundry facilities and garage access are nearby.
- The lavish master suite with a fireplace and a state-of-the-art bath is privately situated in the left wing.
- Three secondary bedrooms have abundant closet space and share two baths on the right side of the home.
- The entire home features expansive 9-ft. ceilings.

Plan DD-3076	
Bedrooms: 4+	**Baths:** 3
Living Area:	
Main floor	3,076 sq. ft.
Total Living Area:	**3,076 sq. ft.**
Standard basement	3,076 sq. ft.
Garage	648 sq. ft.
Exterior Wall Framing:	2x4
Foundation Options:	
Standard basement	
Crawlspace	
Slab	

(All plans can be built with your choice of foundation and framing. A generic conversion diagram is available. See order form.)

BLUEPRINT PRICE CODE:	E

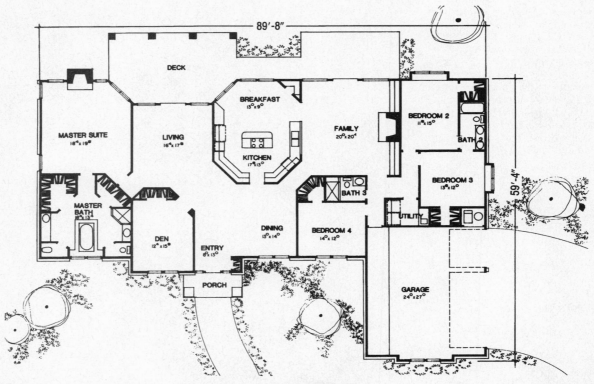

MAIN FLOOR

 TO ORDER THIS BLUEPRINT, CALL TOLL-FREE 1-800-820-1283 Plan DD-3076 *PRICES AND DETAILS ON PAGES 12-15*

Bright and Airy Spaces Abound!

- An arched brick entry and a high, arched window set the tone for the bright, airy spaces this home offers.
- An 11-ft.-high barrel-vaulted ceiling highlights the living room and adds to the striking effect of the arched window. The living room's openness to the dining room further enhances the feeling of spaciousness.
- The kitchen is designed as an integral part of the family room and nook. The angled snack counter allows the cook to keep in touch with family activities.
- The nook features dramatic solarium windows that flood the area with natural light. The family room has sliding glass doors that open to a backyard patio.
- The master bedroom includes a private, skylighted bath and a walk-in closet. Another full bath lies between the two secondary bedrooms.

Plan R-1067

Bedrooms: 3	Baths: 2
Living Area:	
Main floor	1,685 sq. ft.
Total Living Area:	**1,685 sq. ft.**
Garage	432 sq. ft.
Exterior Wall Framing:	2x6

Foundation Options:

Crawlspace
(All plans can be built with your choice of foundation and framing. A generic conversion diagram is available. See order form.)

BLUEPRINT PRICE CODE: **B**

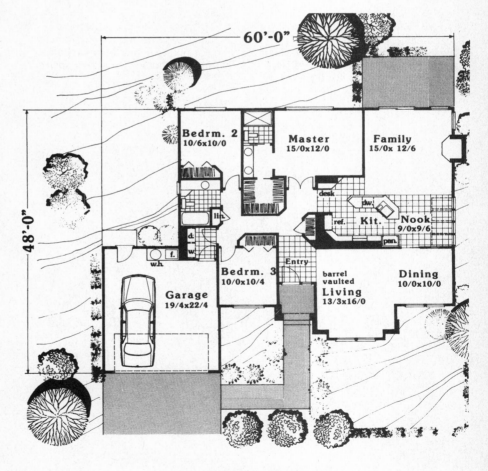

MAIN FLOOR

TO ORDER THIS BLUEPRINT,
CALL TOLL-FREE 1-800-820-1283

Plan R-1067

PRICES AND DETAILS
ON PAGES 12-15

201

Captivating Design

- This captivating and award-winning design is introduced by a unique entry landscape that includes striking columns, an exciting fountain courtyard and a private garden.
- The beautiful, open interior commands attention with expansive glass and ceilings at least 10 ft. high throughout.
- The foyer's 15-ft. ceiling extends into the adjoining dining room, which is set off by a decorative glass-block wall.
- A step-down soffit frames the spacious central living room with its dramatic entry columns and 13-ft. ceiling. A rear bay overlooks a large covered patio.
- The gourmet kitchen shows off an oversized island cooktop and snack bar. A pass-through above the sink provides easy service to the patio's summer kitchen, while indoor dining is offered in the sunny, open breakfast area.
- A warm fireplace and flanking storage shelves adorn an exciting media wall in the large adjacent family room.
- The secondary bedrooms share a full bath near the laundry room and garage.
- Behind double doors on the other side of the home, the romantic master suite is bathed in sunlight. A private garden embraces an elegant oval tub.

Plan HDS-99-185

Bedrooms: 3+	Baths: 2½
Living Area:	
Main floor	2,397 sq. ft.
Total Living Area:	**2,397 sq. ft.**
Garage	473 sq. ft.
Exterior Wall Framing:	2x4

Foundation Options:

Slab

(All plans can be built with your choice of foundation and framing. A generic conversion diagram is available. See order form.)

BLUEPRINT PRICE CODE: C

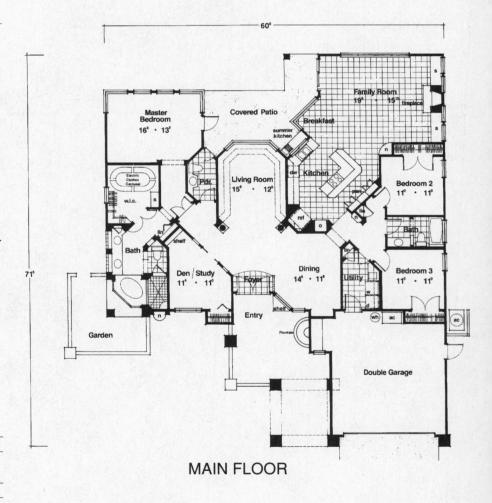

MAIN FLOOR

Plan HDS-99-185

PRICES AND DETAILS
ON PAGES 12-15

Impressive Columns

- Impressive columns and striking stucco give this home a distinguished look.
- Inside, a 14-ft. ceiling extends above the foyer, the formal living and dining rooms and the inviting family room.
- The stunning raised dining room is set off by decorative wood columns that support a wraparound overhead plant shelf. A two-way fireplace is shared with the family room, which also features built-in shelves and arched windows that overlook a large deck.
- The study includes built-in bookshelves and a ceiling that vaults to 13½ feet.
- The kitchen has an angled counter bar and a corner pantry while the breakfast nook provides deck access. Both rooms are enhanced by 10-ft. ceilings.
- The large master suite shows off a bayed sitting area and a roomy, private bath. Ceilings heights here are 10 ft. in the sleeping area and 9 ft. in the bath.
- Two secondary bedrooms with 12-ft. vaulted ceilings share a nice hall bath.

Plan DW-2342

Bedrooms: 3+	Baths: 2
Living Area:	
Main floor	2,342 sq. ft.
Total Living Area:	**2,342 sq. ft.**
Standard basement	2,342 sq. ft.
Garage	460 sq. ft.
Exterior Wall Framing:	2x4

Foundation Options:

Standard basement

Crawlspace

Slab

(All plans can be built with your choice of foundation and framing. A generic conversion diagram is available. See order form.)

BLUEPRINT PRICE CODE:	C

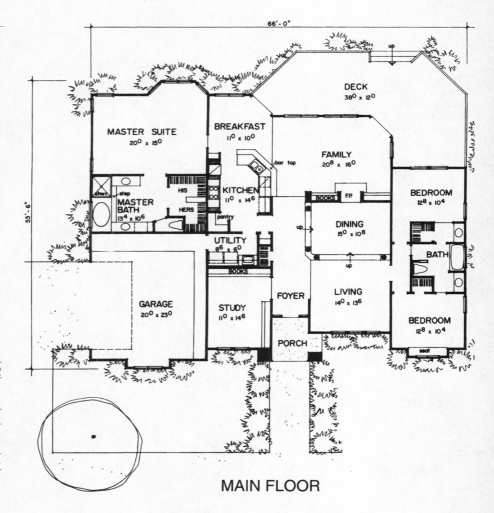

MAIN FLOOR

Vaulted Ceiling in Large Living Room

AREAS

Living	1912 sq. ft.
Carport & Storage	492 sq. ft.
Porches	204 sq. ft.
Total	2608 sq. ft.

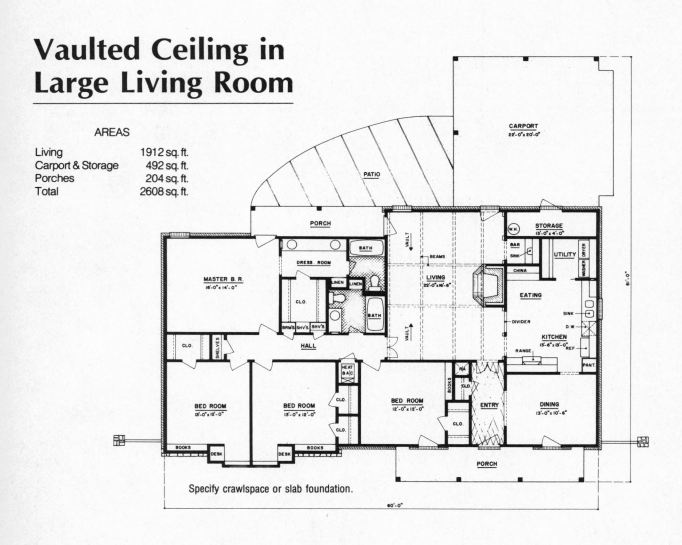

Specify crawlspace or slab foundation.

TO ORDER THIS BLUEPRINT,
CALL TOLL-FREE 1-800-820-1283

Blueprint Price Code B
Plan E-1903

PRICES AND DETAILS
ON PAGES 12-15

Lap of Luxury

- Entering this stunning, feature-filled one-story estate means entering a world of luxury and comfort.
- The open foyer is brightened by an arched transom window. Introduced by an archway, the adjacent formal dining room features a unique ale bar.
- The bright and airy parlor offers French doors to a covered backyard veranda. An outside stairway accesses the partial daylight basement.
- The island kitchen includes a menu desk, a pantry and a panoramic morning room.
- Inviting and spacious, the Gathering Room is enhanced by a media center

and a handsome fireplace with a built-in wood box.
- Double doors lead into the luxurious master suite, which features built-in bookshelves and cabinets. A sitting room provides private outdoor access. The master bath showcases a corner garden tub, a separate shower, dual vanities and roomy his-and-hers walk-in closets.
- A second bedroom, a guest suite, and a library or fourth bedroom complete the home's innovative floor plan.
- For added spaciousness, ceilings in the main living areas and in the master bedroom are 12 ft. high. Ceilings in the other bedrooms, the library and all three baths are 9 ft. high.

Plan EOF-63	
Bedrooms: 3+	**Baths:** 3
Living Area:	
Main floor	3,316 sq. ft.
Total Living Area:	**3,316 sq. ft.**
Partial daylight basement	550 sq. ft.
Garage	496 sq. ft.
Exterior Wall Framing:	2x6

Foundation Options:

Partial daylight basement
(All plans can be built with your choice of foundation and framing. A generic conversion diagram is available. See order form.)

BLUEPRINT PRICE CODE:	E

MAIN FLOOR

Designed with the Master in Mind

- This elegant stucco home is designed with the master of the home in mind.
- Over 600 sq. ft. has been reserved for the master bedroom with an angled sitting area and patio access and a private bath with a large Jacuzzi, a private toilet room, dual dressing areas and an elegant double-doored entry.
- The formal living areas extend from the foyer. The central living room features a vaulted ceiling and a spectacular window wall overlooking the adjoining covered patio with a summer kitchen.
- The large gourmet kitchen merges with a breakfast area and a spacious family room. The breakfast area boasts a fascinating curved glass wall and opens to the patio. A handy snack bar serves refreshments to guests in the family room, which features a volume ceiling and a warming fireplace.
- Two secondary bedrooms, a den or guest room, and a hall or pool bath complete this unique floor plan.

Plan HDS-99-178

Bedrooms: 3-4	**Baths:** 3
Living Area:	
Main floor	2,931 sq. ft.
Total Living Area:	**2,931 sq. ft.**
Garage	703 sq. ft.
Exterior Wall Framing:	8-in. concrete block

Foundation Options:

Slab

(Typical foundation & framing conversion diagram available—see order form.)

BLUEPRINT PRICE CODE: D

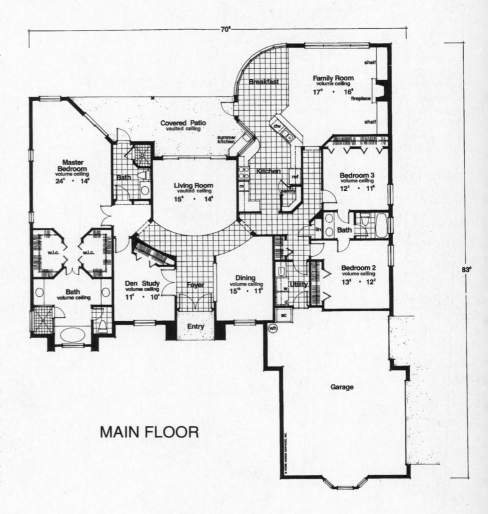

MAIN FLOOR

Plan HDS-99-178

Cozy Bungalow

- This pleasing L-shaped design packs a lot of living space into its floor plan.
- The large family room at the center of the home extends to two outdoor living spaces: a screened porch and a big patio or deck. For colder days, the warm fireplace will come in handy.
- Formal occasions will be well received in the spacious living/dining room at the front of the home. Each area offers a nice view of the front porch.
- The airy kitchen includes a pantry, a windowed sink and lots of counter space. Attached is a cozy breakfast bay and, beyond that, a laundry room.
- Secluded to the rear of the sleeping wing, the master suite boasts a private symmetrical bath with a garden tub, a separate shower and his-and-hers vanities and walk-in closets.
- Two secondary bedrooms and another full bath complete the sleeping wing.

Plan C-8620

Bedrooms: 3	Baths: 2
Living Area:	
Main floor	1,950 sq. ft.
Total Living Area:	**1,950 sq. ft.**
Daylight basement	1,950 sq. ft.
Garage	420 sq. ft.
Exterior Wall Framing:	2x4

Foundation Options:

Daylight basement

Crawlspace

Slab

(All plans can be built with your choice of foundation and framing. A generic conversion diagram is available. See order form.)

BLUEPRINT PRICE CODE: B

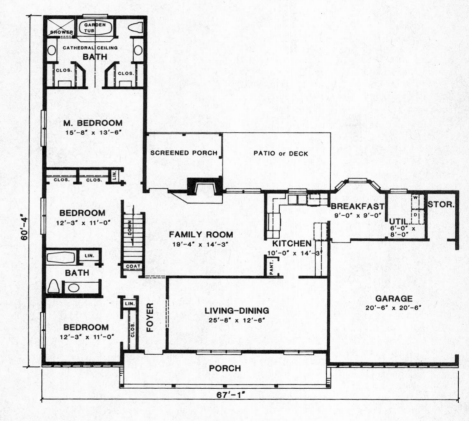

MAIN FLOOR

TO ORDER THIS BLUEPRINT,
CALL TOLL-FREE 1-800-820-1283

Plan C-8620

PRICES AND DETAILS
ON PAGES 12-15

207

Sunny Entry

- A dramatic columned entry highlighted by a sunny window arrangement greets visitors to this glorious home.
- Double doors open to the tiled foyer, which shares a 12-ft. ceiling with the formal living and dining rooms. A tray ceiling tops the dining room, and sliding glass doors in the living room open to a tranquil covered patio.
- The secluded family room boasts a fireplace flanked by bookshelves, plus sliding glass doors to the backyard.
- An island serving bar links the family room to the kitchen and the breakfast nook. A desk and a walk-in pantry are some of the kitchen's features. A wall of windows bathes the nook in sunlight.
- Two bedrooms nearby include private access to a separated bath.
- Across the home, beautiful French doors open to the master suite, which flaunts patio access and two walk-in closets. The master bath boasts a garden tub and two vanities.
- A quiet study off the foyer could accommodate overnight guests. A hall bath nearby features patio access.
- All rooms are enhanced by 10-ft. ceilings, unless otherwise noted.

Plan HDS-99-207

Bedrooms: 3+	Baths: 3
Living Area:	
Main floor	2,593 sq. ft.
Total Living Area:	**2,593 sq. ft.**
Garage	508 sq. ft.

Exterior Wall Framing:

2x4 and 8-in. concrete block

Foundation Options:

Slab

(All plans can be built with your choice of foundation and framing. A generic conversion diagram is available. See order form.)

BLUEPRINT PRICE CODE:	D

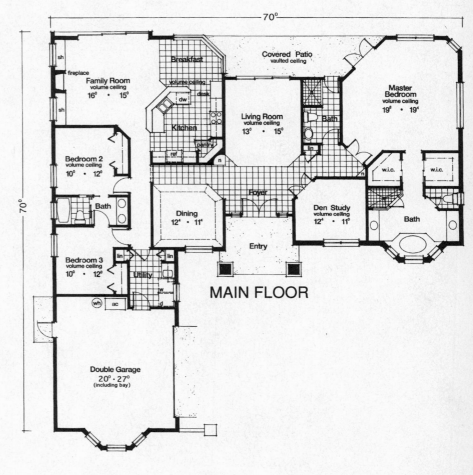

MAIN FLOOR

Plan HDS-99-207

Luxurious Interior

- This luxurious home is introduced by an exciting tiled entry with a 17½-ft. vaulted ceiling and a skylight.
- The highlight of the home is the expansive Great Room and dining area, with its fireplace, planter, 17½-ft. vaulted ceiling and bay windows. The fabulous wraparound deck with a step-up hot tub is the perfect complement to this large entertainment space.
- The kitchen features lots of counter space, a large pantry and an adjoining bay-windowed breakfast nook.
- The exquisite master suite flaunts a sunken garden tub, a separate shower, a dual-sink vanity, a walk-in closet and private access to the deck area.
- The game room downstairs is perfect for casual entertaining, with its warm woodstove, oversized wet bar and patio access. Two bedrooms, a full bath and a large utility area are also included.

Plan P-6595-3D

Bedrooms: 3	Baths: 2½
Living Area:	
Main floor	1,530 sq. ft.
Daylight basement	1,145 sq. ft.
Total Living Area:	**2,675 sq. ft.**
Garage	462 sq. ft.
Exterior Wall Framing:	2x6

Foundation Options:

Daylight basement
(All plans can be built with your choice of foundation and framing. A generic conversion diagram is available. See order form.)

BLUEPRINT PRICE CODE: D

MAIN FLOOR

DAYLIGHT BASEMENT

Photo by Mark Englund/HomeStyles

Extraordinary Estate Living

- Extraordinary estate living is at its best in this palatial beauty.
- The double-doored entry opens to a large central living room that overlooks a covered patio with a vaulted ceiling. Volume 14-ft. ceilings are found in the living room, in the formal dining room and in the den or study, which may serve as a fourth bedroom.
- The gourmet chef will enjoy the spacious kitchen, which flaunts a

cooktop island, a walk-in pantry and a peninsula snack counter shared with the breakfast room and family room.
- This trio of informal living spaces also shares a panorama of glass and a corner fireplace centered between TV and media niches.
- Isolated at the opposite end of the home is the spacious master suite, which offers private patio access. Dual walk-in closets define the entrance to the adjoining master bath, complete with a garden Jacuzzi and separate dressing areas.
- The hall bath also opens to the outdoors for use as a pool bath.

Plan HDS-99-177	
Bedrooms: 3+	**Baths:** 3
Living Area:	
Main floor	2,597 sq. ft.
Total Living Area:	**2,597 sq. ft.**
Garage	761 sq. ft.
Exterior Wall Framing:	2x4
Foundation Options:	

Slab
(All plans can be built with your choice of foundation and framing. A generic conversion diagram is available. See order form.)

BLUEPRINT PRICE CODE:	D

NOTE:
The above photographed home may have been modified by the homeowner. Please refer to floor plan and/or drawn elevation shown for actual blueprint details.

MAIN FLOOR

Covered Patio
vaulted ceiling

Master Bedroom
volume ceiling
18⁰ · 16⁰

Bath

Living Room
volume ceiling
14⁰ · 10⁰

Family Room
volume ceiling
20⁰ · 17⁸

tv

fireplace

m

Breakfast

volume ceiling

Kitchen

dw

wh

ac

ref

Garage

pantry

Utility

d

ac

w

w.i.c.

w.i.c.

n

desk

Bath
volume ceiling

s

up

Den / Study
Bedroom 4
volume ceiling
13⁴ · 11⁰

Foyer

Dining
volume ceiling
13⁰ · 11⁰

linen

Bedroom 2
volume ceiling
11⁰ · 11⁰

Bath

Bedroom 3
volume ceiling
11⁰ · 11⁰

Entry

sh

96⁶

50⁰

TO ORDER THIS BLUEPRINT, CALL TOLL-FREE 1-800-820-1283

Plan HDS-99-177

PRICES AND DETAILS ON PAGES 12-15

Full of Surprises

- While dignified and reserved on the outside, this plan presents intriguing angles, vaulted ceilings and surprising spaces throughout the interior.
- The elegant, vaulted living room flows from the expansive foyer and includes a striking fireplace and a beautiful bay.
- The spacious island kitchen offers wide corner windows above the sink and easy service to both the vaulted dining room and the skylighted nook.
- The adjoining vaulted family room features a warm corner woodstove and sliding doors to the backyard patio.
- The superb master suite includes a vaulted sleeping area and an exquisite private bath with a skylighted dressing area, a large walk-in closet, a step-up spa tub and a separate shower.
- Three secondary bedrooms are located near another full bath and a large laundry room with garage access.

Plans P-7711-3A & -3D

Bedrooms: 4	Baths: 2
Living Area:	
Main floor (crawlspace version)	2,510 sq. ft.
Main floor (basement version)	2,580 sq. ft.
Total Living Area:	**2,510/2,580 sq. ft.**
Daylight basement	2,635 sq. ft.
Garage	806 sq. ft.
Exterior Wall Framing:	**2x6**
Foundation Options:	**Plan #**
Daylight basement	P-7711-3D
Crawlspace	P-7711-3A

(All plans can be built with your choice of foundation and framing. A generic conversion diagram is available. See order form.)

BLUEPRINT PRICE CODE:	**D**

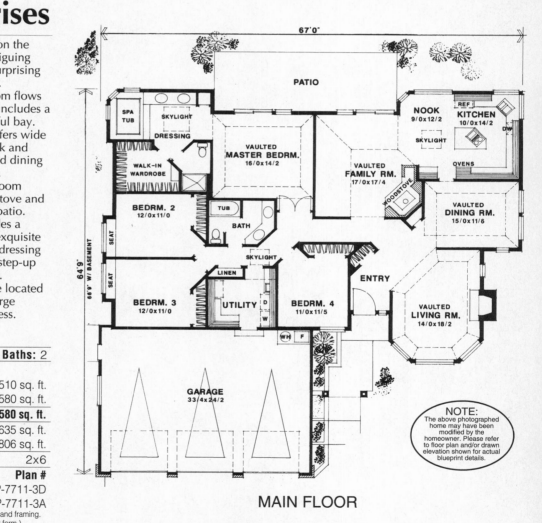

MAIN FLOOR

NOTE:
The above photographed home may have been modified by the homeowner. Please refer to floor plan and/or drawn elevation shown for actual blueprint details.

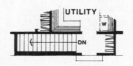

BASEMENT
STAIRWAY
LOCATION

Masterful Master Suite

- This gorgeous home features front and rear covered porches and a master suite so luxurious it deserves its own wing.
- The expansive entry welcomes visitors into a spacious, skylighted living room, which boasts a handsome fireplace. The adjacent formal dining room overlooks the front porch.
- Designed for efficiency, the kitchen features an angled snack bar, a bayed eating area and views of the porch. An all-purpose utility room is conveniently located off the kitchen.
- The kitchen, eating area, living room and dining room are all heightened by 12-ft. ceilings.
- The sumptuous and secluded master suite features a tub and a separate shower, a double-sink vanity, a walk-in closet with built-in shelves and a compartmentalized toilet.
- The two secondary bedrooms share a hall bath at the other end of the home. The rear bedroom offers porch access.
- The garage features built-in storage and access to unfinished attic space.

Plan E-1811

Bedrooms: 3	Baths: 2

Living Area:

Main floor	1,800 sq. ft.
Total Living Area:	**1,800 sq. ft.**
Garage and storage	634 sq. ft.
Exterior Wall Framing:	2x6

Foundation Options:

Crawlspace
Slab
(All plans can be built with your choice of foundation and framing. A generic conversion diagram is available. See order form.)

BLUEPRINT PRICE CODE:	**B**

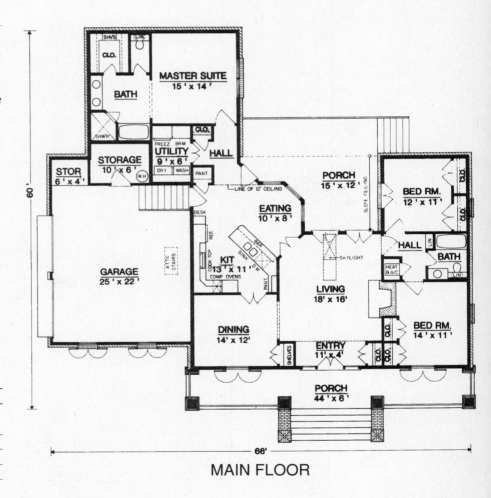

MAIN FLOOR

TO ORDER THIS BLUEPRINT, CALL TOLL-FREE 1-800-820-1283

Plan E-1811

PRICES AND DETAILS ON PAGES 12-15

Fresh Air

- With its nostalgic look and country style, this lovely home brings a breath of fresh air into any neighborhood.
- Past the inviting wraparound porch, the foyer is brightened by an arched transom window above the front door.
- The adjoining formal dining room is defined by decorative columns and features a 9-ft., 4-in. stepped ceiling.
- The bright and airy kitchen includes a pantry, a windowed sink and a sunny breakfast area with porch access.
- Enhanced by an 11-ft stepped ceiling, the spacious Great Room is warmed by a fireplace flanked by sliding glass doors to a covered back porch.
- The lush master bedroom boasts an 11-ft. tray ceiling and a bayed sitting area. The master bath showcases a circular spa tub with a glass-block wall.
- The two remaining bedrooms are serviced by a second bath and a nearby laundry room. The protruding bedroom has a 12-ft. vaulted ceiling.
- Additional living space can be made available by finishing the upper floor.

Plan AX-93308

Bedrooms: 3+	Baths: 2

Living Area:

Main floor	1,793 sq. ft.
Total Living Area:	**1,793 sq. ft.**
Standard basement	1,793 sq. ft.
Unfinished upper floor	779 sq. ft.
Garage and utility	471 sq. ft.
Exterior Wall Framing:	2x4

Foundation Options:

Standard basement
Crawlspace
Slab

(All plans can be built with your choice of foundation and framing. A generic conversion diagram is available. See order form.)

BLUEPRINT PRICE CODE:	B

VIEW INTO GREAT ROOM

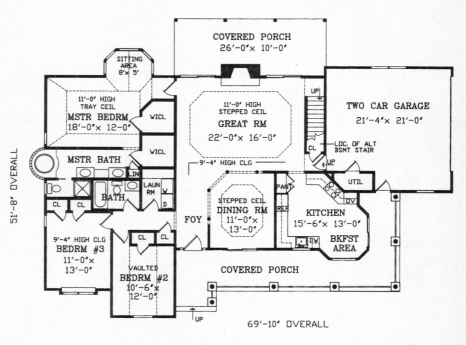

MAIN FLOOR

Versatile
Sun Room

- This cozy country-style home offers an inviting front porch and an interior just as welcoming.
- The spacious living room features a warming fireplace and windows that overlook the porch.
- The living room opens to a dining area, where French doors access a covered porch and a sunny patio.
- The island kitchen has a sink view, plenty of counter space, and a handy pass-through to the adjoining sun room. The bright sun room is large enough to serve as a formal dining room, a family room or a hobby room.
- The private master suite is secluded to the rear. A garden spa tub, dual walk-in closets and separate dressing areas are nice features found in the master bath.

Plan J-90014

Bedrooms: 3	**Baths:** 2½
Living Area:	
Main floor	2,190 sq. ft.
Total Living Area:	**2,190 sq. ft.**
Standard basement	2,190 sq. ft.
Garage	465 sq. ft.
Storage	34 sq. ft.
Exterior Wall Framing:	2x6

Foundation Options:

Standard basement
Crawlspace
Slab

(All plans can be built with your choice of foundation and framing. A generic conversion diagram is available. See order form.)

BLUEPRINT PRICE CODE:	C

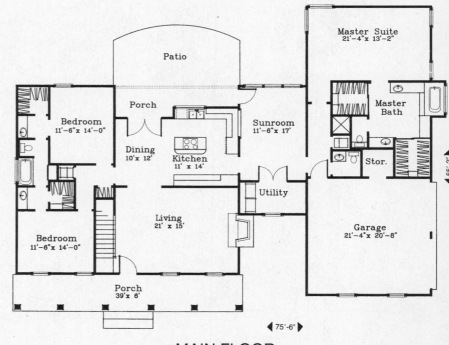

MAIN FLOOR

Tradition Updated

- The nostalgic exterior of this home gives way to dramatic cathedral ceilings and illuminating skylights inside.
- The covered front porch welcomes guests into the stone-tiled foyer, which flows into the living spaces.
- The living and dining rooms merge, forming a spacious, front-oriented entertaining area.

- A large three-sided fireplace situated between the living room and the family room may be enjoyed in both areas.
- The skylighted family room is also brightened by sliding glass doors that access a rear patio.
- The sunny island kitchen offers a nice breakfast nook and easy access to the laundry room and the garage.
- The master suite boasts a walk-in closet and a skylighted bath with a dual-sink vanity, a soaking tub and a separate shower. Two additional bedrooms share another full bath.

Plan AX-90303-A

Bedrooms: 3	Baths: 2
Living Area:	
Main floor	1,615 sq. ft.
Total Living Area:	**1,615 sq. ft.**
Basement	1,615 sq. ft.
Garage	412 sq. ft.
Exterior Wall Framing:	2x4

Foundation Options:

Daylight basement
Standard basement
Crawlspace
Slab
(All plans can be built with your choice of foundation and framing. A generic conversion diagram is available. See order form.)

BLUEPRINT PRICE CODE: **B**

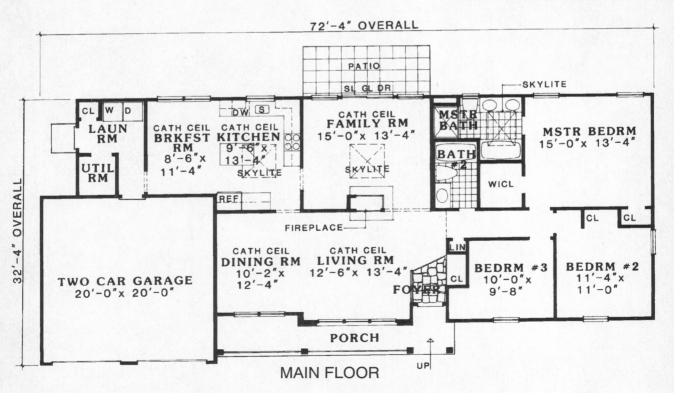

MAIN FLOOR

Friendly Country Charm

- An inviting front porch welcomes you to this friendly one-story home.
- The porch opens to a spacious central living room with a warm fireplace and functional built-in storage shelves.
- The bay window of the adjoining dining room allows a view of the backyard.

The dining area also enjoys an eating bar provided by the adjacent walk-through kitchen.
- The nice-sized kitchen also has a windowed sink and easy access to the laundry room and carport.
- Three bedrooms and two baths occupy the sleeping wing. The oversized master bedroom features a lovely boxed-out window, two walk-in closets and a private bath. The secondary bedrooms share the second full bath.

Plan J-8692

Bedrooms: 3	**Baths:** 2

Living Area:

Main floor	1,633 sq. ft.
Total Living Area:	**1,633 sq. ft.**
Standard basement	1,633 sq. ft.
Carport	380 sq. ft.
Exterior Wall Framing:	2x4

Foundation Options:

Standard basement
Crawlspace
Slab
(All plans can be built with your choice of foundation and framing. A generic conversion diagram is available. See order form.)

BLUEPRINT PRICE CODE: B

UTIL
7-6 x 9-6

KITCHEN
15-6 x 9-6

DINING
13-6 x 12-6

MBR
15 x 12-6

CARPORT

LIVING
18-6 x 18

BR
12-9 x 11-6

BR
13 x 11-6

PORCH

39'-0"

66'-8"

MAIN FLOOR

Plan J-8692

PRICES AND DETAILS ON PAGES 12-15

Rustic, Relaxed Living

- The screened porch of this rustic home offers a cool place to dine on warm summer days. The covered front porch provides an inviting welcome and a place for pure relaxation.
- With its warm fireplace and surrounding windows, the home's spacious living room is ideal for unwinding indoors. The living room unfolds to a nice-sized dining area that overlooks a backyard patio and opens to the screened porch.
- The U-shaped kitchen is centrally located and features a nice windowed sink. A handy pantry and a laundry room adjoin to the right.
- Three large bedrooms make up the home's sleeping wing. The master bedroom boasts a roomy private bath with a step-up spa tub, a separate shower and two walk-in closets.
- The secondary bedrooms share a compartmentalized hall bath.

Plan C-8650	
Bedrooms: 3	**Baths:** 2
Living Area:	
Main floor	1,773 sq. ft.
Total Living Area:	**1,773 sq. ft.**
Daylight basement	1,773 sq. ft.
Garage	441 sq. ft.
Exterior Wall Framing:	2x4
Foundation Options:	
Daylight basement	
Crawlspace	
Slab	

(All plans can be built with your choice of foundation and framing. A generic conversion diagram is available. See order form.)

BLUEPRINT PRICE CODE: B

MAIN FLOOR

Wonderful Detailing

- The wonderfully detailed front porch, with its graceful arches, columns and railings, gives this home a character all its own. Dormer windows and arched transoms further accentuate the porch.
- The floor plan features a central living room with a 10-ft.-high ceiling and a fireplace framed by French doors. These doors open to a covered porch or a sun room, and a sheltered deck beyond.
- Just off the living room, the island kitchen and breakfast area provide a spacious place for family or guests. The nearby formal dining room has arched transom windows and a 10-ft. ceiling, as does the bedroom off the foyer. All of the remaining rooms have 9-ft. ceilings.
- The unusual master suite includes a window alcove, access to the porch and a fantastic bath with a garden tub.
- A huge utility room, a storage area off the garage and a 1,000-sq.-ft. attic space are other bonuses of this design.

Plan J-90019

Bedrooms: 3	Baths: 2½
Living Area:	
Main floor	2,410 sq. ft.
Total Living Area:	**2,410 sq. ft.**
Standard basement	2,410 sq. ft.
Garage	512 sq. ft.
Storage	86 sq. ft.
Exterior Wall Framing:	2x6

Foundation Options:

Standard basement
Crawlspace
Slab

(All plans can be built with your choice of foundation and framing. A generic conversion diagram is available. See order form.)

BLUEPRINT PRICE CODE:	C

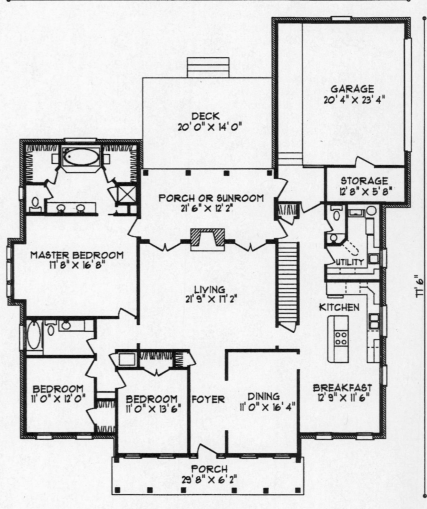

MAIN FLOOR

Plan J-90019

Rustic Welcome

- This rustic design boasts an appealing exterior with a covered front porch that offers guests a friendly welcome.
- Inside, the centrally located Great Room features an 11-ft., 8-in. cathedral ceiling with exposed wood beams. A massive fireplace separates the living area from the large dining room, which offers access to a nice backyard patio.
- The galley-style kitchen flows between the formal dining room and the bayed breakfast room, which offers a handy pantry and access to laundry facilities.
- The master suite features a walk-in closet and a compartmentalized bath.
- Across the Great Room, two additional bedrooms have extra closet space and share a second full bath.
- The side-entry garage gives the front of the home an extra-appealing and uncluttered look.
- The optional daylight basement offers expanded living space. The stairway (not shown) would be located along the wall between the dining room and the back bedroom.

Plan C-8460

Bedrooms: 3	**Baths:** 2
Living Area:	
Main floor	1,670 sq. ft.
Total Living Area:	**1,670 sq. ft.**
Daylight basement	1,600 sq. ft.
Garage	427 sq. ft.
Exterior Wall Framing:	2x4

Foundation Options:
Daylight basement
Crawlspace
Slab
(All plans can be built with your choice of foundation and framing. A generic conversion diagram is available. See order form.)

BLUEPRINT PRICE CODE: B

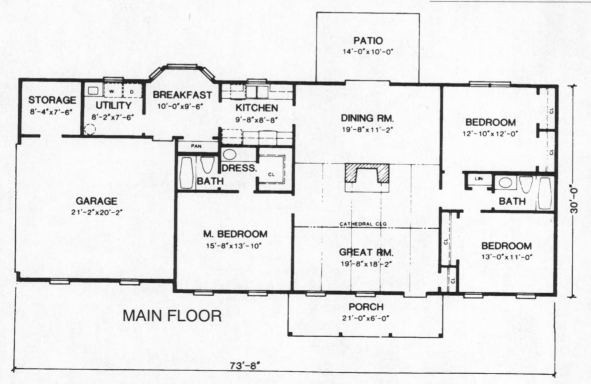

MAIN FLOOR

Photo by Mark Englund/HomeStyles

Elaborate Entry

- This home's important-looking covered entry greets guests with heavy, banded support columns, sunburst transom windows and dual sidelights.
- Once inside the home, the 15-ft.-high foyer is flanked by the formal living and dining rooms, which have 10½-ft. vaulted ceilings. Straight ahead and beyond five decorative columns lies the spacious family room.
- Surrounded by 8-ft.-high walls, the family room features a 13-ft. vaulted ceiling, a fireplace and sliding doors to a covered patio. A neat plant shelf above the fireplace adds style.
- The bright and airy kitchen has a 13-ft. ceiling and serves the family room and the breakfast area, which is enhanced by a corner window and a French door.
- The master suite enjoys a 13-ft. vaulted ceiling and features French-door patio access, a large walk-in closet and a private bath with a corner platform tub and a separate shower.
- Across the home, three secondary bedrooms share a hall bath, which boasts private access to the patio.

Plan HDS-90-806

Bedrooms: 4	Baths: 2
Living Area:	
Main floor	2,041 sq. ft.
Total Living Area:	**2,041 sq. ft.**
Garage	452 sq. ft.
Exterior Wall Framing:	
2x4 or 8-in. concrete block	
Foundation Options:	
Slab	

(All plans can be built with your choice of foundation and framing. A generic conversion diagram is available. See order form.)

BLUEPRINT PRICE CODE:	C

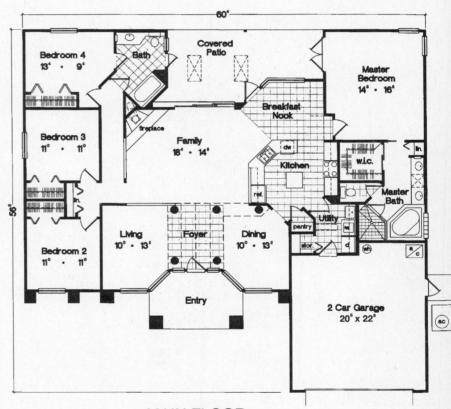

MAIN FLOOR

NOTE:
The above photographed home may have been modified by the homeowner. Please refer to floor plan and/or drawn elevation shown for actual blueprint details.

Plan HDS-90-806

PRICES AND DETAILS ON PAGES 12-15

Design Fits Narrow Lot

- This compact, cozy and dignified plan makes great use of a small lot, while also offering an exciting interior design.
- In from the covered front porch, the living room features a warm fireplace and a 13-ft., 6-in. cathedral ceiling.
- The bay-windowed dining room joins the living room to provide a spacious area for entertaining.
- The galley-style kitchen has easy access to a large pantry closet, the utility room and the carport.
- The master suite includes a deluxe bath and a roomy walk-in closet.
- Two secondary bedrooms share another bath off the hallway.
- A lockable storage area is located off the rear patio.

Plan J-86161

Bedrooms: 3	Baths: 2
Living Area:	
Main floor	1,626 sq. ft.
Total Living Area:	**1,626 sq. ft.**
Standard basement	1,626 sq. ft.
Carport	410 sq. ft.
Storage	104 sq. ft.
Exterior Wall Framing:	2x4

Foundation Options:

Standard basement
Crawlspace
Slab
(All plans can be built with your choice of foundation and framing. A generic conversion diagram is available. See order form.)

BLUEPRINT PRICE CODE: B

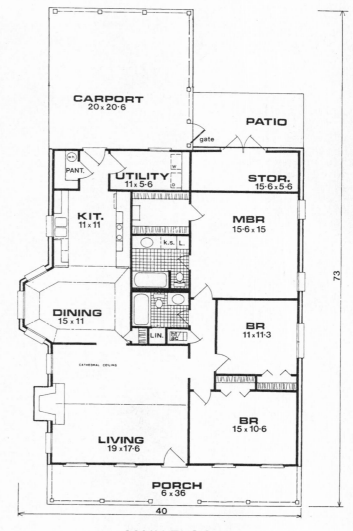

MAIN FLOOR

TO ORDER THIS BLUEPRINT,
CALL TOLL-FREE 1-800-820-1283

Plan J-86161

PRICES AND DETAILS
ON PAGES 12-15

221

A Real Original

- This home's round window, elegant entry and transom windows create an eye-catching, original look.
- Inside, high ceilings and tremendous views let the eyes wander. The foyer provides an exciting look at the expansive deck and the inviting spa through the living room's tall windows. The windows frame a handsome fireplace, while a 10-ft. ceiling adds volume and interest.
- To the right of the foyer is a cozy den or home office with its own fireplace, 10-ft. ceiling and dramatic windows.
- The spacious kitchen/breakfast area features an oversized snack bar island and opens to a large screen porch. Within easy reach are the laundry room and the entrance to the garage.
- The bright formal dining room overlooks the deck and boasts a ceiling that vaults up to 10 feet.
- The secluded master suite looks out to the deck as well, with access through a patio door. The private bath features a dynamite corner spa tub, a separate shower and a large walk-in closet.
- A second bedroom and bath complete the main floor.

Plan B-90065

Bedrooms: 2+	Baths: 2
Living Area:	
Main floor	1,889 sq. ft.
Total Living Area:	**1,889 sq. ft.**
Standard basement	1,889 sq. ft.
Garage	406 sq. ft.
Exterior Wall Framing:	2x6

Foundation Options:

Standard basement

(All plans can be built with your choice of foundation and framing. A generic conversion diagram is available. See order form.)

BLUEPRINT PRICE CODE: **B**

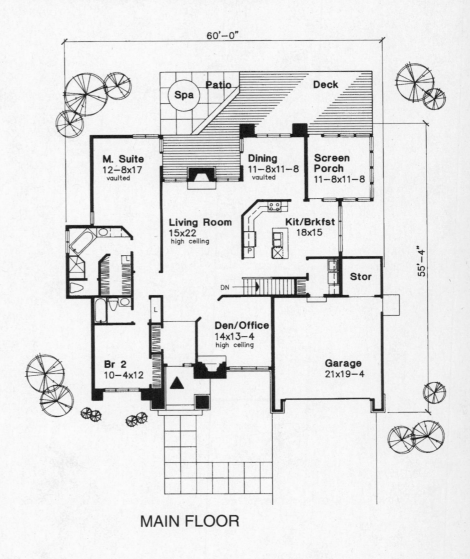

MAIN FLOOR

TO ORDER THIS BLUEPRINT, CALL TOLL-FREE 1-800-820-1283   Plan B-90065   *PRICES AND DETAILS ON PAGES 12-15*

Easy-Living Atmosphere

- Clean lines and a functional, well-designed floor plan create a relaxed, easy-living atmosphere for this sprawling ranch-style home.
- An inviting front porch with attractive columns and planter boxes opens to an airy entry, which flows into the living room and the family room.
- The huge central family room features a 14-ft. vaulted, exposed-beam ceiling and a handsome fireplace with a built-in wood box. A nice desk and plenty of bookshelves give the room a distinguished feel. A French door opens to a versatile covered rear porch.
- The large gourmet kitchen is highlighted by an arched brick pass-through to the family room. Double doors open to the intimate formal dining room, which hosts a built-in china hutch. The sunny informal eating area features lovely porch views on either side.
- The isolated sleeping wing includes four bedrooms. The enormous master bedroom has a giant walk-in closet and a private bath. A compartmentalized bath with two vanities serves the remaining bedrooms.

Plan E-2700

Bedrooms: 4	**Baths:** 2½

Living Area:

Main floor	2,719 sq. ft.
Total Living Area:	**2,719 sq. ft.**
Garage	533 sq. ft.
Storage	50 sq. ft.
Exterior Wall Framing:	2x6

Foundation Options:

Crawlspace
Slab
(All plans can be built with your choice of foundation and framing. A generic conversion diagram is available. See order form.)

BLUEPRINT PRICE CODE: **D**

MAIN FLOOR

Picture-Perfect!

- With graceful arches, columns and railings, the wonderful front porch makes this home the picture of country charm. Decorative chimneys, shutters and quaint dormers add more style.
- Inside, the foyer shows off sidelights and a fantail transom. The foyer is flanked by the dining room and a bedroom, both of which boast porch views and arched transoms. All three areas are expanded by 10-ft. ceilings.
- The living room also flaunts a 10-ft. ceiling, plus a fireplace and French doors that open to a skylighted porch. The remaining rooms offer 9-ft. ceilings.
- The L-shaped kitchen has an island cooktop and a sunny breakfast nook.
- A Palladian window arrangement brightens the sitting alcove in the master suite. Other highlights include porch access and a fantastic bath with a garden tub and a separate shower.
- The upper floor is perfect for future expansion space.

Plan J-9401

Bedrooms: 3+	Baths: 2½
Living Area:	
Main floor	2,089 sq. ft.
Total Living Area:	**2,089 sq. ft.**
Upper floor (unfinished)	878 sq. ft.
Standard basement	2,089 sq. ft.
Garage and storage	530 sq. ft.
Exterior Wall Framing:	2x4

Foundation Options:

Standard basement
Crawlspace
Slab

(All plans can be built with your choice of foundation and framing. A generic conversion diagram is available. See order form.)

BLUEPRINT PRICE CODE: C

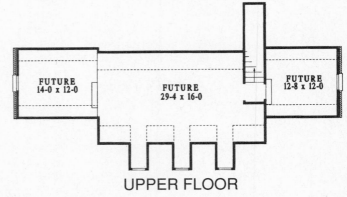

UPPER FLOOR

MAIN FLOOR